JOHN HOPTON

JOHN HOPTON

A FIFTEENTH CENTURY
SUFFOLK GENTLEMAN

COLIN RICHMOND

Senior Lecturer in History,
University of Keele

CAMBRIDGE UNIVERSITY PRESS

Cambridge

London   New York   New Rochelle

Melbourne   Sydney

Published by the Press Syndicate of the University of Cambridge
The Pitt Building, Trumpington Street, Cambridge CB2 IRP
32 East 57th Street, New York, NY 10022, USA
296 Beaconsfield Parade, Middle Park, Melbourne 3206, Australia

First published 1981

Printed in Great Britain by
Western Printing Services Ltd, Bristol

British Library Cataloguing in Publication Data
Richmond, Colin
John Hopton.
1. Hopton, John
2. Great Britain – History – Wars of the Roses,
1455–1485 – Biography
3. Suffolk, Eng. – Biography
I. Title
942.6′4′0430924   DA247.H/   80–40920
ISBN 0 521 23434 4

CONTENTS

for
Clara Gissing

PREFACE

I would like first to thank those archivists and their staffs who over the years have been so helpful. To William Serjeant at Ipswich I am particularly grateful for seeing to the deposit of some Blois MSS at Cambridge University Library in the summer term 1971; to Arthur Owen, archivist there, I am grateful for receiving them, and to the staff of the Anderson Room for their courtesy. At the Suffolk Record Office I would also like to thank Patricia Woodgate and Marion Allen. At Norwich I am grateful to Jean Kennedy, at Stafford to Freddie Stitt, Margaret O'Sullivan, and Isobel Morcom. At Magdalen College, Oxford, Gerald Harriss and his capable deputies (Jasper Scovil and Pamela Colman) always welcomed my visits. Especially I want to thank the staffs in the Manuscripts Department of the British Museum and the Round Room of the Public Record Office: their skills have not gone unappreciated.

To my friends I am also grateful. To Bernard Finnemore for the index, to Mary Harris for help with my Latin, to Norman Scarfe for detailed criticism, to Carolyn Busfield for typing many drafts including the final one, to Peter and Margaret Spufford for constant enthusiasm, to David Morgan for interest, encouragement, expert advice, and innumerable references, to Rees Davies for reading a draft and making suggestions which without exception improved it: he has given more time and attention to this book than it deserves, certainly more than I deserve.

It is fitting that a study which began in earnest at Cambridge should be completed there: to William Davies and his colleagues at the Press I am most grateful.

vii

A NOTE ON SOURCES

The collection of MSS on which this study depends is the Blois Family Deposit at the Suffolk Record Office, Ipswich. The documents from it relating to John Hopton and his family, almost all estate accounts and associated papers, I have described below (pp 32–4). These were supplemented by Easton Bavents estate accounts in the Redstone Collection, for which see also below (p 33). Various other collections at Ipswich provided information for chapter 4.

At Magdalen College, Oxford, are MSS concerning Sir John Gra, most of whose Lincolnshire property was purchased by William Wainfleet for the college; these and other documents there were used in chapter 1.

In the British Library MSS section there are some deeds and other random documents concerning Thomasin Barrington, the Knevet family, and others, as well as a handful of seventeenth century transcripts of important Hopton documents. There are perhaps others which I have not come across.

From the Public Record Office I have mainly used *inquisitions post mortem*, but have also found other classes of document useful here and there.

At the Staffordshire Record Office, Stafford, among the Stafford Collection the Jerningham and Sulyard Papers produced material relevant to chapter 4.

The Bradfer-Lawrence and Townshend Collections in the Norfolk Record Office, at Norwich, were helpful, while at Lincoln, in the

Lincolnshire Record Office, I used the Ancaster Deposit for the Willoughbys.

Yet, after the Blois papers I have made most use of wills: those proved in the Prerogative Court of Canterbury, at the Public Record Office; those proved in the Bishop of Norwich's Consistory Court, at the Norfolk Record Office; and those proved in the Suffolk Archdeaconry Court, at the Suffolk Record Office, Ipswich. Occasionally wills from other sources including printed wills, particularly those in *Testamenta Eboracensia*, have been useful.

Beside wills the *Paston Letters* are my major source. I have deployed them throughout but especially in chapter 4. They reveal what other material only hints at; without them I could not have explored Hopton's world, indeed I only carried on, once I had set out, because I had them as my companions.

Beyond this the scraps I have used come from a wide variety of printed sources; these I have made clear in the notes. One further source of evidence which I hope makes its own impact is the visible, the tombs, churches, and what remains of the houses of the men and women I have discussed. Scant as this is, it frequently still has a power to move us which even the most exciting written record does not always have.

ABBREVIATIONS

BIHR	*Bulletin of the Institute of Historical Research*
BL	British Library
Blomefield	F. Blomefield, *Topographical History of Norfolk* (5 vols, Kersfield and Lynn, 1739–75)
C	Chancery
Cal Anc Deeds	*Calendar of Ancient Deeds*
CCR	*Calendar of Close Rolls*
CFR	*Calendar of Fine Rolls*
CIPM	*Calendar of Inquisitions Post Mortem*
CPR	*Calendar of Patent Rolls*
Copinger	W. A. Copinger, *Manors of Suffolk* (7 vols, 1905–11)
CP	*The Complete Peerage*, ed. V. Gibbs and others (1910–59)
Davis	*Paston Letters and Papers of the fifteenth century*, ed. Norman Davis, I (1971), II (1976)
E	Exchequer
Ec H R	*Economic History Review*
EHR	*English Historical Review*
Emden, *Biog Reg Camb*	A. B. Emden, *A Biographical Register of the University of Cambridge to 1500* (1963)
Gairdner	James Gairdner, *The Paston Letters* (6 vols, Library edition, 1904)
HMC	Historical Manuscripts Commission
Magd. Coll.	Magdalen College, Oxford

NRO	Norfolk Record Office
PCC	Prerogative Court of Canterbury
Parr	Robert T. L. Parr, 'Yoxford Yesterday' (8 typescript vols, begun in 1907 and not completed before 1947, unpublished; in the Borough Library, Ipswich)
Pevsner	Nikolaus Pevsner, *The Buildings of England* (1951–74)
PRO	Public Record Office
Rot Parl	*Rotuli Parliamentorum* (1767–77)
A Royalist's Notebook	*A Royalist's Notebook, the Commonplace Book of Sir John Oglander of Nunwell, 1622–1652*, ed. Francis Bamford (1936)
SRO	Suffolk Record Office
Staffs RO	Staffordshire Record Office
The Stonor Letters and Papers	*The Stonor Letters and Papers*, ed. C. L. Kingsford, Camden Society, Third Series (2 vols, 1919)
Test Ebor	*Testamenta Eboracensia*, ed. James Raine and others, Surtees Society (1836–1902)
VCH	Victoria County History
Walberswick Churchwardens Accounts	*Walberswick Churchwardens' Accounts, A.D. 1450–1499*, ed. R. W. M. Lewis (1947)
Wedgwood	J. C. Wedgwood, *History of Parliament, Biographies of the Members of the Commons House 1439–1509* (H.M.S.O., 1936)

Thorp Perrow
YORK
LEEDS
Swillington
Mirfield Ackworth
Thornhill
Castle Carlton Saltfleetby
Tibshelf Ingleby
South Wingfield LINCOLN
Crich
NOTTINGHAM Gonalston
Bunny Widmerpool
Kirby Bellars
LEICESTER
Great and
Little Stretton

See Map 2
NORWICH
Walbersw
Blythburgh
Yoxford Westle
IPSWICH

LONDON

Map 1

NORWICH

GREAT
YARMOUTH

Pirnhow Ellingham

LOWESTOFT

BECCLES

COVEHITHE

HARLESTON   Westhall

Wissett   Easton Bavents

HALESWORTH   SOUTHWOLD

EYE   Blythburgh   Walberswick
            Thorington

                        DUNWICH
         SIBTON

              Westleton
FRAMLINGHAM   Yoxford Middleton

WICKHAM MARKET

                    ORFORD

WOODBRIDGE

IPSWICH

Map 2

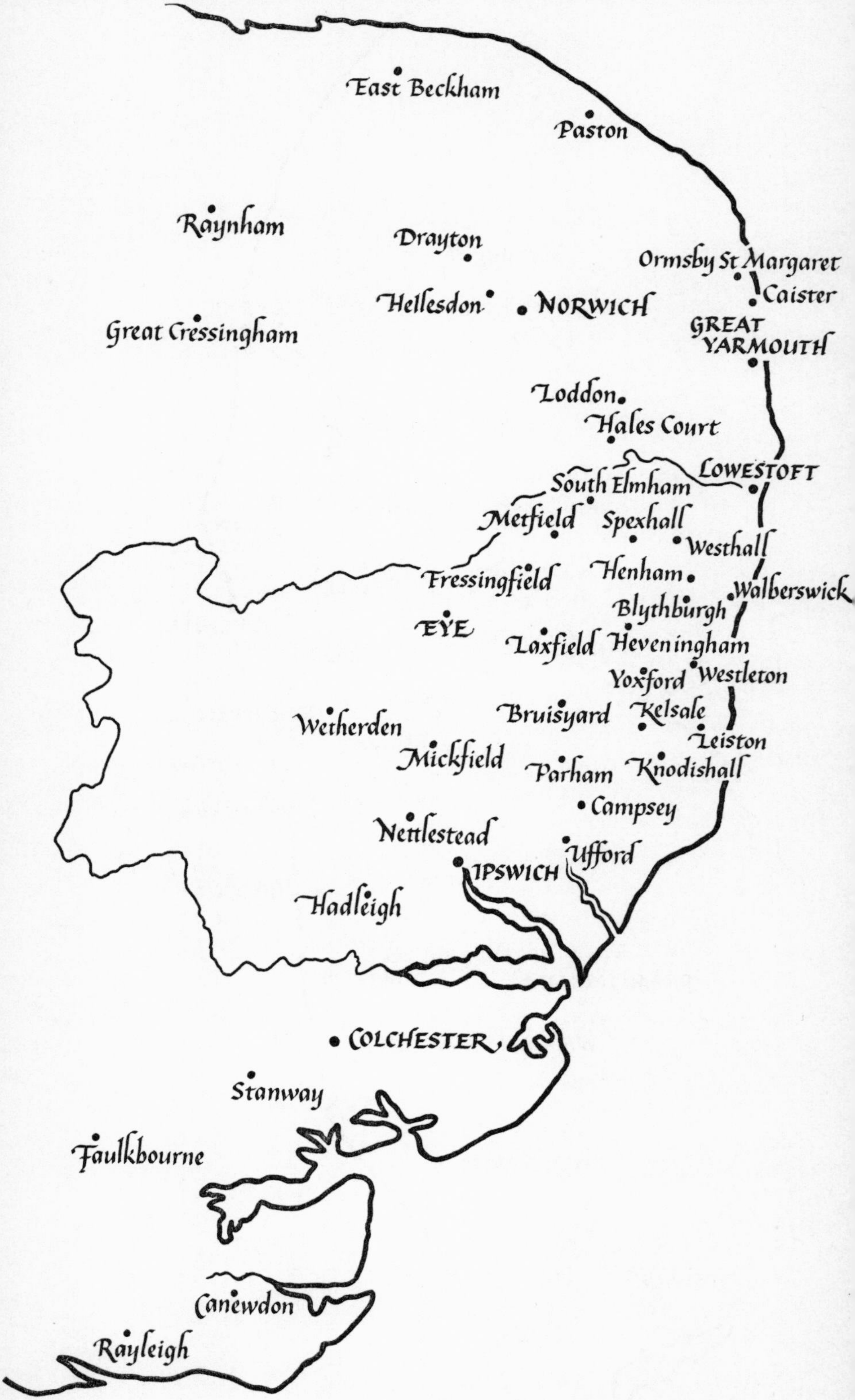

East Beckham

Paston

Raynham

Drayton

Ormsby St Margaret

Hellesdon   NORWICH   Caister

Great Cressingham   GREAT
YARMOUTH

Loddon

Hales Court

LOWESTOFT

South Elmham

Metfield   Spexhall

Westhall

Fressingfield   Henham   Walberswick

EYE   Blythburgh

Laxfield   Heveningham

Yoxford   Westleton

Wetherden   Bruisyard   Kelsale

Mickfield   Leiston

Parham   Knodishall

Campsey

Nettlestead

Ufford

IPSWICH

Hadleigh

• COLCHESTER

Stanway

Faulkbourne

Canewdon

Rayleigh

Map 3

INTRODUCTION

> I have composed the text of this present book as I best might...
> the beginning I have put in the beginning, and the end at the end.
>
> From the prologue to *The Anglo-Saxon version of the Life of
> St Guthlac*, trans and ed. C. W. Goodwin (1848), p7

I stumbled on John Hopton one summer in the late 1960s. At the
Suffolk Record Office, Ipswich, I had out the rough account
book of Hopton's Blythburgh bailiff, Nicholas Greenhagh.[1]
Later that summer or the next I looked at other fifteenth century
documents in the collection from which it came, the Blois Family
Deposit, and in no considered way pondered the possibility of
working on the gentleman whom they concerned, John Hopton.
At Christmas 1970 I sat down to discover something about him
from the ordinary, published sources. I was surprised at what I
found.

I had expected, had been looking for indeed, a typical figure,
one of 'those gentlemen whose aggressive self-confidence, intem-
perate acquisitiveness and blatant family pride set the tone of
English history between the fourteenth and eighteenth centuries'.[2]
Such a man is worth studying because I happen to think the
inscription of 1633 on Leominster old town hall is accurate for
the later Middle Ages: 'Like columnes do upprop the fabrik of a
building, so noble gentry dos support the honor of a kingdom.'[3]
The gentry's political importance is not to be denied, and politically active I had found most of them to be; for example, if they
were worth anything (in wealth, status, influence) they sat in
parliament. I anticipated that John Hopton would fall into this
pattern: playing a part in local government and local affairs,

[1] For which see chapter 2, pp33–4.
[2] *Social History*, vol 3, no. 1 (Jan. 1978), p122.
[3] Pevsner, *Shropshire*, p228.

sometimes (perhaps often) at odds with his neighbours, prone to throw his weight about, and politically involved, either through a connection with a local magnate or by some affiliation made at the heart of political life at Westminster – for his adult life spanned most of the Wars of the Roses. He turned out differently.

For one thing, as my views on fifteenth century gentry and the fifteenth century generally were altered by what I 'found' John Hopton to be, so how I wanted to present them changed. What became important to describe now was not just John Hopton but also the society in which he lived; for that society, which was as much a product of my assumptions as John Hopton previously had been, might, from an angle of vision starting at him, be rather different. Hence chapter 4 soon became what I was working towards. It was also a necessity. The amount of material on John Hopton himself was limited, even more limited by the fact of his being the man he turned out to be; moreover, most of it concerned his estates and I did not want to lose him in a study of his property. If I was going to keep him in view I had to see him beside his 'acquaintances, neighbours and friends'. Only a description of his context would bring him out. It is a local and a Suffolk context because I believe that is his context, but two criticisms might be (and have been) made: he ought perhaps to be seen against a broader social background and in a wider geographical one – the West Riding of Yorkshire and London should figure more than they do.[4] Maybe so. Indeed his being a Yorkshireman living in Suffolk, and his being a wealthy Yorkshireman at that, could be the reasons why he is not the typical gentleman I had expected; on the one hand he was an outsider, on the other a rich one: possibly obliged to be independent, certainly he could afford to be.

My having come across this particular fifteenth century gentleman (I nearly put this particular type of gentleman) has produced another peculiarity of the book he has led me to write. There is not much, hardly any comparative material in it. I have not gone looking for other John Hoptons in counties other than Suffolk, nor have I used him as a means to ask general questions about the

4 Here I am grateful to Rees Davies.

gentry and their society; as to whether he is in some or many aspects typical, more or less so than for instance the image I once had of a gentleman in that century, and to what extent the local world he lived in is one discernible elsewhere have been none of my business. I have left that to others. The presentation of as near as I could get to the real particularity of one gentleman at one place at one time is all I have tried to achieve.

One generalization I will venture on. If John Hopton is to fifteenth century politics as Rosencrantz and Guildenstern are to Hamlet, then we ought possibly to consider rewriting the play. Ten years' association with John Hopton has not only made me fond of him,[5] but also makes me think I know him and his society: I feel I can say as William Worcester wrote to John Paston, 'I am of hys contrey and know hys rysyng and maryages aswell as hymsylf.'[6] I may be deceiving myself, but if I am not, John Hopton and his like (presuming there are any) are more important than I had assumed. English fifteenth century life might not so much bear Huizinga's 'mixed smell of blood and roses'[7] as the odour of Hoskins' 'very small beer'.[8] I believe it does. Alongside Borges' single marvellous line 'over us looms atrocious history' I would like to set this book.

[5] 'Attempts to write biographies without empathy for the subject of the work...are schoolboys' jokes or exercises in sleights of mind.' Julia Namier, *Lewis Namier* (1971), p306.
[6] Davies II, p178.
[7] *The Waning of the Middle Ages* (Penguin ed., 1955), p26.
[8] 'But real life at any time is mostly very small beer (only some historians contrive to inflate it).' W. G. Hoskins, *English Local History, the Past and the Future*, an inaugural lecture delivered in the University of Leicester, 3 March 1966 (Leicester 1967), p8.

THE SWILLINGTONS
and JOHN HOPTON

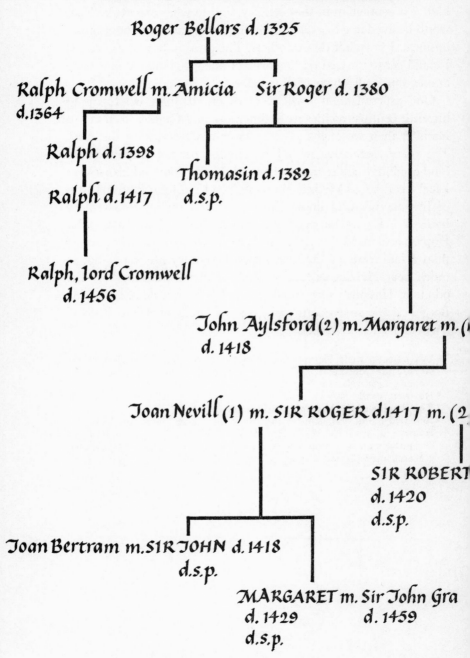

Roger Bellars d. 1325

Ralph Cromwell m. Amicia   Sir Roger d. 1380
d. 1364

Ralph d. 1398

Ralph d. 1417   Thomasin d. 1382
d.s.p.

Ralph, lord Cromwell
d. 1456

John Aylsford (2) m. Margaret m. (
d. 1418

Joan Nevill (1) m. SIR ROGER d. 1417 m. (2

SIR ROBERT
d. 1420
d.s.p.

Joan Bertram m. SIR JOHN d. 1418
d.s.p.

MARGARET m. Sir John Gra
d. 1429   d. 1459
d.s.p.

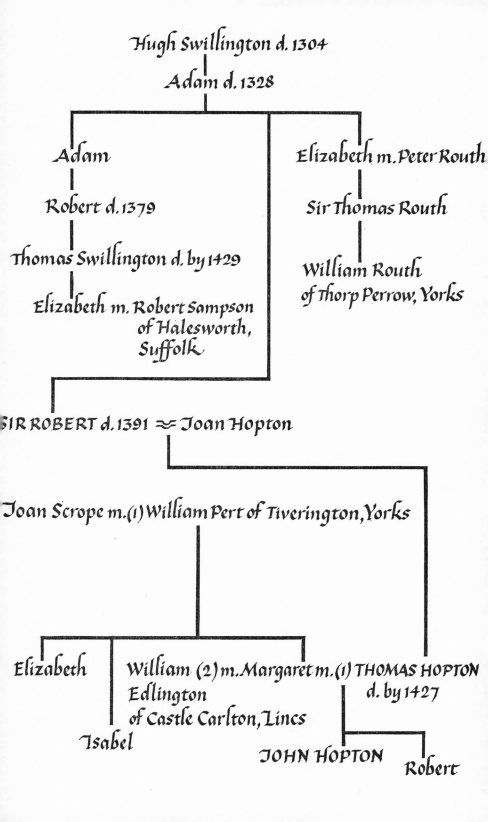

Hugh Swillington d. 1304

Adam d. 1328

Adam

Robert d. 1379

Thomas Swillington d. by 1429

Elizabeth m. Robert Sampson
of Halesworth,
Suffolk

Elizabeth m. Peter Routh

Sir Thomas Routh

William Routh
of Thorp Perrow, Yorks

SIR ROBERT d. 1391 ≈ Joan Hopton

Joan Scrope m.(1) William Pert of Tiverington, Yorks

Elizabeth

William (2) m. Margaret m.(1) THOMAS HOPTON
Edlington   d. by 1427
of Castle Carlton, Lincs

Isabel

JOHN HOPTON

Robert

I

HOW JOHN HOPTON OBTAINED HIS LIVELIHOOD

...for it is resonable a gentilman to know his pedegre and his possibilyte: seynt Poule foryete nat to write to the Romayns of what lynage he was descended, Ad Romanos xj.

> Thomas Gate to Thomas Stonor,
> 5 October between 1460 and 1474
> *The Stonor Letters and Papers* I, p136

'A most interesting dinner. There was a M. de la Raspelière there who kept us spell-bound with his explanation of how that Mme de Saint-Loup with the pretty daughter is not really a Forcheville at all. It was as good as a novel.'

> Marcel Proust,
> *Remembrance of Things Past*, vol 12 (Chatto and Windus paperback edition, 1967), p354

John Hopton was a fortunate man. On 7 February 1430 the escheators of various counties were ordered to hand over to him numerous estates which had been found to be his by virtue of enfeoffments made some seventeen years previously by Sir Roger Swillington, the half-brother of John's father Thomas Hopton.[1] Such a windfall was not entirely unexpected in 1430. Three years before, on 26 February 1427, in an indenture between Thomas Saville of Thornhill, Yorks, and the guardians of John Hopton (then styled John Swillington) for the marriage of Saville's daughter Margaret to John, mention was made of 'what time of good fortune any of the reversions falle'.[2] The young man clearly had good, albeit still unsettled, prospects. At any rate Thomas Saville thought them worth taking a risk for; his gamble on the

---

[1] *CFR 1422–30*, pp313–19. The first court held in his name at Westwood, for his two chief Suffolk properties, Blythburgh and Walberswick, was on 22 February 1430: SRO, HA 30/312/194.

[2] BL, Lansdowne MS 255, f242 (new numbering), a copy made 17 April 1642 from the original in the possession of William Saville bart of Thornhill. See Parr III, pp220–1.

quality of his daughter's future life paid off in 1430. Still, if Hopton's own future looked bright in 1427, at the time of the actual enfeoffments a dozen years earlier that future was barely worth consideration at all.

Sir Roger Swillington had made careful provision for the descent of the bulk of his property; indeed it was just his care to leave nothing to chance that led directly to John Hopton's dramatic enrichment in 1430. His fortune stemmed not from some oversight or omission in the schemes of men, but from death, infertility, and the incompatibility of husband and wife, to which the best laid plans have perforce to yield. Sir Roger had settled his estates on his son John and the heirs male of his body, with remainders successively to his second son Robert and the heirs male of his body, to the daughters of John and their heirs, to the daughters of Robert and their heirs, to Margaret his daughter and the heirs of her body, to Thomas Hopton and his sons, to Sir Thomas Routh and his sons. Between 1417 and 1429 Sir Roger, his wife Joan (who held certain of these properties for her life), Sir John and Robert Swillington, and Margaret (married to Sir John Gra of Ingleby, Lincs.), all died. Sir John, Robert and Margaret left no children. During that time Thomas Hopton too had died.[3] His son John was therefore the final beneficiary of the original settlement. The wheel of fortune had spun dizzily, then come to rest where Sir Roger Swillington was not likely to have expected it; it was his thoughtful preparation for eventualities which he could not have seriously contemplated that made out of a bastard's son a substantial country gentleman. It was a startling conversion, and to grasp it fully we must trace John Hopton's story back a long way before 1430.

We have to begin where John Hopton began, in Yorkshire; for while the greater part of his life was spent in Suffolk, he was a Yorkshireman, as were his predecessors at Blythburgh, the Swillingtons. They came from the village of that name which lies a few miles to the south east of Leeds in the valley of the Aire, where they had been long established. By the late thirteenth

[3] *CFR 1422–30*, pp313–19; see also *CCR 1492–35*, p101, *CPR 1413–16*, p55.

century they had added to their Yorkshire properties estates in Suffolk and Norfolk; these Hugh Swillington, who died in 1304, had obtained by his marriage to Helewise Pirnhow.[4] Adam, the second surviving son of Hugh, was a retainer of Thomas of Lancaster,[5] and was summoned to parliament in the first year of Edward III's reign. He died in 1328. This promise of a wider than merely provincial importance went unfulfilled in the main line of the family; Adam's eldest son, also Adam, died young and his son Robert, who died in 1379,[6] was of little consequence. It was his uncle Sir Robert, the second son of Adam (d. 1328), who was the successful member of the family. He obtained from his nephew the greater part of the family estates in Yorkshire and East Anglia,[7] under what terms we do not know, but it was entirely in keeping with the grand figure cut by the representative of the junior branch, and the sorry one cut by that of the main line, that Sir Robert should acquire the patrimony. For Sir Robert Swillington was undoubtedly a man of ability, whose talents for war and qualities as administrator and counsellor were recognised and made use of by king and Duke of Lancaster alike. To trace the career of this serviceable younger son is not our purpose here; indeed it would require a chapter to itself. His career followed a not unusual pattern for the fourteenth century, and is in no way remarkable save in its degree of achievement. John of Gaunt's retainers were a group of all the talents, and Sir Robert Swillington, holding most of his Yorkshire properties of the Duchy of Lancaster honour of Pontefract, of which he was steward, found his niche there, among his near neighbours and friends, Sir John Saville of Elland, Sir William Scargill of Thorpe Stapleton, and Hugh Waterton of Methley; yet he clearly was the brightest of stars even in that brilliant firmament, being Gaunt's chamberlain of the household and one of his councillors.[8] To John of Gaunt,

[4] *CP* XII, 578; see also the Rev. Canon Beanlands, 'The Swillingtons of Swillington', Thoresby Society, xv, *Miscellanea* (1909), pp185–211.
[5] G. Holmes, *The Estates of the Higher Nobility in Fourteenth Century England* (1957), p71.
[6] *Test Ebor* I, p107.
[7] Beanlands, p205.
[8] *John of Gaunt's Register 1372–76*, ed. S. Armitage-Smith, Camden Society, Third Series, XXI (1911), *passim* (*sub* index); *The Controversy*

arguably the most successful politician of the English Middle Ages (William the Marshal always excepted), Swillington rendered steady service and gave (no doubt) wise counsel; and Gaunt's success was both the product of such advice and the cause of his advisor's prosperity. Never out of royal favour, Gaunt throughout his long career could always secure for his followers the patronage at the disposal of the king; this, and not only his own vast wealth, was the key to his power, and he and his councillors never lost sight of it. He never made, or was never allowed to make, the mistake of his wife's grandfather Thomas: Gaunt died in his bed surrounded by a large and loyal retinue, he was not struck down, a failed because deserted leader.

It was a major contribution to this happy and stable situation that so many of Gaunt's retainers were also retained by the king. Swillington was one of these. He was retained as a yeoman by Edward III as early as 1350, with an annuity of £10 per annum for his good service and for his staying in the king's service; this fee and other subsequent royal favours were confirmed by Richard II in February 1378.[9] He had long been in Gaunt's service by that time, having received from the duke in August 1362, for example, lands for life over and above the value of £60 a year in lieu of an annual cash payment of that amount.[10] Of the opportunities this service offered him Sir Robert made much. Of the profits (if any) of his military service we have no sure record: their assistance to his prosperity must remain an open question. An advantageous marriage – 'the beginning of worldly wisdom'[11] – was however one opportunity he did not miss. He took as second wife[12] Margaret, daughter and co-heiress of Sir Roger Bellars of Leicestershire; on the death of her father in 1380 and her sister in

between Sir Richard Scrope and Sir Robert Grosvenor, ed. Sir N. H. Nicolas (1832), I, pp58, 112, 203; II, pp190, 214, 302; Robert Somerville, History of the Duchy of Lancaster, I (1953), p112, and sub index.

9 CPR 1348–50, p541; CPR 1377–81, pp134–5.

10 CPR 1361–4, p397.

11 K. B. McFarlane, Lancastrian Kings and Lollard Knights (1972), p172. See Anthony Trollope, Doctor Thorne (Everyman edition, 1908, reprinted 1975), passim, especially pp198–9.

12 He seems to have made an early first marriage in 1348: Beanlands, pp204–5. He was married to Margaret by autumn 1375: CIPM xiv, pp111–12; CFR 1368–77, pp319–20.

1382, she brought him substantial properties in Derbyshire, Nottinghamshire and Leicestershire.[13] That he benefited in all the innumerable other ways open to such a valuable and valued servant is finally and most obviously demonstrated by his will and in his *inquisition post mortem*. The generosity of his bequests to the men of his own household and to the women of his wife's, the 500 marks for his daughter's marriage, the £100 to his younger son Richard, speak for themselves: he had the means to be munificent. His landed property was the basis for this liberality; his 35 manors were concentrated in Yorkshire, the central Midlands, and Suffolk. In the absence of estate documents there is little reason to doubt the general accuracy of Sir Arthur Hopton's statement to Leland over a century later, that the 'Swillingtons. . . sum tyme were menne of 2000. markes of landes by the yere or more',[14] and that this was the time at which they were. How important his marriage had been to him is shown not only by the number of properties of his wife – and their comparative valuation in relation to the other properties – listed in his inquisition, but also by the fact that he made his will at Stanford, Notts, one of her estates, and desired to be buried in Kirby Bellars Priory rather than at Swillington. Nor did he forget his master, the Duke of Lancaster: Gaunt was made an overseer of his will and he left him his best goblet of gold and silver and his best horse. He died in July 1391.[15] It is with some reluctance that we leave him.

We cannot leave him quite yet. It was a measure of the man that he should at his death remember his bastard: he left £20 'a Thomas de Hopton bastardo'. And too that he did not forget the woman who was (it seems likely) Thomas' mother: to Joan Hopton he left an annuity of £2 for life.[16] There is no reason to doubt that Thomas Hopton was Sir Robert's son, and every reason to believe it: the evidence of the will, the association of

---

[13] *CIPM* xv, pp130–4, 195–6; PRO, C136/73/61; *CCR 1377–81*, p435; *CFR 1377–83*, pp245–6.
[14] *Itinerary*, ed. L. T. Smith (Centaur Press edition, 1964), II, p19.
[15] His will: PRO, PCC 8 Rous (Probate 11/1) printed in *Early Lincoln Wills, 1280–1547*, ed. A. A. Gibbons (Lincoln 1888), p77; dated 7 July, proved 22 July. 11 July is given as the date of his death in his *IPM*: PRO, C136/73/61.
[16] PRO, PCC 8 Rous.

Thomas Hopton with Sir Roger Swillington, Sir Robert's son and heir and the enfeoffments of Sir Roger with their remainders to Thomas and his male heirs. Moreover, there was the later and successful attempt of the Hoptons to obscure the manner in which they obtained the bulk of the Swillington properties, for the Hoptons by the sixteenth century had fabricated a pedigree and tampered with the quarterings of their arms to disguise their descent from a bastard line. They achieved their purpose for as long as it mattered.[17] It seems that Thomas' mother was of gentle birth, from a family which was near neighbour to the Swillingtons; the Hoptons of Armley, Mirfield and Ackworth, in their various branches are not easy to disentangle, but it appears that Joan was of this local family. The young John Hopton in 1427 had lands in Ackworth and thereabouts, and it is probable that he had inherited these from his father, as his guardians were enfeoffed in them to his use; how these had come to Thomas is not clear. His half-brother Sir Roger had granted him a small property in Ufton, Derbyshire, for his life, but it was to revert to the Swillington family on his death.[18] All this was small beer indeed; nevertheless it was more than most bastards ever got. Sir Robert and Sir Roger's concern for the welfare of Thomas Hopton – he may have been a useful man for Sir Roger to have in Yorkshire, and he was one of his feoffees for Swillington itself[19] – shows that the relationship between them was a close and enduring one. Thomas' illegitimacy was no bar to friendship with his half-brother and with Sir Roger's substantial Yorkshire neighbours, for William Scargill was one of the guardians of his son and Thomas Saville was ready enough to marry a daughter to that son. By then of course the Swillington lands were in prospect and John Hopton had changed his name to be ready for them, a change that was curiously impermanent, yet is a witness, as are the enfeoffments that engendered it, to the nearness of Hoptons and Swillingtons. Surely none of this could have been if Thomas' mother had not been a gentlewoman.

[17] Beanlands, p208. Parr I, p218; *Visitations of Suffolk 1561, 1577, 1612,* ed. W. C. Metcalfe (1882), p43. Davy's MSS collection of Suffolk pedigrees has the correct Hopton descent: BL, Add MS 19136 f100.
[18] *CFR 1422–30,* p316.   [19] *CCR 1422–29,* p347.

We must now, however, return to Sir Robert's son and heir Roger. He had been knighted by the summer of 1396[20] but there is no evidence of his activity, official or otherwise, before the usurpation of September 1399. Then the family's link with the new royal house of Lancaster was restored, if indeed it had ever been broken. On 25 February 1400 Henry IV granted Sir Roger an annuity of £40 for life: he was styled a king's knight.[21] He was still so styled in Henry's V's reign,[22] yet Sir Roger in no way emulated his father; while he was a useful Lancastrian servant in local government he never sought, or was required, to exercise his talents beyond that limited sphere. His summons to attend the Great Council at Westminster in August 1401 had no sequel.[23] He appears to have been a quiet and dependable supporter of the new regime with no pretensions. Only in one respect perhaps did he render Henry IV a more than routine service: he went to live on his Suffolk estates. This of course could have been his own inclination, for his mother (who had married John Aylsford by 1396,[24] and who survived her son by almost a year) held some Midland estates including Kirby Bellars during her lifetime.[25] Yet while his move from the West Riding can only have been by choice, the king may well have been the prompter or promoter of that choice. In the West Riding Lancastrian influence was powerful, in Suffolk it was not; to have Sir Roger there, if not a necessity, was certainly an advantage. He made the move some time in or shortly after 1403. While in December 1399 and May 1402 he was on Yorkshire commissions, by September 1403 he was a commissioner of array both in the West Riding and in Suffolk, and in May 1406 for Suffolk alone; and while on the commission of the peace for the West Riding from May 1401 to February 1407, his service then ceased there, but continued in

[20] *CPR 1391–6*, p723.
[21] *CPR 1399–1401*, p221.
[22] *CCR 1413–19*, p215.
[23] *Proceedings and Ordinances of the Privy Council of England*, ed. Sir N. H. Nicolas (Record Commissions 1834–7), I, pp157, 159.
[24] *CPR 1391–6*, p723. Margaret had been assigned dower in the Suffolk estates; Sir Roger bought her and her husband out for a rent of 100 marks per annum: see PRO, C136/73/61 and C138/28/46.
[25] *CPR 1399–1401*, p213; *CPR 1401–5*, pp129, 288–9.

Suffolk, where he had been first appointed in November 1403, into Henry V's reign, albeit intermittently.[26] It was at Blythburgh that he took up residence, and between 1404 and 1408 he obtained various confirmations of his rights there, including that of holding a weekly market on Thursdays and three fairs yearly,[27] and got a charter of free warren.[28] More important, in terms of the royal favour to himself and to his tenants at Blythburgh and at Walberswick, a long quarrel between the burgesses of Dunwich and the Swillingtons over the use of the continually shifting harbour mouth that served these ports was settled, at least for the time being, with the royal licence. Sir Roger and his tenants were the beneficiaries.[29] Manifestly there was now a resident lord at Blythburgh.

Sir Roger also married again. His first wife had been Joan, daughter of Sir Robert Nevill of Hornby, Lancs. She had died by 1407, as by that year Sir Roger was married to Joan, daughter of Stephen Scrope, widow of William Pert of Tiverington, Yorks. This marriage brought him the manor of Castle Carlton, Lincs,[30] and (somewhat unusually) a son-in-law who was his own half-brother, Thomas Hopton. Or it was shortly to bring him such a son-in-law, for Thomas Hopton at some point married Margaret, Joan's third daughter by William Pert.[31] That marriage cannot have been long after, and may have been before Sir Roger's own marriage, for Margaret Pert was the mother of our John Hopton, and John was certainly of age in 1429 (even if his age, as then given by the jurors of the *inquisition post mortem* on Margaret Gra as twenty-four, does not altogether tally with the fact of his having guardians two years previously). This would, however, suggest that the half-brothers were both married by 1407, the one

26 *CPR 1399–1401*, pp213, 567; *CPR 1401–5*, pp129, 288, 289, 519, 521; *CPR 1405–8*, pp231, 497, 500; *CPR 1413–16*, p423; *CPR 1416–22*, p460.
27 *CPR 1401–5*, p353; *CPR 1405–8*, p455.
28 SRO, HA 30/312/1.
29 *CCR 1405–9*, pp336–8; BL, Add Charter 40673, see SRO, HA 30/369/327; *CPR 1408–13*, pp206–7, see SRO, HA 30/50/22/27/1.
30 *CCR 1405–9*, p174. Stephen Scrope was (according to Nicolas) the fourth son of Sir Geoffrey Scrope of Masham: *Scrope and Grosvenor Controversy* II, p332.
31 *CFR 1461–7*, p190 and *CFR 1422–30*, p207.

to the mother, the other to the daughter: one wonders whether both unions were arranged together and took place at the same time. It would help us better to understand this rather curious episode if we knew the relative ages of the half-brothers; Sir Roger was said to be twenty-two years old at his father's death in 1391 and, if that statement has any accuracy, he died before his fiftieth year in 1417. Thomas Hopton was dead by February 1427, and his widow had taken a second husband by December of that year. But the fact that Thomas survived his half-brother, though by how long is uncertain,[32] tells us nothing about his age: he could have been an old man who married a young wife *c.* 1407, or he may have still been young himself. If his conception had been a youthful venture of Sir Robert, before his probable first marriage in 1348, Thomas would have been a very old man to have taken such a wife in the first decade of the fifteenth century and to have fathered two sons, John and Robert. All in all it seems more likely that Thomas was a bastard of Sir Robert's maturity and that Sir Roger and he were pretty close in age. They were evidently close enough in other respects, for Sir Roger must have been the matchmaker for his half-brother. Thomas was not likely to have aspired to such a bride on his own account: he cannot have had much to offer. He had at any rate now achieved respectability.[33]

The other testimony of that intimacy between the half-brothers was the series of enfeoffments made by Sir Roger, and it is to the complicated story of the working out of these that we must now turn. That Thomas Hopton and his male heirs were preferred ahead of the representatives of the former main branch of the Swillingtons – in Sir Roger's view (though not in the view of Chancery some years later) Sir Thomas Routh and his male heirs – does demonstrate that Sir Roger held his illegitimate brother in

[32] Presumably he did not die until after October 1420, for Ufton, which he held for life, descended directly to Margaret Gra; whereas if Thomas had died before October 1420 it would have gone to her brother Robert, who died in that month.

[33] Joan Pert's other two daughters had as their husbands respectable enough Yorkshire gentlemen: in 1427 Elizabeth was married to Roger Aske and Isobel to Robert Conyers: *CFR 1422–30*, p207.

9

high favour, even if he can hardly have imagined that the remainders would ever reach him. On 4 July 1413 Sir Roger made his enfeoffment of the manor of Wissett, Suffolk; on the following day he obtained the royal licence to settle Blythburgh after the same fashion.[34] That Sir Roger made similar arrangements for the bulk of his other estates – where he was able to do so – we know from the evidence of the *inquisition post mortem* on Margaret Gra of 1429, where it was discovered that John Hopton was the beneficiary under the terms of certain enfeoffments of those estates. The feoffees in these other estates, however, were different to those for Wissett and Blythburgh, being altogether far grander folk including as they did Robert, lord Willoughby of Eresby, Henry, lord Fitzhugh, and the Swillingtons' Suffolk neighbour, Sir John Heveningham. It seems certain nonetheless that the enfeoffments, if not the feoffees, were all of a piece, though most were probably later than 1413.[35] No one was, after all, much concerned with Thomas Hopton during Sir Roger's lifetime. It was not until he and his sons were dead that Thomas or his son John began to feature in the calculations of others. Meanwhile Sir Roger and his two sons died in a short space of time.

Sir Roger made his will at London on 24 and 26 November 1416.[36] Among other bequests he left a cup worth 10 marks and 10 marks in money to both Robert, lord Willoughby and Henry, lord Fitzhugh, and he left a cup of similar value and 5 marks in cash to John Heveningham the elder. To Richard Daniel, parson of Swillington and his executor, whom we shall meet again, he left 20 marks for his good and faithful service and to see to the carrying out of his will; and to Robert Sampson, whom we shall

---

[34] *CCR 1429–35*, p101; *CPR 1413–16*, p55; and see above pp1–2.
[35] In Margaret Gra's *IPM* the enfeoffments are not dated. Sir Roger made enfeoffments of his chief Yorkshire estates in December 1416 and February 1417 – after he had made his will: Lord Fitzhugh was then one of the feoffees (*CCR 1413–19*, pp404–6); he also had the same group of feoffees for the remainder of his Suffolk properties (*CCR 1413–19*, pp400–2); but we are not of course told of the full scope of the settlements on these occasions. The descent as outlined in the Blythburgh and Wissett enfeoffments, and inferred for the other properties, was complicated between 1417 and 1427 by Joan Pert, Sir Roger's widow, holding many of the estates in dower or because they had been settled on her for life.
[36] Will; PRO, Probate 11/2B (PCC 38 Marche).

also soon encounter, he left 2 marks. To Thomas Hopton and to his cousin Thomas Swillington, the last in the direct male line of the main branch of the family, he left indifferently 10 marks each. Most of his religious bequests were to London friaries, or to houses and churches on or near his Suffolk estates – such as Blythburgh Priory which received £5, the parish church of Blythburgh which received his best missal and best antiphoner, and the parish church, 'quondam capella', of Walberswick – while at Dunwich the friars were to sing for his soul. Most of the men who got small gifts were also from the Suffolk he knew: John Paynell of Westleton, John Keswick of Wissett and an officer of his, William Wolsey of Blythburg, John Croxton, 'serviens Garnarie mee apud Hyngton', and Thomas Northales. He left 8s 4d for the repair of the bridge at Blythburgh. There is no doubt that, Yorkshireman though he was, he had turned his back on the shires and had become a Suffolk gentleman. He also left £10 to Kirby Bellars Priory, but unlike his father he did not wish to be buried there; it was in the house of friars at Ludgate in London that he desired burial.

Sir Roger did not die, according to his *inquisition post mortem*, until 6 August 1417; his will was proved on 12 August and his widow Joan and Richard Daniel were given administration of it. It may be that Sir Roger made his will as a preliminary to his taking part in Henry V's campaign to conquer Normandy; preparations were under way for that enterprise by the autumn of 1416. There is, however, no record of him serving in the expedition which sailed in July 1417. But Sir Roger's son and heir John, who had been on the Agincourt campaign,[37] did serve in the expedition of 1417.[38] When he made his indenture in February 1417 he was an esquire; when he took possession of his father's lands in October he was a knight.[39] He was then said to be twenty-five years old and had less than a year to live. He died in April

---

[37] With 4 men at arms and 11 archers; his brother-in-law Sir John Gra also served: Sir N. H. Nicolas, *The Battle of Agincourt* (1832), pp380, 385; see PRO, E 404/31/228 and Gra E 404/31/379, E 101/69/3/375.
[38] PRO, E 101/70/2/593, with one other man at arms and 6 archers; Sir John Gra served on the same terms: E 101/70/3/624.
[39] *CFR 1413–22*, p212.

1418, leaving no children by his wife Joan, daughter of Sir John Bertram.[40]

On the very day the writ for his *inquisition post mortem* was issued, so was another for his grandmother, Margaret Bellars. He had died on 2 April, she on 9 April.[41] She had not held much property during her second marriage (to John Aylsford), having made over to Sir Roger almost all her valuable Nottinghamshire and Derbyshire manors in return for an annual rent of 210 marks; she retained only Bunny, Notts, and Kirby, Leics.[42] As, however, she also received 100 marks a year from Sir Roger for her Suffolk dower interests, she and her second husband enjoyed a comfortable income – with none of the disadvantages of having to collect it – from these rents alone. Just over £200 a year, with no family to support, allowed Margaret an affluent old age, and should have made John Aylsford a contented man. Equally that £200 must have bitten deeply into Sir Roger's resources; having to find such a sum every year – and it was he who had all the trouble of raising it – may have been one of the reasons for the apparent difference in status and influence between him and his father. Having a long lived dowager in the family could be a real handicap in the late Middle Ages. A second wife, for example, might be a joy and a solace to an ageing parent, but the sons of his first wife would have mixed feelings about her.[43] However, Margaret was Sir John's own mother; and John died almost as soon as he had taken possession of his patrimony and he had too little time to

[40] Perhaps Wigston Magna, Leics, was settled on them by her father: *CCR 1413–19*, p492.
[41] *CFR 1413–22*, p238; dates of death as given in their *IPMs*: PRO, C138/31/24, C138/32/26.
[42] *CCR 1413–19*, pp400–2; PRO, C138/32/26.
[43] There were problems also for sons-in-law, if they had married daughters who were heiresses. The emotional complexities of having a stepmother-in-law and 'a bouncing stepmother' are examined at brilliant length by Henry James in *The Golden Bowl*. The phrase is Charlotte's describing herself: 'it can't in the least have appeared to him hitherto a matter of course that you should give his wife a bouncing stepmother' (Penguin ed.), p184. While we are given to understand that the Prince has married Maggie for her money, the dramatic potentiality of any settlements Adam Verver might have made in favour of his second wife is not, so far as I noticed, even alluded to.

find out just how that patrimony had been depleted by the life interests in it of his stepmother, Joan Pert.

It was her son, his half-brother Robert, who was Sir John's heir. Even though he was her son this did not alter the fact that the estates she held for life were denied to him as they had been to Sir John. Moreover, Sir John's wife survived him and she also was assigned her dower from the Swillington lands.[44] Robert, however, was not to enjoy for long even those properties he did have. He was barely twenty-one when his half-brother died in 1418, and he was already involved in the war in Normandy. In 1419 he was serving at Pontoise[45] and had been knighted, but he was killed at the siege of Melun in October the following year.[46] He had not married. His heir was his older half-sister Margaret, married to Sir John Gra of Ingleby, Lincs; she was given livery of Sir Robert's lands in March 1421.[47] The male line of the Swillingtons had come to a sudden end. Yet even though the young John Hopton assumed the name Swillington at this time – for after all his paternal grandfather had been a Swillington – his chance of gaining the estates which went with the name was still slim: Margaret Gra was about thirty years old[48] and had a husband. But fortune contrived to smile upon him, indeed one wonders if she were not wearing – on one side of her face at least – a wide and malicious grin, for by October 1423 Margaret and her husband were living apart, she with her aunt Margaret Nevill, the wife of Sir William Harrington of Hornby, Lancs.[49] No longer in her first youth, her prospect of having children by Sir John Gra was now even more remote. Sir John, a combative man by all accounts, had in 1424 to be constrained under a bond of 500 marks to keep the peace towards her and to treat her honourably

[44] *CCR 1413–19*, pp477, 492.

[45] *Deputy Keeper of the Public Records, 41st Report* (1880), pp690, 711, 793.

[46] The Commission to array his retinue at Melun was dated 2 October (*ibid.*, *42nd Report* (1881), p391); dates of death given by the jurors at his *IPM* held in January 1421 were 5 and 12 October: PRO, C138/48/71.

[47] *CFR 1413–22*, pp355–6. They were married by 13 August 1411: Magdalen College, Oxford, Multon Hall 54 and 61. He also called himself Graa, but as he preferred Gra I have used that.

[48] According to Sir Robert's *IPM*: PRO, C138/48/71.

[49] J. S. Roskell, *The Commons in the Parliament of 1422* (1954), p81.

and peaceably.[50] If he had been attempting to drag her back it was no doubt because he would stand to lose so much if she died childless before him; he had property of his own but it was little compared to what she had.[51] This he now enjoyed with her; if, however, she were to die before he did and they had produced no children, he would have no right to it by courtesy. And that, despite his violence in 1424, was how it turned out: Margaret died childless in 1429 and Sir John was left to fight for another thirty years for what he could salvage from his barren marriage.

It was this unhappy union and Sir John's dilemma which make the marriage agreement of February 1427 between Thomas Saville and John Hopton's guardians so much more understandable. By that time there was little likelihood of Margaret Gra having any heirs of her body: she was in her late thirties and still (presumably) estranged from her husband. Thomas Saville was not after all taking such a gamble: 'John Hopton was a youth of great expectations'.[52] What Thomas was gambling on was not whether the reversions in young John's favour would fall in (there was little risk there), but when.[53] He bound himself in the indenture to find John and Margaret in all things according to their degree; this arrangement was to lapse if and when the reversions fell in. Within six months of that looked for and happy occurrence John was to make a settlement of those properties on himself and Margaret and their children. In return for this Saville agreed to pay 400 marks within four years after the settlement was made. From that 400 marks, however, was to be subtracted all that he had spent on the young couple in the time between their marriage

[50] CCR 1422–9, p189.
[51] See, for instance, the figures in Roskell, p81.
[52] So Parr III, p222.
[53] Was Margaret poorly as well as childless? After all she was probably still short of 40 when she died. Even so, a sickly woman might recover *and* bear a child, as did Isobel the youthful wife of Robert Hylle. So ill was Isobel at 11 years old it was thought she could not live long. Robert therefore took what measures he could to secure for himself her inheritance in the event of that predicted early death; for £50 her next heir granted him a life interest in her lands. Then within five years Isobel recovered and had a son. 'And thus Robert had nothing for his £50 but ease of heart in the meanwhile': *The Hylle Cartulary*, ed. R. W. Dunning, Somerset Record Society, lxviii (1968), pp8–9. I am grateful to Graham Kent for bringing this reference to my notice.

and the drawing up of the settlement.[54] Clearly there might have come a point where, with the reversions still unripe and John and Margaret still living at his expense, Saville had exceeded his 400 marks, though he left himself plenty of time to manoeuvre and we would like to know precisely what degree it was to which John and Margaret were entitled in their maintenance: perhaps it would have deteriorated the nearer Thomas got to spending his 400 marks. As it was that situation cannot have arisen. Death came quickly to remove the remaining obstacles in Hopton's path, so neither he nor his father-in-law were kept waiting long. Sir Roger Swillingtons' widow, Joan Pert, was dead within seven months of the sealing of the marriage indenture: she died on 20 September 1427.[55] Her rich dower lands fell to Sir John and Margaret Gra.[56] They enjoyed them for barely two years before Margaret died on 7 October 1429.[57] That which had been unthinkable hardly more than a dozen years before had nevertheless occurred: Sir Roger Swillington's heirs, male and female, had all died, leaving not one child between them[58] and John Hopton came into what was, only by the widest use of the phrase, his own.

Any description of what lands he got in 1430 must necessarily involve a narrative of how he secured them against those who challenged his title, for with so much at issue such were not wanting, and must also include some mention of those lands

---

[54] BL, Lansdowne MS 255 f242.
[55] Thus her *IPM*: PRO, C139/35/52.   [56] *CCR 1422–9*, pp357–60.
[57] Thus her *IPM*: PRO, C139/46/40.
[58] Sir Roger Swillington is one of the 29 names collected by William Worcester of those lords and knights of Norfolk and Suffolk who had died without male issue in the reigns of Henry V and Henry VI. This was a continuation of his list of those who had died without male issue between the coronations of Edward III and Henry V, and who had been commemorated for that reason by Sir Thomas Erpingham in the East window he had given to the church of the Austin Friars at Norwich in 1419: Norwich Public Library MS 7197 f306. William was not of course being strictly accurate; when Sir Roger died in 1417 he left two sons. Nonetheless Swillington is properly on his list, as within three years of Sir Roger's death the family was extinct in the male line. Sir Thomas Erpingham (who would have known Sir Robert Swillington (d. 1391), as he too was a retainer of John of Gaunt, as well as Sir Roger) would no doubt have noted the end of yet another East Anglian family, even as the window, which displayed his interest in such things – he himself having no children – was going up: see K. B. McFarlane, *The Nobility of Later Medieval England* (1973), pp145–6.

which did not come to him. These last were principally the Bellars inheritance which Margaret Bellars had brought into the Swillington family by her marriage to Sir Robert (d. 1391); now, in 1429 on the death of Margaret Gra, the last of that branch of the family, they fell to Margaret Bellars' own right heir, the influential Midland magnate Ralph, lord Cromwell.[59] These were substantial properties, as we shall see. Cromwell had no difficulty in securing Kirby, Leics; this manor, along with those of South Wingfield and Tibshelf, Derbys, and Widmerpool and Gonalston, Notts, the escheators of those counties were required to deliver to him on 24 February 1430.[60] But these four other estates were in the hands of a group of men who were clearly the feoffees or agents of Sir John Gra. Cromwell undertook litigation in the Court of Common Bench against them in Easter and Trinity terms 1430. Final concords and fines dating from Edward II's reign were brought in evidence to demonstrate the justice of Cromwell's claim to be the heir of Margaret Bellars, and, the defendants not appearing, all four estates were awarded to him.[61] Without doubt the reason for the suits going by default to Cromwell was a private arbitration made on 25 February 1430 – just a day after livery had been given to Cromwell – between him and Gra, which awarded the four manors to Cromwell as heir of Margaret Gra. In return for his acquiescence in the loss of these estates Gra was to receive an annual rent charge from Cromwell of 40 marks. This then was the price Cromwell was willing to pay to prevent any further litigation, which would no doubt have been an expensive nuisance, even though Gra did not have a legal leg to stand on. By the award Gra was also allowed to sue out livery of the manors of Bunny, Notts, and Crich, Derbys, the two remaining Bellars estates.[62] This Gra promptly did, and they were ordered

[59] Cromwell's great-grandfather had married Amicia Bellars, Sir Roger Bellars' sister. Sir Roger had left another daughter besides Margaret – Thomasin – but she had died a minor in royal wardship in February 1382: PRO, C139/46/40; *CIPM* xv, pp130–4, 195–6.
[60] *CFR 1422–30*, pp310–12.　　　　[61] *CPR 1429–36*, pp290–2.
[62] Magdalen College, Cartae Regiae 91. The arbitrators were Edmund Winter, Roger Hunt and Robert Southwell. For the first two, see Roskell, pp193, 237; Robert Southwell was the father of the Mowbray dukes of Norfolk's councillor, Richard: Wedgwood, p783.

to be delivered to him by the escheators on 3 March 1430.[63] Not that this did him any good, for he had no better claim to these estates than to the others, and Cromwell had already initiated pleas against him in Common Bench for them as well. Both properties Sir John and Margaret had (quite improperly) settled on themselves and their heirs in the autumn of 1424 and, these being estates held in chief, they had paid £40 for entry into them under these terms in February 1425.[64] Cromwell was prompt in his attack on Gra's possession of Bunny: on 14 October 1429, just a week after Margaret's death, he sued out a writ of *novel disseisin* against him. The justices did not, however, meet at Nottingham until 28 July 1430. Sir John did not appear and the jury found for Cromwell, awarding him £210 in damages and costs, which Cromwell remitted to his opponent.[65] A few weeks previously he had also secured Crich: on 2 July before the justices at Westminster, Sir John once again having failed to appear (having defaulted before), Cromwell recovered the manor by writ of entry, the writ in this suit having been sued out on 1 January 1430.[66] Thus Ralph, lord Cromwell made secure the Bellars properties. They were well worth securing. A valuation of 1429–30 puts their clear annual value at just over £164. This was only a trifle less than a sixth of the estimated total clear annual value of all Cromwell's lands. He had, however, to make payment of £18 13s 8d a year to Joan Bertram, the widow of Sir John Swillington, for her dower from these estates.[67] Their high value makes Sir John Gra's attempts to get something out of them more understandable.

Nor was it merely a feeling of being so near and yet so far that impelled him to fight tooth and nail for these lands he had so briefly and so fortuitously held in right of his now dead wife. He was also in debt: for if ever a man needed money it was Sir

[63] *CCR 1429–35*, p10.
[64] *CCR 1429–35*, p10; *CPR 1422–9*, p270. Was it over this that Sir John was harsh with his wife?
[65] *CPR 1429–36*, pp293–4.
[66] *CPR 1429–36*, pp290–2.
[67] *HMC, Report on the Manuscripts of Lord De L'Isle and Dudley*, 1 (1925), p208. For valors, see R. R. Davies' outstanding paper 'Baronial Accounts, Incomes and Arrears in the Later Middle Ages', *EcHR* xxi (1968).

John. Not that he should have done. He was the son and heir[68] of Thomas Gra, merchant and mayor of York, ambassador to Prussia, member of parliament a dozen times or more.[69] William, Thomas' father, had been a great York burgess too, but John, like so many representatives of the third generation of English merchant families was a gentleman and, in his case anyway, a soldier. Did his gentlemanly tastes prove too grand for his lands, which his father had so carefully acquired in Lincolnshire and Yorkshire,[70] to bear? Or was it his soldiering which in some way encumbered him? Perhaps both. He succeeded his father in 1405; by 1413 he was mortgaging Saltfleetby and other property in Lincolnshire.[71] He would continue to mortgage one estate or another almost for the rest of his life. Yet he served on the Agincourt expedition and the campaign that opened in 1417; he was at the battle of Verneuil in 1424; in 1435 he was in the retinue of the Duke of Bedford and captain of Younins;[72] in 1436 he served in the Duke of Gloucester's raid into Flanders.[73]

It would be ironic, I think, if it was Gra's military service which ruined him, for ruined he was in the end, selling off the reversion of many of his Lincolnshire estates in 1459 to Sir Gervaise Clifton. Clifton sold out to Bishop Wainfleet, who settled these properties on his foundation at Oxford, Magdalen College.[74]

[68] Descents in Magdalen College, Multon Hall, 106A, 143; Saltfleetby 17; Cartae Misc. 63, 173.
[69] K. B. McFarlane, *The Nobility of Later Medieval England*, pp295–6; May McKisack, *The Parliamentary Representation of the English Boroughs during the Middle Ages* (1932), p103.
[70] Magdalen College, Multon Hall, 16, 143; Saltfleetby 20, 31A; Cartae Misc. 63, 77, 64–8, for example.
[71] Magdalen College, Saltfleetby 10, 33A, 35; and thereafter Saltfleetby 18, 57 (draft only), 9A.
[72] *The Wars of the English in France during the reign of Henry VI*, ed. Rev. J. Stevenson, Rolls Series 22, II, part 2 (1864), pp394, 436, for example.
[73] Magdalen College, Saltfleetby 36A.
[74] Magdalen College, Multon Hall 77, 68A, 60 for instance; Saltfleetby 1, 3, 14, 15, 16. These properties, Saltfleetby, Multon Hall, and Somercotes, were worth together about £50 per annum. Wainfleet bought the reversion to them from Clifton for £800: see now John Mills, 'The Foundation, Endowment and early administration of Magdalen College, Oxford', unpublished Oxford BLitt dissertation, 1977, pp36–7. The deeds, with the estates themselves, came to the college on the death of Thomasin, Sir John's widow, in 1475; 'all such evidenz being in my ward and kepying

A few years later Wainfleet secured many of the estates which had belonged to Sir John Fastolf, estates which that clever and dogged warrior had purchased out of the profits of war. It is in the possibility of this conjunction that the irony might lie: Magdalen's endowment stemming from war losses as well as war profits. If that were the case Sir John Gra would deserve to be remembered there as well as Sir John Fastolf.

Whatever their cause however, he was undoubtedly in financial difficulties in the 1430s. He married again within three years of Margaret's death;[75] his second wife was Thomasin, daughter of Thomas Fauconer, mercer and alderman of London, and (as Professor Roskell notes)[76] 'he probably found his second wife's father useful in his troubles'. He also continued to borrow. One of those who endeavoured to take advantage of his reliance on loans and mortgages was – it is no surprise to learn – Ralph, lord Cromwell. At the very time in 1430 that Cromwell was fighting off and buying off Gra's challenge to the Bellars inheritance, he was also taking over property Gra had mortgaged. In May 1430 Sir John granted Multon Hall, Lincs, to Thomas Morstead; the condition for recovery was that he should pay him within ten years 400 marks, less ten times the annual value of the manor. Inside a month Morstead had released his right to Cromwell.[77] As we might expect of such an arrangement in such circumstances, relations between Gra and Cromwell grew strained. In February 1434 some straightening out was attempted. On 7 February Cromwell took over Gra's debt to Morstead and was enfeoffed with Multon Hall on new terms: he was to be paid 280 marks in seven years, less each year the clear annual value. Morstead acknowledged payment by Cromwell on 26 February. Meanwhile on 14 February (an auspicious day for undertakings to be reached) not only did Sir John acknowledge the enfeoffment of Cromwell in Multon Hall, he also undertook to give him first

concernying to the manors of Saltfleetby, Somercotes and Frenyngton that my said executors inordinent after my decease make deliverance therof unto my lord Bishop of Wynchester'; as indeed did Thomasin's will from which this instruction is taken: Multon Hall 47, dated 30 January, proved 30 April 1475.
[75] Magdalen College, Saltfleetby 5.
[76] Roskell, p81.   [77] Magdalen College, Multon Hall, 1, 59, 8, 9.

refusal (after the Duke of Gloucester) of any other Lincolnshire lands he should wish to dispose of, and he prayed 'to excuse hymself of anythyng reported that he should have saide or wrought in noysing of the saide lorde, and of that he cannot be excused to knowlech it and submitte hym, knowledging all his mysgovernance in that partie and of forgiveness'.[78] What Gra had noised abroad about Cromwell, we learn from a later document,[79] was that he was a usurer. This taunt must have hurt Cromwell the more for its being, one suspects, the truth: an image of the Treasurer of England as loan shark is not wide of the mark. Be that as it may: he had Sir John Gra on the hook; Multon Hall almost, it would seem, in the bag. But for once the victim, and to our mind born loser, eventually escaped. In St Paul's cathedral on 18 May 1437, in the presence of creditable witnesses, Sir John laid down the balance of his debt, just over 269 marks.[80] Cromwell of course did all he could to avoid the consequences of that proffer: he denied it, kept control of Multon Hall, and maintained that he did so rightfully as Gra had not performed his other undertakings of February 1434. He took Gra to law over these broken promises and judgment was duly given for him. Yet in this instance, despite the law, justice of a sort prevailed, for Gra eventually recovered Multon Hall and received compensation, though perhaps not in Cromwell's lifetime.[81]

One of the agreements Cromwell alleged Sir John had not fulfilled was the delivery to him of 'alle the dedes and evidence

---

[78] Magdalen College, Multon Hall 136, 101A, 3, 70; 67, 72A (seisin to Cromwell, March 1434); CCR 1429–36, pp304–5; PRO, C1/11/441 (Gra's petition to Chancery).

[79] Cromwell's answer to Gra's bill in Chancery: Magdalen College, Cartae Misc. 317.

[80] Magdalen College, Multon Hall 10; see also 90A.

[81] Magdalen College, Cartae Misc. 317. The legal proceedings are to be dated around 1440, as on 22 June 1440 the witnesses of Gra's proffer in St Paul's in May 1437 set their seals (9 survive, 5 are lost) to the declaration of that event drawn up by Robert Kent, public notary: Multon Hall 10. There is however another, later petition of Gra's to the Chancellor: Cromwell was still denying him possession. It dates from after 1449 (the latest date mentioned in it): PRO, C1/19/262. Multon Hall was not back in Gra's hands until June 1456 – or so the surviving deeds at Magdalen College suggest: Multon Hall 62, 63, 64, 68A, 49. For the compensation paid by Cromwell's executors, see Mills, p37.

that he had in kepying longyng to the heire generale of Swylyng-ton'.[82] Were Cromwell and John Hopton in alliance? Gra was, as we shall shortly see, Hopton's most determined opponent, just as he was Cromwell's. Certainly he did not forget his claim to the Bellars estates; we would indeed be surprised if he had. Cromwell died in February 1456; in April 1459 his much exercised executors – Ralph was another nobleman who died without issue – came to some accommodation with the aged but persistent Sir John.[83]

There was one other challenger whom Cromwell's executors and John Hopton had in common: Elizabeth Swillington, married to Robert Sampson of Halesworth, Suffolk. Elizabeth was the daughter and heir of Thomas Swillington of the main line of that family. He, still alive in 1417, was dead by 1429, so that Elizabeth then remained as the last representative of the family and the right heir of Margaret Gra, though her claim here does not go unchallenged either – as we shall see. As late as 1459 Cromwell's executors were involved in a suit with her;[84] she was, however, much less of a nuisance to Hopton: she and her husband made a release to him of the properties which were his under Sir Roger's enfeoffments in May 1431, and in the following July Hopton made a release to them of all actions real and personal.[85] By this time all their energies were probably engaged in obtaining those Swillington properties which had not been enfeoffed and which, therefore, fell to Elizabeth as Margaret Gra's heir. They were few and far between, but nonetheless were worth having for Robert Sampson was not a man of any substance. At Margaret Gra's *inquisition post mortem* it was found that Elizabeth was her heir in a messuage at East Greenwich and a messuage and some small plots in the town of Nottingham.[86] The jurors had however found

[82] Magdalen College, Cartae Misc. 317.
[83] HMC, *De L'Isle and Dudley MSS*, I, p211. He died later the same year: writ of *diem clausit extremum* 5 December 1459 (*CFR 1452–61*, p245). No *IPM*.
[84] HMC, *De L'Isle and Dudley MSS*, I, pp186, 211.
[85] *CCR 1429–35*, pp130, 120.
[86] PRO, C139/36/40. The property at East Greenwich was, however, delivered to Gra on 3 March 1430, by virtue of a fine of 1421–2: *CFR 1429–35*, p10; no doubt this was in error, like the delivery to him of Bunny and Crich on the same day.

that Margaret's heir in a messuage and two rent charges in the city of York, in the manor of Shelf, Yorks, and in $3\frac{1}{2}$ acres of land in Nottinghamshire, was William Routh of Thorp Perrow, Yorks, son of Sir Thomas Routh, who was the son of Elizabeth (wife of Peter Routh), sister of Sir Robert Swillington (d. 1391). Elizabeth Routh was a daughter of Adam Swillington who had died in 1328. There was evidently confusion and difficulty here, although clearly Routh's claim was weaker than that of Elizabeth Sampson, as he had descended through a less senior line and a female one at that. But it was not on these grounds that he was challenged. The Sampsons cut through the confusion by claiming that Adam's daughter Elizabeth was a bastard (born at Forncett, Norfolk), and that therefore William Routh had no title at all. Routh did not take up the challenge, failing to appear in Chancery, and on 1 April 1432 the disputed lands were awarded to Elizabeth and Robert Sampson.[87]

William Routh meanwhile was not idle on another front. He was taking issue with John Hopton over the enfeoffed Swillington properties in Yorkshire, including the manor of Thorp Perrow itself, although the ownership of this estate seems to have been raised as part of a counter attack by John Hopton, as it was not a Swillington estate after 1391 and by 1429 had been securely with the Routh family for many years.[88] Almost immediately after the inquisition on Margaret Gra had been taken, Routh and Hopton put their dispute over the manors of Swillington, Rodes and Thorp Perrow to the arbitration of Richard Nevill, earl of Salisbury. On 29 November 1429 at London Nevill made the award.[89] Routh was simply to proceed at law against Hopton for

---

87 PRO, C139/46/40; *CFR 1430–37*, pp89–90; for Peter Routh, see the genealogy in Beanlands, pp192–3.
88 Beanlands, p205.
89 For the award see BL, Lansdowne MS 255 f237 new numbering. This is also a seventeenth century copy, uncharacteristically missed by Parr. For Nevill's recent earldom, see *CP* xi, p395 footnote O. He was, at least on a geographical view of things, the 'natural' lord of both of them; he may have been more directly the patron of William Routh: 30 years later, in 1458–9, William was retained by him: A. J. Pollard, 'The Northern Retainers of Richard Nevill, Earl of Salisbury', *Northern History*, xi (1976 for 1975), pp59, 68.

the manors of Swillington and Rodes, and Hopton was to respond at law making 'no default nor lag protection nor no delay take'. The parties were bound under obligations of 500 marks. There was no mention of Thorp Perrow; it remained with Routh and was presumably no longer to be in dispute. To let the law take its course was sound and entirely proper advice (given to him, as the Earl said, by council indifferent and learned of the law); it hardly represents this great – albeit newly great – nobleman exerting his influence to deny or warp the law, or shows him ignoring it: quite the contrary. After all in their passionate pursuit of security for themselves and their property men had sooner or later to find that security in the law. For Hopton at any rate Nevill's award was the beginning of victory, for at law there was to be no overthrowing of the enfeoffments. On 17 March 1435 William Routh confirmed to Hopton all the properties that fell to him by Sir Roger Swillington's enfeoffments.[90]

Routh was not the last of John's opponents to capitulate. That was of course to be Sir John Gra. We have seen – in the case of the manors of Bunny and Crich – how he attempted to insure himself against the evil day when his wife should die childless and her lands would necessarily be lost to him: by settling them on himself and his wife. That illegal procedure had been easily thrust aside by Ralph Cromwell. The method by which Sir John hoped to hang onto Wissett in Suffolk was more blatantly unlawful.[91] He had forged, in the name of Sir Roger Swillington's last surviving feoffee and faithful servant, Richard Daniel, parson of Swillington and sometime Sir Roger's steward in Suffolk,[92] a release of the manor to Gra and his wife. This expedient availed him no better than the other. Daniel denounced this writing and made a quit-claim to John Hopton of the manor of Wissett on 17 February

---

[90] SRO, HA 30/369/371 is however only a draft indenture. There is no trace that it has ever been sealed.

[91] He had perhaps gone in for sharp practice even earlier: on the death of Sir John Swillington in 1418 Margaret (not Robert) was declared his heir and seisin was granted to her and her husband Sir John Gra (*CFR 1413–22*, p263). The fragment of a petition to the Chancellor by Sir Roger's feoffees (in PRO, E28/32) must relate to this episode.

[92] SRO, HA 30/50/22/20/9/11, Westhall account 1394–5.

1430.[93] The fact that he had been the Gras' receiver in Norfolk and Suffolk as late as 1428–9[94] did not deter him from his duty, and he moved easily into Hopton's service: he was his receiver general in 1435.[95] We hear no more of Sir John's attempts on Hopton's Suffolk estates. This early defeat possibly compelled him to move his ground. By autumn 1432 he was disputing Hopton's right to Swillington itself. On 3 October 1432 he entered into an indenture with two men by which he undertook to pay them £20 over a period of two years; if, however, he should receive the arrears of the rent charge he had got out of the settlement made with Cromwell over the Bellars inheritance in February 1430, or if there was to be a settlement between him and John Hopton over Swillington by which a large sum of money be paid to him, then he was to pay them from whichever of these monies should come first into his hands.[96] It is here made abundantly obvious what he was after in his challenge to Hopton: a large sum of money. Whether he achieved that aim we do not know, but it was not until over three years later, on 6 December 1435, that he quit-claimed to Hopton all the enfeoffed properties, and made a release to him of all actions real and personal.[97] Perhaps during that interval he had won some monetary compensation for the disaster which had overtaken him in 1429. For just as surely as the death of Margaret Gra was the making of John Hopton, so had it been a calamity for her bereaved husband. Some idea of the dimension of his loss can be gained from figures alone: Hopton would enjoy a clear revenue of at least £200 per annum from the Swillington estates in Suffolk and Norfolk; Swillington itself and the other Yorkshire estates may have doubled or more than doubled that figure.[98] If we also add the £164 per annum which Cromwell received from the Bellars inheritance we gain a vivid impression of what Sir John Gra lost on the death of his wife, and we can

93 *CCR 1429–35*, p94. On 22 February he was present at Hopton's first court at Westwood: SRO, HA 30/312/194.
94 SRO, HA 30/50/22/9/12, Westhall account.
95 SRO, HA 30/22/8/3, list of arrears Michaelmas 1435. Was this part of the price for his earlier support?
96 Magdalen College, Saltfleetby 23.
97 *CCR 1435–41*, p43.
98 See chapter 2, p95.

better understand his determination to get something from those who gained all this.

We must now turn to John Hopton, the bridegroom at the feast, and describe what exactly was delivered to him in February 1430, and to which he secured his right in the following years. In Yorkshire he had the manors of Oldhall and Newhall in Swillington, the neighbouring manor of Preston, the manors of Cuthworth and Rodes or Rodeshall, with rents and land in some twenty other places.[99] In Suffolk he had the manors of Blythburgh and Walberswick; Wissett and Wissett Roos; Yoxford, Stricklands, Meriells, Middleton and Brendfen, all in Yoxford; Lembaldes, Claydons and Risings in Westleton; Westhall; and Thorington. And across the Suffolk border just inside Norfolk there were the manors of Ellingham and Pirnhow.[100] In addition to these important estates Hopton also obtained as a result of Sir Roger Swillington's enfeoffments some small properties at Stanton, Hickling, Sutton Bonnington, and West and East Leake in Nottinghamshire, the manors of Great and Little Stretton, and lands at Lubbersthorpe, Ibstock, Dadlington and elsewhere in Leicestershire, and in Derbyshire the small estate at Ufton, which his father Thomas Hopton had held for his life.[101] Now of Ufton we hear no more, but these other outlying estates in the central Midlands soon were in Ralph, lord Cromwell's possession; the Nottinghamshire lands appear in his accounts for 1444–5 where, as the lands late of Sir John Swillington, acquired of John Hopton esquire, they had their own bailiff,[102] and the Leicestershire properties, stated as 'lately of John Hopton', appear as a unit in an undated valor of his estates.[103] These were scattered and miscellaneous properties of no great value, and they were distant from the two main concentrations of Hopton's estates in Suffolk and

[99] PRO, C139/46/40, Margaret Gra's *IPM*. All these manors, save one half of Oldhall, were held of the Duchy of Lancaster honour of Pontefract; that remaining half was held of William Scargill, for whom see chapter 4.
[100] For Pirnhow between Ellingham and Ditchingham, see Beanlands, p191.
[101] PRO, C139/46/40; *CFR 1422–30*, pp313–19. There was also a wood and a small rent in Lincs.
[102] HMC, *De L'Isle and Dudley MSS*, I, p217.
[103] PRO, SC11/822. They were valued at just under £11. I owe this reference to Graham Kent.

Yorkshire; they were, however, near Cromwell's own properties, including those Bellars lands he had obtained in 1430 – with which, so to speak, they naturally belonged. It was logical, therefore, for Hopton to have disposed of them to Cromwell, but when and for how much (if for anything) we do not exactly know. It may be that Hopton handed them over to Cromwell for his help against Sir John Gra. We have no evidence of this, yet that great ally[104] may have made them the price for his support. Or, it is possible that it was only around 1440, when Hopton himself was rounding out his estates at Yoxford by the purchase of the manor of Cockfield Hall, that he sold these Midland properties to Cromwell. Whatever the circumstances, he had soon disposed of them. They may after all have been something of an embarrassment to him, for their relatively small yield may not have been worth the cost of management and collection, distant and dispersed as they were.

It was thus the Swillington lands in Yorkshire and Suffolk which formed the basis of John's landed wealth throughout his life. We have no evidence for the Yorkshire estates and how he ran them, but some – albeit fragmentary – for the Suffolk estates. To these he added by purchase, though not on any large scale. He acquired first, in 1440, Cockfield Hall, the only manor in Yoxford which the Swillingtons had not owned. It had been held by a branch of the Norwich family (founders of Mettingham College, Suffolk), and John Norwich, who succeeded to Cockfield Hall in 1374, was the last direct representative of his line. He died

104 Not apparently, as we have observed, great enough to beat down for good Sir John Gra where Multon Hall was concerned. Yet Lady Fitzhugh's sentiment (expressed during her dispute with Cromwell over the estate of Quinton, Glos (at arbitration in July 1429): Magdalen College, Quinton 59, 74), sounds rather like whistling in the wind: 'Nevertheless my said Lady, blessed be God, has divers fair evidence and thing so substantial and many to prove that the said release is the said Robert's deed, the which they be heard and known, in good faith I trust to God no gentleman for his own worship will say with Cromwell' (Quinton 57). Self-respect presumably warred with self-interest in gentlemen's hearts as often in the fifteenth as in any other century, with no doubt proportionately the same victories and defeats: Lord and Lady Fitzhugh released their right in Quinton to Cromwell in 1441 (Quinton 5); Maud Willoughby sold it to Cromwell's executors of whom Wainfleet was one in 1475 (Quinton 67, 65); it was securely in the college's hands by 1480 (Quinton 1 and 42).

a childless widower in 1428 after a long and unpretentious life. In his will he required his feoffees to sell all his lands in Norfolk and Suffolk; they and his executors were to employ the money so raised on various pious works and in bequests to local churches and religious houses. A generous benefactor of Yoxford church, he was buried there beside his wife; their brasses still survive.[105] Richard Daniel was one of his executors, Sir John Fastolf (whose situation a generation later was so much like John Norwich's) was perhaps one of his feoffees, for it was Fastolf and John Linford of Stalham who granted the manor of Cockfield Hall, with the advowson of the church of St Margaret, Westwick in Norwich, to John Hopton in August 1440. Hopton held his first court there on 22 August.[106]

His acquisition of the manor of Easton Bavents, then on the coast north of Southwold but now mostly lost to the sea, was altogether a more complicated affair. Easton Bavents was held in 1431 by Ela, widow of Roger Shardlow, for her life; their son Sir John Shardlow, however, died childless in 1433, and Ela in December 1435 sold the reversion to Hopton for 400 marks. He was farming the manor from her in 1436–7 at £20 a year, and Richard Daniel was busy there on his behalf.[107] In July 1451 Hopton settled the reversion on himself with remainder to his younger son Thomas, and in October that year Ela granted him the manor outright in return for a yearly pension of 20 marks.[108] This early provision for his younger son became effective on John's death in 1478, but Thomas did not enjoy the estate long as he died some time between 1484 and 1486.[109] To Easton Bavents with its good series of accounts we will return.

One small property which John obtained late in his life came to him from his mother Margaret Pert; this was her third share of Castle Carlton, Lincs. She had inherited this on the death of

---

[105] Inscriptions lost. He died 15 April 1428; his will (NRO, Norwich Consistory Court, Reg. Surfleete, f29v) of 15 March 1428 was proved 22 September 1428: Parr II, pp210–12; III, p4.
[106] SRO, HA 30/369/180, with a fine seal of Fastolf; HA 30/369/124.
[107] SRO, V5/19/1/14.
[108] Copinger, II, pp62–3.
[109] His will, dated 17 April 1484 proved 3 July 1486: *Test Ebor* IV, pp5–6.

her mother in 1427; Margaret had by then married William
Edlington; he survived her and continued to hold the estate by
courtesy until his death in April 1466. In his will he styled himself
William Edlington esquire of Castle Carlton,[110] and although he
made a number of bequests to the church there as well as to the
neighbouring churches of Saltfleetby and South and North
Riston, it was 'at my chamber door within Frere Austyns in
London' that he desired to be buried. His funeral was to be
without ceremony: 'it is my will that noon interement be donn for
me in fest makyng for it is but a vayn glorie of the warlde'.
Instead the money was to be distributed to the poor of Castle
Carlton and other villages round about. He left nothing to the
Austin Friars of London. He was chiefly concerned for his widow
Christina, his two sons and his three daughters. Christina was to
have all his goods 'forto fynde my children as gentlemen ight to
be founde to the tyme that they be xxiiij yere of age and than she
forto rewarde them as she thinkes worthy'. One is left with the
impression that she might have found this a difficult task, more
particularly as, although he desired her to have Castle Carlton if
she would remain a widow, that property in fact went (as it
rightly ought to have done) to John Hopton.[111] His far more
wealthy stepson had remained in communication with him: a few
years before William's death John was paying him an annuity of
£13 10s 0d.[112] William did not remember John in his will.

John Hopton remained content with these few additions to the
Swillington properties in Yorkshire and East Anglia. By marriage
he gained no landed advantage; from his first wife Margaret
Saville he received nothing but respectability and, although his
second wife Thomasin Barrington did bring property to their
marriage in 1457, she was to administer it for the maintenance of
her children by her previous husbands: such was the content of a

[110] So he was also called in 1436, when his income was recorded as
£26 13s 4d: H. L. Gray, 'Incomes from land in England in 1436', *EHR*
xlix (1934), p635. Was it derived chiefly, perhaps solely, from this estate?
[111] *CFR 1422–30*, p208; PRO, C140/20/32; *CFR 1461–71*, p190. His *IPM*
gives 23 April 1466 as the date of his death. His will (PRO, Probate 11/5,
PCC 13 Godyn) is dated 11 June 1465 and proved 21 May: it says the
same year but this is presumably a slip for 1466.
[112] SRO, HA 30/314/18 m1.

careful agreement made between them before they went to their wedding. Nor did he seek a career in royal or aristocratic service, and hence to augment his income through the patronage involved. His ambition seems to have been amply satisfied by the windfall of 1430. He never had to seek his fortune, it had fallen ripe into his hands, and he apparently saw no reason to do other than peaceably enjoy it. Such ambition as he did have was for his children; for himself the life of an independent country gentleman was enough. To achieve that position he had had to exercise no talent, exert no influence, make no decision. He was beholden to no one: father, friend or patron. Least of all had he himself to thank: no strenuous efforts in the arts of peace or war had made him what he was. He is for that reason an untypical figure. Made neither by birth, nor service, nor marriage, he is in this respect unlike many of his better known East Anglian neighbours, some of whom we shall encounter later. And above all so different from John Paston.

Hopton's chance came to him as a young man; it was his for the taking. Paston's came late. In 1459, on the death of Sir John Fastolf, there was the opportunity to gain a landed fortune and Paston made every effort, used every means to secure it. Hopton certainly had his opponents in Gra, Sampson and Routh, but the trouble they caused him was trifling compared with that which Paston endured from the opposition of Fastolf's other executors and their allies. What made the difference was the nature of their title. Hopton had an undoubted legal right to the Swillington lands: Sir Roger's enfeoffments were unambiguous and Hopton's title was clear. Paston had no such luck and perhaps did not deserve it. His claim to Fastolf's estates was (at the very least) questionable, based as it was on a Paston edition of the old man's *nuncupative* will. To maintain and defend that claim John Paston had to fight fiercely in and out of court. Where Hopton won without a battle Paston never saw victory, even though he employed every tactic open to him. For some seven years he never relaxed his campaign, yet at his death in 1466 he was no nearer success. When another ten years later the long conflict ceased, it was only after Sir John Paston had agreed to a compromise, by which in order to secure some of Fastolf's properties he had to surrender others. He gained much but he had not won all.

That is far from John Hopton's experience of nigh on fifty years of undisturbed possession in the same local society over the same period. In this respect it is he perhaps who is more typical. For the Pastons', and for that matter Sir John Fastolf's, continual vigilance in the defence of lands to which they had unclear title, has left us a wealth of evidence. They are familiar figures, easily accessible, readily available for us to cite as representatives of the society they inhabited. But are their careworn, troubled lives any more characteristic of fifteenth century England than John Hopton's carefree days at Blythburgh? He spoiled for no fight, legal or otherwise, and once he had made fast the Swillington lands, avoided, so far as ever he could (and that in fact was very far), the law and the law courts. He is far more difficult to know than John Paston or Sir John Fastolf. Indeed he is impossible to know in the way they can be known: his unembattled life has necessarily left fewer traces. So much the more do we need him to redress the balance of our view of fifteenth century society: a man of trivial virtues and trifling vices, amicable and amiable.[113]

He had no reason to be otherwise. With the acquisition of the Swillington estates in 1430 this young Yorkshireman settled to his good fortune and lived a prosaic, but seemingly an harmonious life at Blythburgh in Suffolk. As these estates gave him the means to lead that life, we must first examine them in a little detail before attempting to come at the man himself.

[113] The very antithesis of the Hon. Mrs Skewton's exclamatory view of this period: ' "Such charming times!" cried Cleopatra. "So full of faith! So vigorous and forcible! So picturesque! So perfectly removed from commonplace! Oh dear!" ' (Charles Dickens, *Dombey and Son* (Oxford Illus. Dickens, 1950), p384.

2
THE ESTATES

'Read all thy ancestors' books of accounts. It may be thou mayest find somewhat out of them that will be worth thy labour.'

Sir John Oglander
A Royalist's Notebook, p229

'my maister...gaf me these wetche woordys: that there was no man of wurship in Norfolk that hath so many auditours of fee as he hadde, and yet cowde he never knowe the certeynté how hise lyvelode was disposed'

Geoffrey Sperlyng writing to John Paston I about Sir John Fastolf, 6 January 1460
Davis II, p202

We lack information for Swillington and the other Yorkshire estates. Just how unfortunate is this gap in our knowledge is demonstrated by the two accounts which survive for Swillington. Even those chance and random survivors do not date from John Hopton's lifetime. Moreover they are not only over a hundred years apart, they are entirely dissimilar. Nonetheless one of them at least is most revealing.

The first account is of Thomas Clerk, described as receiver of monies from the sale of grain and stock. It is for 1408–9.[1] All we need notice from it here is that such sales fetched over £70,[2] while the costs of production were £11, and other payments £12. Liveries of cash to Sir Roger Swillington at Westwood, the manor house which stood on the boundary between Blythburgh and Walberswick, were over £60.

---

[1] It is in the National Coal Board deposit at Leeds City Archives Department, an uncatalogued collection which bears the call number MX. I am most grateful to Mr W. J. Connor, Senior Assistant Archivist, for responding to my enquiries with a copy of the document. I should also at this point like to thank Mr Stuart Raymond, Librarian of the Yorkshire Archaeological Society, for his good offices in this piece of detection.

[2] Throughout this chapter I have frequently rounded figures out to the nearest £.

The second account is of William Dinley, bailiff, for 1522–3.[3] The charge was very simple: arrears and profits of courts were nil, sales of wood were £26, rents and farms were £396. The discharge was hardly more complicated: outgoing rents £13, fees and wages £24, repairs £9, other expenses, including William's Christmas journey to Yoxford to present his account, £5. The one complication, so far as we are concerned, is a slight one. Cash liveries to Sir Arthur Hopton, and payments to merchants and others on his warrant are recorded for times beyond the period of account, some two years beyond it in fact. They total £378.

These two remnants leave us question begging. All we ought to say, I think, is that Swillington was a valuable property, probably a very valuable property, and leave it at that. One other thing: if it was as productive an estate for John Hopton as it evidently was for his great grandson, then it was worth as much as, if not more than, all his Suffolk estates put together. Thus we have a real clue to what otherwise is something of a mystery: Hopton's ability to find large sums of money when required to do so, for instance for the purchase of Easton Bavents and for his daughter Elizabeth's marriage portion.

We are rather better served by the surviving evidence for the Suffolk estates, though here too we cannot move with any great certainty for the accounts that do remain are few and far between. Leaving aside Easton Bavents for the moment, Blythburgh, which formed one accounting unit with Walberswick, has the fullest series: apart from an isolated account for 1419–20, there are four accounts in sequence from 1463 to 1467, two in the next decade (1477–9), three in the 1480s (1480–1, 1483–5), and one for 1490–1. Westleton, which also included the manors of Lembaldes, Claydons and Risings, has the next best set of accounts: for 1469–70, 1477–8, 1478–9, 1481–2 and 1490–1. Then comes Yoxford, which included also Cockfield Hall, Meriells and Brendfen,[4] with

---

[3] SRO, HA 30/369/64.
[4] Brendfen was in the joint parish of Middleton and Fordley, actually lying in Fordley (*The Chorography of Suffolk*, ed. D. MacCulloch, Suffolk Record Society, XIX (1976), p42. I owe this reference to Norman Scarfe). This accounts for the fact that Middleton always appears among the

accounts for 1443–4, 1445–6, 1483–4 and 1492–3. For Westhall there are three early accounts, for 1376–7, 1394–5 and (badly damaged) for 1428–9, and one late, for 1481–2. This last account includes Thorington[5] and the two Norfolk manors of Pirnhow and Ellingham, the only accounts we have of these estates. There are no accounts for Wissett. Easton Bavents stands rather apart from these ultimately poor fragments of evidence,[6] for there are some fourteen accounts before 1451, when Hopton acquired the property, most of them of the fourteenth century, beginning in 1330–1.[7] There is then one for 1459–60 and, in one bundle,[8] fourteen accounts from the reign of Edward IV; finally there is a detached account of 1465–6. Thus for the years between 1459 and 1481 there is a long though not complete series of accounts.[9] In addition to the accounts there are a number of rentals and extents for Blythburgh, Westleton and Yoxford,[10] two lists of arrears covering all the East Anglian estates, of 1435 and 1479,[11] and a briefer list of what was owing to Thomasin Hopton, John's wife, out of the monies assigned from Yoxford and Wissett for the expenses of the household, dating from 1473.[12] Lastly there is a rough account book of the bailiff of Blythburgh, which has not

lands held by Hopton in inquisitions: those of 1430 and 1478, for instance. The main estate at Middleton, however, that of Middleton with Fordley, was held at this time by the Audley family: Copinger II, p125. Strick-lands, which also appears among Hopton's properties in 1430 and again in 1478, is something of a mystery; it certainly lay in Yoxford but it does not feature as a separate unit in the accounts; in the terrier of 1471 it does feature, but only in the title, not elsewhere: SRO, HA 30/369/1. It was presumably small enough to have lost its identity when Hopton, by purchasing Cockfield Hall, possessed all the manors of Yoxford.

[5] This manor was apparently Thorington Hall: Copinger II, p167.
[6] The Easton Bavents accounts are not in the Blois Family Deposit, from which the Hopton material at Ipswich derives, but in the Redstone collection (also at Ipswich), and they came to it from the Duke of Bedford.
[7] Including one for 1348–9 headed 'quo anno pestilencia hominum regnavit in Anglia': SRO, V5/19/1/3.
[8] SRO, V5/19/1/16.
[9] The sixteen accounts are for 1459–60, 1461–2, 1464–5, 1465–6, 1467–8, 1468–9, 1470–1, 1471–2, 1472–3, 1473–4, 1474–5, 1475–6, 1476–7, 1477–8, 1479–80, 1480–1.
[10] There are two terriers or drags: one of 1471 for Yoxford, the other of 1478 for Westleton: SRO, HA 30/369/1 and HA 30/50/22/27/7(1).
[11] SRO, HA 30/50/22/8/3 and HA 30/369/31.
[12] SRO, HA 30/369/294.

only rents collected from that estate over the period 1444–56, but also his expenditure – or part of it – during those years. As he acted as Hopton's cofferer, these casual jottings of his own and his master's expenses are an invaluable supplement to the information of the accounts: they also reveal a little of Hopton himself.[13]

Blythburgh with Walberswick was a large estate on the sandy soils of the Suffolk coastal plain. It comprised the small town of Blythburgh, which with its priory lay inland on the river Blyth, and the newer and more flourishing fishing village of Walberswick on the coast, where not only the Blyth but also the Dunwich river entered the sea. Then, as now, there were wide tracts of heath and marsh as well as the arable fields. At Westwood, on the rise midway between Blythburgh and Walberswick, the Hoptons had their house: it faced south east towards the port of Dunwich, now lost under the sea, but in the fifteenth century still a place of some consequence.

Rents formed the major item of account. They were not completely static during the century but almost so, at between £24 and £25 a year. Even more stable were farms (or leases) which were £6 for Blythburgh and Hinton, a hamlet in the south part of Blythburgh parish, and £6 for Walberswick.

It was a different story so far as the demesne was concerned. In 1419–20 the demesne had been farmed out to two men for £11 6s 8d. In December 1429, when the estate was briefly in the hands of the crown and custody had been granted to Sir William Phelip (later Lord Bardolf), the demesne was leased to William Reve and Robert his son for £8.[14] In 1463–4 Henry Brown was farming demesne arable and pasture and Hall meadow for £13 10s 0d; the great close called le Haughe was, however, in the lord's hands. So the situation remained in the following three years of account. By 1477–8 there had been important changes. The only demesne still leased out was part of that pertaining to the tenement Burghards; Henry Brown continued to farm this for

---

13 It is a small pocket book of 104 folios bound in leather. With it this long study of John Hopton began. It is SRO, HA 30/369/46.
14 SRO, HA 30/312/194: first court after Margaret Gra's death 1 December 1429.

£3 6s 8d a year. The remainder of the demesne was being directly exploited by Hopton, le Haughe being pastured by his beasts, the other lands of Burghards tenement being reserved for his sheep.[15] In the subsequent year all the demesne seems to have been in the lord's hands; nothing at all was received for demesne leases, Henry Brown was not mentioned. John Hopton's death in November 1478 brought no immediate alteration: in 1480–1 all but 9 enclosed acres, lying in the south part of the lord's new close in Blythburgh, continued in the hands of the new lord, William Hopton; those 9 acres were leased for 9s to Henry Goodwin and his wife Marion. Such was also the situation in 1483–4. William Hopton's death in February 1484 did however initiate change, for in 1484–5 much of the demesne was once more leased out. The Goodwins retained their 9 acres, Thomas Herlewin leased le Haughe for 30s, and John Deynes farmed 92 arable acres for just over £3, though he may in fact have been in control of more demesne land than that. By 1490–1 all the demesne was once more at farm. Robert Copping now held the Goodwins' 9 acres, John Raningham and Thomas Reve paid £2 4s 0d for le Haughe, and Henry Everard and John Dade leased all the rest of the demesne (arable and pasture) as well as the lord's two fold courses ('ac pro cursu ij faldarum') for £18 per annum.[16] Included in Everard and Dade's lease were the demesne fen and marsh in North End and the tenement called Stronders, for these it was noted were part of the fold course.[17]

These fold courses hold the key to any understanding (however dim) of the demesne at Blythburgh, and the fen and the marsh evidently played an important if shifting role within them. For while we have seen that by 1477–8 the demesne as such was being used for the lord's animals, the fen and the marsh clearly were not; they were then leased out to three men, and had been since

[15] It was stated that these lands now in hand had previously been farmed for a total of £17 10s 0d including le Haughe at £2 10s 0d: SRO, HA 30/314/18 m5.
[16] In 1505–6 the demesne lands (or what were called simply 'the shepys pasture') were still farmed out for £18 a year, and le Haughe at £2: SRO, HA 30/369/44 f29 (this is another rough account book of the bailiff of that date).
[17] SRO, HA 30/369/281.

1467–8, for £10 a year.[18] By 1480–1, before its due time, their fifteen-year lease had been terminated, and the fen, the marsh and Stronders tenement were being used by the lord.[19] They continued in the lord's hands in 1483–4 and 1484–5, when they were being pastured by his sheep. It seems, therefore, that use of demesne fen and marsh in the operation of the fold courses was not made until sometime after demesne arable and pasture had been put to such service. If we knew how many sheep there were at Blythburgh between the late 1470s and the mid-1480s we might be able to interpret this evidence in terms of an increased demesne flock; but we have no detailed information of that sort and so must continue to wonder how the fold courses worked.

The one figure for that flock which we do have comes from 1477–8. On the back of the account for that year there is, for the one and only time, a curious and brief grange account dealing with rabbits, reeds, the sheep and their wool. It records that on 8 December 1478 Thomas Dalby, the shepherd, had 721 sheep in his care.[20] It may be, however, that the Easton Bavents flock of 200 sheep was numbered among these, as in spring 1478 it was no longer at Easton, while in the woolhouse at Westwood in December 1478 there was the tithe wool of Easton which John Hopton had purchased. Autumn 1478 was of course an unusual time; John Hopton died in November: hence, I believe, our one indication of how many sheep there were, and how much wool there was at Westwood. There are other references to the flock and its custody in the accounts of 1477–8: Robert Payn, a household officer who was (we shall discover) much else besides, was paid 6s 8d for his office of sheep reeve, shearing costs amounted to 19s, the shepherd Thomas Dalby received his stipend in the form of cash and a house in the park, and there was another shepherd waged from 24 June until Michaelmas, perhaps another indication of an increased flock from that date. The prior of Blythburgh apparently had sheep at Blythburgh that year too: he paid 6s 8d for pasturing them in le Haughe. Later accounts are not at all helpful. By 1484–5, however, when part at least of the demesne

18 SRO, HA 30/314/18 m5.   19 SRO, HA 30/314/18 m7.
20 SRO, HA 30/134/18 m5d.

was being leased out again, it is likely that the flock was not what it had been: in 1478–9 214 sheep had been sold,[21] in 1480–1 John Seman and Robert Payn bought sheep to the value of £11.[22] Moreover John Deynes, who leased some of the demesne in 1484–5, pastured his sheep there. It seems possible therefore that the demesne flock was being broken up almost from the time that we have any sure information of its size, that is in December 1478. At any rate by 1490–1, when the lord's fold courses were leased out, we can be sure that it was no more.

Nor do we have any useful information as to demesne arable husbandry. In 1477–8 Henry Haven received 3s 6d for ploughing the lord's new close two years previously with his own plough. That is all the accounts ever reveal to us. There are no grain accounts. Perhaps such husbandry was none of the bailiff's business: Henry Haven's ploughing was a special case and required Thomasin Hopton's witness before it was eventually paid for.[23] Just as there was a sheep reeve, who presumably kept some accounts of his own, no doubt there was also someone in charge of arable farming. However it was the bailiff who accounted in 1477–8 for the sums received from tenants for the manuring of their lands, presumably by the lord's folded sheep, at 1s 4d an acre. He accounted under this heading for £1 6s 8d.

One thing at least seems clear: policy as regards the management of the demesne varied. This our other fragments of information also appear to suggest. In 1435, for instance, there was a flock of 700 sheep at Blythburgh, as the arrears list of that year fortunately tells us.[24] The bailiff's rough account book of 1444–56 also reveals a few details of demesne cultivation and of the demesne animals. He records payments for weeding and 'erying', and for binding corn, for the purchase of bullocks at Harleston, sixty on one occasion in 1447–8, for buying ploughs and hurdles, sheep and lambs, for the costs of sheep-keeping, for washing

---

[21] 114 to Richard Bingle the local butcher (whom we will encounter shortly) for £8 10s 0d; 100 to John Smith for £10 0s 0d: SRO, HA 30/314/18 m6.
[22] Robert Payn was also a butcher: SRO, HA 30/314/18 m7.
[23] SRO, HA 30/314/18 m5.
[24] SRO, HA 30/50/22/8/3.

and shearing them. In 1454-5 he noted his delivery to the shepherd of 236 wethers, 232 ewes and 118 lambs. There were expenses for foldage and for carrying the fold hurdles from one place to another, and in 1453-4 he noted the 'delyverans of the colet', listing eight persons with figures against their names: probably these were the cullet sheep, that is tenants' sheep which were allowed to feed with the lord's animals in his fold course.[25] Haymaking was a frequent item. These jottings from the years around 1450 suggest that then too Hopton's husbandry was of importance.[26] Our accounts of the early 1460s, on the other hand, show no sign of any such husbandry, arable or pastoral; nor for that matter do the accounts of 1419-20. Evidently ideas as to how the demesne should be managed changed over the years, and changed again.

Our scattered odds and ends of information about the exploitation of the demesne do not at all enable us, even if we wished, to discuss the profitability of direct farming at Blythburgh. We know of the existence of the fold courses, but we know nothing of how they worked. Even what actually constituted demesne land at any particular time is hard to determine, for it seems to have been increasing throughout the period.[27] One demesne source of profit, however, is easier to grasp: the rabbit warren.

The warren was farmed out in 1473-4 to John Walker for £2 13s 4d and an annual delivery to the household of 200 rabbits.[28] In 1480-1 a new nine-year lease was made to John Warner (perhaps the same man) for a straightforward payment of £8 a year. By 1505-6 the warren was being farmed out for £6 13s 4d a year.[29] How much was it worth when it was in the lord's hands?

[25] K. J. Allison, 'The Sheep-Corn Husbandry of Norfolk in the Sixteenth and Seventeenth Centuries', Agricultural History Review, v (1957), p21. For fold courses, cullets and marshes, see also Davis II, pp326, 583.
[26] SRO, HA 30/369/46. There is considerable uncertainty about which years the various entries refer to. My examples come from fs21, 22, 30, 30v, 39v, 46, 46v, 61v, 62, 77, 77v, 87v, 101v, 102, 103.
[27] See below, pp45-6.
[28] The account of 1477-8, the fourth year of the lease: SRO, HA 30/314/18 m5.
[29] SRO, HA 30/369/44 f29.

First what did it cost to maintain? In 1419–20 the warrener received £3 0s 8d; during the 1460s his stipend was £3 1s 4d. His and his helpers' expenses at the yearly or twice yearly capture and killing of the rabbits was never more than £1, and usually less. The cost of new nets amounted to three or four shillings each year, while there were also, from time to time, other maintenance costs, also of a few shillings. Once the carriage of rabbits to Ipswich came to 7s 5d,[30] and in 1464–5 the expenses of William Hopton and the lord's supervisor, while assessing the allowances which had to be made to tenants as a result of damage done by the rabbits, were 8s; we ought also to count as a charge the allowances they arrived at, nearly £2.[31] The yearly costs of the warren were therefore between £4 and £6.[32]

What did it bring in by way of rabbit sales? Over a thousand rabbits were killed each year. For 1464–5, 1465–6 and 1466–7 the bailiff drew up an account of where these rabbits went. In 1464–5 there were 1507 rabbits; just over 100 were given to the prior of Blythburgh, the warrener had 58 as part of his fee, another 286 were freely distributed to various men, and the household took about 250. The remaining 800 were sold for £7 17s 0d. In 1465–6 there were 1249 rabbits to be accounted for: the prior of Blythburgh had 92, the household at Yoxford (the other Hopton residence in Suffolk) took 318, that at Westwood (the chief seat) 40, the warrener and his assistants at the winter slaughter had 66, other men received as gifts a further 100, and Henry Brown, the demesne farmer, got 30 as a recompense for damage done to his growing corn by these rabbits. The remaining 600 or so were sold for just over £5 17s 0d, 500 of them to John Harpenden, a London poulterer, for £4 10s 0d. In 1466–7 there were 1505 rabbits; 82 went to the prior (stated specifically this time to be for tithe), 385 went to the Yoxford household, 92 to the warrener and his deputies at the winter slaughter, Henry Brown had 17 for the same reason as in the previous year, and 41 went as

30 SRO, HA 30/314/18 m1.
31 SRO, HA 30/314/18 m2.
32 In 1465–6 a John Bunting was paid 6d 'pro predicibus capiend'; the skins of these were not, presumably, for wrapping his baby in: SRO, HA 30/314/18 m3.

gifts to other men. The remaining 900 were sold, 724 of them to John Harpenden again, total receipts being £8 os 2d. Earlier sales had produced like sums. In 1463–4 900 rabbits had fetched just over £8; in 1419–20 1410 had sold for £10 15s od. Such then are the figures. All in all John Hopton would surely have agreed, where conies were concerned, with Robert Reyce, writing of the county in the early seventeenth century:

Of the harmless Conies, which do delight naturally to make their aboad here, I must say somewhat more, for their great increase, with rich profitt for al good house keepers, hath made every one of any reckoning to prepare fitt harbour for them, with great welcome and entertainment, from whence it proceeds that there are so many warrens here in every place, which do furnish the next marketts, and are carried to London with noe little reckoning, from whence it is that there is none who deeme their houses well seated, who have nott to the same belonging a commonwealth of Conies, neither can hee bee deemed a good house keeper that hath not plenty of these at all times to furnish his table.[33]

We should also mention the dovehouse and the mill. The windmill was leased out for £2 3s 4d in 1419–20. In 1463–4 William Mason leased it for only £1 6s 8d; he and Hopton shared responsibility for repairs to it and the cottage attached. By 1477–8 Mason's widow held the lease, and in 1480–1 John Buck, miller, was the lessee on the same terms as before; he was still there in 1490–1. In 1505–6 the lease of the mill was at the same figure it had been over forty years before: £1 6s 8d.[34] The dovehouse was farmed out for 6s in 1419–20; in the 1460s and 1470s it was in the lord's hands;[35] in 1484–5 the bailiff John Baret appears to have been farming it for 10s. In 1490–1 it was bare of pigeons.[36]

Sales of wood were hardly more important. No doubt both timber and underwood came from the park at Westwood, which in the 1460s and 1470s the bailiff managed at a fee of 13s 4d a

33 *Suffolk in the XVIIth Century, the Breviary of Suffolk by Robert Reyce, 1618*...ed. Lord Francis Hervey (1902), p35.

34 SRO, HA 30/369/44 f27.

35 It was repaired in 1463–4, for example; grain was purchased for the birds in 1477–8.

36 The swannery, empty in 1419–20, is never mentioned thereafter. The fishponds were farmed by John Baret in 1490–1 for 1s 8d.

year. In 1463–4, for example, a cartload of firewood was sold for
1s 8d, an old, rotten oak for 2s 3d, while pannage for pigs brought
in 10s. In 1464–5 700 staves fetched a little over 10s, and faggots
and wood for fuel not only went to the household but were also
sold. In 1466–7 John Hoo paid £1 18s 4d for 23 cartloads of oak
called 'ship tymber de lez toppis quercuum', and £2 2s 8d was
received from various men for 800 faggots made from the same
oaks. Oak for ships was also an item, along with charcoal, in
1480–1. Thereafter, however, there appear to have been no wood
sales.[37] Such sales had usually only amounted to a few shillings,
had sometimes reached a pound or two, but the £4 of 1466–7
seems to have been exceptional.[38]

More regular sources of income were the tolls at the fair (held
three times a year at the feasts of the Annunciation (25 March),
Assumption (15 August) and Nativity (8 September) of the Virgin
Mary), the profits of the market, the fees for anchorage in
Walberswick harbour from vessels of other ports,[39] the farm of
the ferry at Walberswick, the fee called 'Breggesilium' (fixed at 3s
per annum by an agreement made between Sir Robert Swillington
and the tenants),[40] and the charge for weighing bushels of salt and
grain at the quay.[41] These were all put together under one heading in the accounts and while individually each was insignificant,
together they brought in annually between £2 and £4.

The ferry had been at farm, it was stated in 1419–20, for a
mere 4s a year.[42] In 1463–4, however, Robert Dolfinby farmed

[37] Also sold were cartloads of 'fenger' (bracken?); it was very cheap: 1s for
12 cartloads in 1477–8, 2s 6d for 30 loads in 1478–9.
[38] SRO, HA 30/314/18 m4.
[39] Chiefly fishing boats (called farecosts); those of Southwold, Easton Bavents
and Covehithe regularly used the harbour. Pedlars of fish were also
charged ¼d for each horseload.
[40] SRO, HA 30/314/18 m1. In 1419–20 2s 8d was received from this source.
It was a charge of some sort levied on boats, presumably connected with
the bridge.
[41] '...pro bussellis domini mensurandis salis et bladi'. In 1477–8 it was
stated that the sum received from this was only 1s 4d because the Bretons
had not come that year with salt: SRO, HA 30/314/18 m5.
[42] Nothing was received that year because the farm had been granted to
Henry Fynk for life. At the close of the account, however, the bailiff
accounted for 30s 2d paid to John Thornton, the lord's receiver, 'per
manus Henry Fynk'; this looks like the farm of the ferry: SRO, HA

ferry and ferryboat (with its anchor and cable) for 30s. He was still in possession in 1478–9, but in 1480–1 Thomas Pigot took on the farm for twenty years at £1 6s 8d per annum. He had gone by 1490–1, as in that year Robert Boswell of Dunwich farmed the ferry *and* all the fees and payments rendered at Walberswick harbour (which we have noticed above) for £3 6s 8d.[43] These dues – here farmed at £2 – had in earlier years never achieved that figure, at least in the bailiff's accounts: perhaps Dolfinby and Pigot had seen to that.[44]

Receipts from the tolls at the fairs were always less than £1 a year. They were at their highest in 1419–20, at their lowest (less than 10s) during the 1460s, and had recovered in the 1480s. The market saw no such revival. In 1419–20 12s was recorded as the profits of the market. In the 1460s and 1470s the sum was less than half that, and by 1490–1 the proceeds were just 3s from one stall: a decayed market indeed.[45]

One item of income only remains to be dealt with summarily. The profits of the manorial court formed an important if variable portion of the receipts, ranging from about £7 to about £13 per annum. They fell to an unusual £5 8s 9d in 1466–7 and rose to an exceptional £16 16s 9d in 1490–1, when eight courts were held.

Having surveyed the individual items of revenue,[46] we ought perhaps to set out the total charge side of the accounts, even if this can reveal very little. Paradoxically it is what it is not shown

---

30/369/78. Probably the 30s recorded against the name of Robert Clerk in a check-list of rents of 1458 was for the farm of the ferry: SRO, HA 30/50/22/10/17(6).

[43] SRO, HA 30/369/281.

[44] That in 1419–20 £2 3s 7d had come from these fees might reinforce this suggestion.

[45] In 1458 there had been four stalls or shops, including Richard Bingle's the butcher: check-list of rents SRO, HA 30/50/22/10/17(6). Richard, who leased the tenement Burghards in the early 1460s (HA 30/369/302) and who bought 114 sheep from Sir William Hopton in 1478–9 (HA 30/314/18 m6) was in business in the market until the 1480s.

[46] There were small profits to be had from time to time out of the coastal situation of the manor; in 1463–4, for instance, the remnants of an old ship were sold off for 30s, and in 1465–6 John Stocker, citizen of London, paid 6s or the right to take away some wine of his which had been washed upon the shore.

that is revealing. For it does not, of course, show what the profits of demesne farming were, save in two years. And those two years, 1478–9 and 1480–1, where the sale of considerable numbers of sheep raise the charge by some £10, even more paradoxically may have been when demesne pastoral farming was beginning to be wound down. In 1478–9 when there were no arrears (because of a new lord) the total charge was £83;[47] in 1480–1 the total charge (less arrears) was £80.[48] In 1490–1, when also there were no arrears because there was a new lord, the charge was again just over £80; exceptional profits from the courts of that year and the high figure of the demesne lease were the reasons for that. In other years (including 1419–20) the current charge ranged between £63 and £73.[49]

We are still far from any assessment of the actual cash Hopton received from his Blythburgh bailiff; in order to come at this we obviously have to examine the discharge side of the accounts. Yet even the most casual survey of the expenditure recorded for Blythburgh is sufficient to show the virtual impossibility of any such assessment, for John Hopton lived at Westwood on the estate and the bailiff acted as his cofferer of the household established there. Hence on the one hand there are payments made and recorded by him as expenses within the manor, which are what we would call household charges, and on the other hand the greater part of the liveries of money consist of the bailiff's payments for provisions of clothing or for other requirements of that household. Liveries of cash there are, but they do not amount to much in any one year and they do not at all reflect what the estate was producing in cash terms. There are also variations in accounting practice which further confuse the situation: in 1477–8, for example, under a new heading of foreign expenses appear items which hitherto have featured under the heading of internal

---

[47] I have here subtracted £13 3s 4d from the total charge of £96 4s 8d as this sum was delivered to the bailiff by the lord.

[48] In this year also the bailiff received drafts both from the lord and from other bailiffs; this £58, together with the arrears of the warren and money handed over by men who owed it to the lord I have excluded from my figure.

[49] Arrears are excluded; the figures are: 1419–20 £73; 1463–4 £69; 1464–5 £73; 1465–6 £70; 1466–7 £73; 1483–4 £63; 1484–5 £68.

expenses, or among the liveries. Moreover, on two occasions (1463–4, 1480–1) the Blythburgh bailiff acted as receiver for all the East Anglian estates. This fluidity both of organization and of accounting is not particularly surprising: the whole body of East Anglian estates was not large and each estate itself was small, while everything in John's time was under the eye of a resident lord. Nevertheless, the conjunction (in our terms) of local and central expenditure on a single account makes extremely hazardous any attempt to arrive at the clear value of the manor.

The first item on the discharge side of the accounts, however, was not of expenditure. This was outgoing rents, decayed rents (that is rents and farms which were not collectable because the tenements were in the lord's hands), and allowances on rents and farms. There was only one major payment in the outgoing rents, that was £1 paid each year to the bailiffs of Dunwich in order that the people of Blythburgh and Walberswick might be free of all tolls and customs at the port of Dunwich. This arrangement had been negotiated by Sir Roger Swillington or one of his sons.[50] By 1477–8 it was no longer being paid; in the 1460s John Hopton had reached a new agreement with the Dunwich authorities.

Decayed rents, not much over £1 in 1419–20, were well over £8 by 1460–1. In the early 1460s various allowances on farms (either because the lands were included in Henry Brown's demesne farm or were in the lord's hands) added nearly £4 to this sum. By 1470–1 decays and allowances together amounted to £13, and in 1490–1 the figure was £14. Thus the actual income from rents and farms, which were charged throughout the period at about £37 a year, ought to have been about £29 in 1460–1, not much over £25 a year by the mid-1460s, £24 a year in the 1470s, and £23 a year thereafter. Decays, which are never given in detail, formed the greater part of this difference between charged and actual (or rather, anticipated) income. There had been (it seems) a heavy fall in the value of rents between 1419–20 and 1460–1. In 1419–20 decays were less than 4% of the total charge of rents and farms; in 1460–1 they were 23%. A rental of

---

[50] The 1419–20 accounts: by the dead lord. It was probably part of the agreement arrived at with Dunwich by Sir Roger during Henry IV's reign.

Michaelmas 1437 and a list of rents of 1458 seem to indicate that the main advance in decays took place after 1437. In 1437 rents and farms totalled just short of £35, still only a couple of pounds less than the total of 1419–20.[51] In 1458 however rents and farms totalled only a little over £30.[52]

What really were these decays? And what did it mean that tenements and lands were in the lord's hands? And why were they? The rental of 1437 gives us one clue: it states that 6 acres of land in various parcels lately leased to Thomas Northales were in the lord's hands for the pasture of his sheep. This suggests that the demesne pasture had been extended; the allowances of the 1460s seem, and those of the early 1480s are specifically stated, to be for this purpose.[53] Moreover, when we compare the accounts of 1419–20 with those of 1490–1 it seems clear that over those eighty years the demesne itself has expanded: in 1419–20 demesne leases totalled £11, in 1490–1 they were £20. We arrive at greater certainty if we compare the overall position – rents, farms, demesne farms *and* decays and allowances – over the eighty years. In 1419–20 rents and farms totalled £37, demesne leases £11. Decays were just over £1. In 1490–1 rents and farms were still £37, but decays and allowances now amounted to over £14; demesne leases were well over £20. In other words, total income from rents, farms and demesne leases *less* decays and allowances was £47 in 1419–20 and about £44 in 1490–1. Surely then what has happened is that there has been a readjustment in the relationship between tenanted land on the one hand and demesne on the other; the latter has gained at the expense of the former, and decays and allowances represent that readjustment, albeit in a clumsy fashion. If we are right and demesne was extended,

[51] SRO, HA 30/50/22/27/6(2); and 6 (1) for Blythburgh; HA 30/369/385 and 314/1 for Walberswick.
[52] SRO, HA 30/50/22/10/17(6).
[53] SRO, HA 30/50/22/27/6(2); HA 30/314/18 ms 7, 8. The lord's new close mentioned in 1477–8, also indicates the creation of demesne, in this case enclosed. So does the history of Burghards tenement. It seems to have been newly acquired by the lord in 1463–4; previously farmed by Richard Bingle, it was in that year included in Henry Brown's demesne farm; it was the one part of the demesne he was left farming in 1477–8; by 1483–4 it was in the lord's hands.

possibly to provide more pasture for the lord's as well as demesne farmers' sheep, was this because Hopton chose this course, or was such a policy thrust upon him by his inability to obtain tenants on good enough terms? Either way he was not a landlord who sat still and wrung his hands. The overall value of the estate did not fall.[54]

How the fold courses worked within this expanded demesne we cannot say. Much of it was pasture: Hall meadow, Burghards tenement (or most of it), and the enclosure called le Haughe; there was also the park, as well as the marsh and the fen of North End. How Hopton farmed, and indeed how his tenants farmed, are important questions. The variety of their landed resources is revealed, for example, by the rental of 1437. There were open fields, at any rate at Blythburgh,[55] and there were enclosures of both arable and pasture; they rented meadow, marsh and fen as well as messuages, curtilages and gardens; they held parcels of the heath at Walberswick, reedbeds and alder groves.[56] We are, however, not concerned here with the communities of Blythburgh and Walberswick, composed not just of farmers, smallholders and agricultural labourers, but also of fishermen and seamen; in such an environment a man and his family were fortunate in that they could turn their hands to a number of occupations. As their landlord, resident landlord though he was, John Hopton was not part of their community: his interests were hardly theirs.

It was at the manorial court that his interests as landlord and theirs as tenants coincided or ran foul of each other. Fines were often the result of this confrontation. However, one of the regular items on the discharge side of the accounts, for which the bailiff received allowance, was that of condoned fines: John evidently

---

54 Sir William Hopton bought a messuage by the cemetery of Blythburgh church: see p77 below. This extension of the demesne through purchase was also undertaken by John Hopton at Westleton and Yoxford: see pp60, 70 below.
55 I take it that land lying 'in campo' denotes this. The only field named is Wildgatefield: SRO, HA 30/50/22/27/6(2).
56 *Ibid.* There were curtilages in the new market ('in novo foro') and Alice Candelar held a curtilage called the Feriyerd. John Burward held the Curpettys with the reedbeds there. 'Bruaria' may denote not so much parcels of the heath as the right to take furze there.

took some notice of the way of life of his tenants, for many were forgiven because of their poverty.[57] These allowed amercements seldom added up to much (in monetary terms) – in the years of which we have record they were between 2s and 12s[58] – but to each person concerned they no doubt counted for a great deal (in monetary terms). In 1477–8 indeed two fines were allowed specifically out of charity: 'tantum via elemosine'. There were other reasons, less humanitarian, for the pardoning of court fines. The prior of Blythburgh, for instance, was not the sort of man one pursued for every penny he owed: good neighbourliness and good sense saw to that. He was pardoned £1 in 1464–5, but was owing 22s again in 1477–8, and by the 1480s the large sum of £6; that was almost certainly wiped from the slate in 1490–1. And, conversely, there were sometimes those who would not, and could not be made to, pay: in 1490–1 two men fined for affrays and Alice Stapleton, fined for keeping a brothel, had fled and the bailiff could not distrain on them –or so he said.[59]

So far as John Hopton and his bailiff were concerned these were trifling matters. We must now turn to what they would have seen as the more substantial items of account. The headings of the discharge which we have not discussed are repairs to the manorial buildings, integral expenses of the estate (as defined in the accounts), the bailiff's fee, and liveries to the lord. As these categories of expenditure intermingle after 1477–8 and in that year foreign expenses appear as a separate heading, it is simpler if we concentrate our attention on the 1460s, only supplementing that study with information from later years where it seems relevant or helpful.

Repairs varied from year to year: in 1463–4 the windows of the hall were mended, the thatched roofs of various rooms and the chapel were seen to, a wall of the park was whitewashed, the dovehouse put in order; in 1466–7 it was the kitchen where all the work was undertaken. Costs were under £2 in each case. In 1465–6

---

[57] See for a good example 1466–7, when three men were thus pardoned: SRO, HA 30/314/18 m4.
[58] An exceptional year was 1464–5 when they amounted to well over £6 and twenty men were involved.
[59] SRO, HA 30/369/281.

however, over £5 was spent, chiefly on an extensive overhaul of the long room 'prope portas manerii', and its kitchen; floors and walls renewed, a new fireplace put in and the roof thatched. In 1464–5, on the other hand, only 14s was required for work done to the barn. As one would expect, the house at Westwood and its outbuildings were kept in good repair; thatching was the most frequent item of expense, there being a plentiful supply of reeds from the marshes and fens of the estate; the thatcher and his mate worked for a week in 1490–1, eating at the bailiff's expense (2d a day), the thatcher getting a wage of 4d a day, his mate 2d.[60] For most other jobs in the 1460s Matthew Hunne, the carpenter, was indispensable, and he worked at other tasks besides those at the house itself; for example, in 1465–6 he built a quay beside the bridge at Blythburgh, and it was he, one day in 1463–4, who went to oversee the cutting of timber at Wissett which was to be used for repairs to the house at Cockfield Hall in Yoxford. These expenses, however, and those for the maintenance of the park palings, an unskilled job which did not concern Matthew Hunne but only mere labourers, are to be found among the general, so called integral manorial expenses.

Under this heading (in the 1460s) there is a great diversity of expenditure. Yearly totals range between £5 and £16. To illustrate the nature of these heterogeneous expenses we shall concentrate on two years, 1463–4, when the total was at its highest, and 1466–7, when it was at its lowest. The costs of the steward, supervisor, bailiff and other officers at the manor courts invariably head the list; these were 18s in 1463–4, 16s in 1466–7.[61] The supervisor's expenses varied from year to year: in 1463–4 they were 9s 6d. but in 1466–7, when Robert Hopton, John's brother, had joined him in his tasks, they were a mere 1s 7d. The cost of the audit in 1463–4 came to 6s 7d: the auditor, the steward, the supervisor and the bailiffs of Yoxford, Westhall and Thorington were busy for two days (and three nights) examining the accounts. No such expenses were recorded in 1466–7: probably that year

60 SRO, HA 30/369/281.
61 In 1490–1, when there were eight courts held, expenses amounted to £3 5s 7d, but these included the costs of the guardians of Arthur Hopton and other gentlemen as well as the officials.

the Blythburgh accounts were audited, along with those of the other East Anglian estates, elsewhere.[62] There were also business expenses of a more general nature. In 1466–7 these were not great: an agreement was reached by Hopton with Dunwich that year and the costs of having the Attorney General in to help thrash out the matter, of drawing up documents and of sealing the final accommodation, came to over 13s. This settlement had been years in the making, for in 1463–4 3s 4d was paid for a copy of the royal charter concerning the lord's rights regarding Dunwich, and in the following two years negotiations continued (and continued to be expensive). Apart from the conclusion of this matter, however, there was little in 1466–7 which was other than strictly manorial expenditure. In 1463–4 there was a great deal.

First there was the cost of taking John's stepfather, William Edlington's annuity to London, and Edmund Medley and Thomas Johnson's costs in riding to Castle Carlton, Lincs, and back again on Hopton's affairs – these must also have involved his stepfather. Johnson and Medley with Elis Lumhals, bailiff of Yoxford, also took money over to John Knevet esquire and his son Thomas Knevet (the husband of Elizabeth, daughter of John Hopton's wife Thomasin by her first husband). There was also business between John and the Duke of Suffolk: a man was paid for going to Wingfield; Robert Banyard of Hopton's council and the auditor, Walter Fulbourne, were at Eye for a couple of days; while Walter was there again for four days discussing matters that lay between the duke and Hopton, though what these were we do not know. Such central (as opposed to local) expenses occur in most of the accounts of the 1460s, though never to the same extent as in 1463–4.[63] Besides this sort of expenditure, in 1463–4 (as in other years) there were also what one would describe as household

[62] In 1465–6 the cost of the Blythburgh audit came to 1s 4d. The general audit was made at Westwood in 1483–4 and 1484–5; it took four days on each occasion.

[63] In 1464–5, for instance, the expenses of John and other justices of the peace holding sessions at Blythburgh amounted to 8s 4d; Edmund Clere, the escheator, was entertained at Westwood, a clerk of Hugh Fenn, Under-Treasurer of England, received 2s reward when John made fine to escape knighthood; and Doctor John Allen was paid 1s 2d for writing and sealing a warrant for the manor court of Meriells, Yoxford.

costs. The bailiff accounted, for example, for the lord's expenses at Blythburgh in October 1463, for those of his son John and others during two days' hunting at Wissett, and for the making of robes for the lord's sons by John Abbot, tailor. Moreover, various provisions for household consumption were purchased from the demesne farmer Henry Brown, including butter, milk and pork.[64]

The great majority of costs which we have not so far dealt with in 1463–4 concerned the upkeep of the estate, in other words manorial expenditure proper: on the warren, the park, the fishponds, the felling of timber and the cutting and preparation of wood. In 1466–7, in addition to routine outlay like this, John Moore, shipwright, built a boat for the lord's use on the river: it took him and his mate ten and a half days and their wages came to just under 8s. Occasionally purchases were made for other estates, wainscot for Cockfield Hall in 1463–4 for instance; in the same year too a ditcher was paid 10s for clearing the pond there, Henry Brown carted hay from Yoxford to Westwood, and rye was taken from Westwood to Yoxford. With the estates lying so close to each other these overlapping charges were bound to occur. Finally, under this heading of estate expenses, John Hoo the bailiff received a reward of £1 a year in the 1460s; this was in addition to his fee of £3, which always featured as a separate item on the account.

Such then was the expenditure at Blythburgh. It embraced far more than mere running costs, including as it did household expenses and payments for the business affairs of the lord, not all of which related specifically to this estate. Here the bailiff's double function as estate official and cofferer to the lord ran together, and in his accounts he did not distinguish between his expenditure under different heads: there was no reason why he should if Hopton and the auditors were content. Hence liveries to the lord also include household expenditure and (at least in 1463–4) payments from the lord's coffers; in that year, for example, William

---

[64] The great variety of expenses – central, household *and* manorial – found this year under this heading is the case again in 1477–8 but this time under the heading foreign expenses: SRO, HA 30/314/18 m5.

Edlington's annuity and the money paid to John and Thomas Knevet.

In the 1440s and 1450s the bailiff Nicholas Greenhagh kept a notebook.[65] In it he simply headed the entries: the expenses of John Hopton paid by Nicholas Greenhagh bailiff. They include estate items, fees and household costs, as well as (from time to time) John Hopton's personal spending. Let us take a few pages in illustration, those for 1444–5 for instance. Nicholas purchased quantities of fish (cod, sprats, ling, salmon, herrings[66] and eels) and meat (mutton, pork and veal); he bought oats, malt, salt, candles, pepper and saffron; he also bought barrels of cloth and haber-dashery, two furs and four dozen pattens from Gervaise Nutkin, which stuff was part of the cargo of the ship *Mary Knight*. There were also household and estate maintenance costs: a rope for the well, a new door for the mill, for leading the gutters at the hall, for mending kettles and pans, for making stands and kelers in the brewhouse, and for carting timber from Rumburgh, lead from Beccles and household stuff from Easton Bavents. The toll house was repaired and thatched; a dovecot was bought. He also recorded the fees paid to William Bondes, Hopton's attorney, and to John Ulveston his supervisor, and the money he had handed over to his master at Ipswich, as well as his own costs of a journey to Norwich 'to bye cheper'.[67] These expenses would no doubt have appeared under various heads in the enrolled accounts of that year, some certainly under that of liveries. With the liveries of the 1460s we can now deal.

In 1464–5, 1465–6 and 1466–7 deliveries of cash were impor-tant but not large: £16 in 1464–5 out of a total under the head-ing of liveries of £46; £19 out of a total of £28 in 1465–6; £20 out of a total of £41 in 1466–7.[68] The year 1463–4 was excep-tional because of receipts of £97 from other bailiffs; hence liveries amounted to over £140, of which 100 marks was handed on to

---

[65] SRO, HA 30/369/46.
[66] He also sold 18000 herring at 5s per 1000 to John Manning: SRO, HA 30/369/46 f15.
[67] *Ibid.*, fs7v, 9–15.
[68] In the different circumstances of 1419–20 all the liveries had been of cash delivered to John Thornton, the receiver: they totalled nearly £54.

the lord in cash at one time, and another £1 while he was at Blythburgh in October 1463. Payments to various people by the lord's warrant were sometimes important. For example in 1464–5 Walter Fulbourne, the auditor, received £1, William Micklefield esquire was paid £5 13s 4d, Eleanor, daughter of William Boliant, had 6s 8d, Doctor John Allen 8s 4d as a gift, and Robert Hopton's wife at Southwold 3s 4d. In 1466–7 Robert Hopton himself received £6 13s 4d. Once again 1463–4 was an exceptional year: William Edlington got his annuity of £13 10s 0d, Richard Chandler of Southwark was paid £10, John Knevet 50 marks, and Thomas and Elizabeth Knevet £3 13s 4d. The remaining liveries were in the form of household purchases or family expenses. In 1464–5 cloth and grain were brought at a cost of £14, and other household expenses incurred at Yoxford but charged on this account amounted to £7. In 1465–6 also, a considerable quantity of cloth was purchased for John and Thomasin, their children and servants, some fish was bought for the household at Yoxford, and the abbot of Leiston received 24s for rabbits he had sold to the lord. The bailiff also accounted for 4s paid to John Hopton, the lord's son – the price of a haircut and perhaps a shave for himself and his brothers.[69] In 1466–7 cloth was a major item too and there were purchases of fish, oysters and wine; cloth, fish and wine were also bought in 1463–4 and the bailiff recorded 34s 1d laid out by him on household stuff provided for the lord and lady when they were 'ad scolas apud Northalis'. Such then was the range of the liveries of the 1460s.

In later years there are complications which render it difficult to make comparison with the earlier situation: the heading of foreign payments in 1477–8, for example, includes Robert Hopton's annuity of £6 13s 4d (which had appeared under liveries in 1466–7), and the payment of £6 to Robert Pilgrim for the celebration of masses at Blythburgh, an item which is later discharged on the Westleton accounts under the heading of liveries. Liveries in 1477–8 comprised only deliveries of cash totalling £10, and there was no entry at all under this head in 1478–9.

There are difficulties too when we turn to the question of

[69] Or was this the price of the razor itself? The word is 'razura'.

arrears. Essentially we do not have a good series of accounts. The four consecutive accounts between 1463–4 and 1466–7 suggest – but only suggest – that the problem of arrears was not an overwhelming one. At the start of the first year arrears were at the comparatively high figure of £24. This was reduced to £15 during the course of the accounting year, and was reduced still further during 1464–5 to a mere £5.[70] This sum was made up of £3 8s 7¾d owed from before 1463–4 by the previous bailiff but one, £1 6s 8d owed by Katherine, wife of John Deynes of Wickham Market, for rabbits bought by her in 1462–3, and an annual rent of 10d for marshland unpaid by Robert Hopton for eight years. By the close of 1465–6 these arrears still stood and in addition Henry Brown owed £6 16s 8d (half his demesne farm of that year), uncollected amercements amounted to 13s 4d and the bailiff himself owed £1 16s 8d. Thus total arrears at the head of the account for 1466–7 had risen again to over £14. During that year Henry Brown paid off his arrears but did not pay his farm for the current year, while the old arrears of the last bailiff but one, of Katherine Deynes and of Robert Hopton remained unpaid, and the uncollected amercements had risen to £1. So at the end of our sequence of accounts arrears stood at £19. The bulk of them was made up of Brown's demesne farm of £13 10s 0d for the immediately preceding year. He had not been at all in arrears before 1465–6 and there is ittle reason to suppose that his farm for 1466–7 would go unpaid for long. In 1477–8, by which time he was only farming part of the demesne (at £3 6s 8d per annum), his arrears at the opening of the account were only £2 6s 8d, which he owed from the previous year. He paid off these arrears in the course of the year. We can, I think, safely assume Henry

70 The £15 was composed of the sums still owing in the following year (viz. £3 8s 7¾d from a former bailiff, Katherine Deynes' £1 6s 8d and the 5s 10d owed by Robert Hopton), £3 12s 0d owed for rabbits from William Jenny, £3 owed by the farmers of Stronders tenement, 9s 9½d owed by John English, bailiff the previous year, £1 13s 4d owed by a former lessee of the ferry, and £2 of unpaid amercements. During 1464–5 this was reduced after this fashion: Jenny paid his debt and so did John English, the £3 for Stronders tenement was allowed as it was in the lord's hands and the amercements were forgiven. I can find no trace of how the arrears of the ferry were eliminated.

Brown was not a problem to the bailiff. On the other hand the debt of the former bailiff was; it looks very much like a straightforward bad debt; perhaps Katherine Deynes' £1 6s 8d should be put in that category also. Robert Hopton's unpaid rent was unimportant, whether it was paid or not.

These desperate debts may have been included in the bailiff's own arrears of nearly £10 at the start of 1477–8. In addition there were unpaid amercements totalling about £7, Henry Brown's £2 6s 8d, and John Walker's arrears of £2 os 4d from his farm of the warren of £2 13s 4d per annum. John paid off part of his arrears and Henry Brown all his during the year. Yet at the close of the account the bailiff owed over £35; unfortunately he gives us no details. This debt was wiped off at the opening of the following year because there was a new lord of the estate: William Hopton. The accounts of the 1480s suggest, however, that arrears in William's time were of no greater concern than they had been in the 1460s. At the beginning of 1480–1 they stood at £14; the prior of Blythburgh owed £6 in amercements, Edward Derykson 14s 9d also in amercements, John Warner, farmer of the warren, owed £5, and Robert Dolfinby, just replaced as farmer of the ferry, £2 12s od. By the close of the year arrears had been reduced slightly to £13: the prior and Edward Derykson owed the same sums as before, John Warner – having paid off his arrears – owed £5 5s 5d out of his new lease of the warren of £8, and the bailiff's own debt was a little over a £1. By 1483–4 arrears were down to £10: the prior still owed £6, Derykson's debt was now over £1, and Thomas Pigot (who farmed the ferry) owed nearly £3. At the close of the year the position was much the same save in one important respect: Pigot's debt now stood at nearly £6. He alleged that this had been paid, but his claim was not allowed as his arrears stood at this figure at the head of the accounts of 1484–5. He apparently paid off £2 in the course of the year, yet at its close he was recorded as owing £6 12s 11d. It was then recorded that he was to pay £1 the following Christmas, £3 before Easter and £2 by the Michaelmas of 1486; this done he would be allowed the old debt of 12s 11d owed to Thomasin. There alas our information fails us. We do not know whether he honoured this undertaking. The other additions to arrears by Michaelmas 1485 – additions that is to Pigot's debt and those of the prior and Derykson – were the new farms of the demesne: just over £3 from John Deynes and 30s from Thomas Harlewin, and £4 owed by the farmer of the warren John Warner, a total of £22. This may have been a large figure, but it was (one feels) only temporarily so. If Pigot duly paid his debt (and the auditors were clearly concerned that he should), then there was little to worry the bailiff here. The demesne farmers and John Warner were not behindhand to any disturbing extent, and the prior of Blythburgh's £6 was the sort of debt which was really not the bailiff's responsibility to see gathered in. All in all this evidence from the 1480s complements that of the 1460s: long term arrears were not a major consideration in the management of the estate. The collection of rents seems to have proved no problem at all.

Our survey has been detailed. The search for answers to some of the more important questions has been, as is so often the case, fruitless; above all we are still a very long distance from an understanding of John Hopton's demesne farming. We do not know how profiitable that farming was, particularly we do not know about his pastoral farming; our ignorance on these points, allied to the other difficulties we have encountered, makes any attempt to arrive at the clear yield of the estate plainly impossible. All we can hope to indicate is a minimum figure. That, in the rough and ready fashion which is the only course open to us, is quickly done. If we take the four accounts of the early 1460s, which are the easiest to handle for this purpose, we discover that the clear potential yield was around £40 a year.[71] There we should let things be.

The equally large estate of Westleton lay immediately to the south of Blythburgh and Walberswick, and surrounded Dunwich on that port's landward side. It comprised perhaps even more heath

---

[71] This has been arrived at by subtracting from the charge, arrears, decays and allowances, local expenses, the bailiff's fee and reward. On this basis the figure in 1419–20 was £52, in 1483–4 £45.

than did Blythburgh, and it too had its marshes.[72] Its handful of accounts from the 1470s and 1480s[73] present us with fewer problems than those of Blythburgh; the story they have to tell is a straightforward one and it should not detain us long. The Westleton estate was composed of four manors: Westleton itself, which included the two manors of Valens and Bovyles always associated with it, Lembaldes, Claydons, and Risings.[74]

The most substantial of the manors was Lembaldes, which also comprised lands outside Westleton in Darsham[75] and Thorington.[76] The rents and farms of Lembaldes at over £32 were greater than those of all the other manors put together, at less than £23. Claydons and Risings were very small manors indeed.[77] Rents and farms of all the manors were virtually the same throughout the twenty years covered by the accounts; the only alteration came after a new rental of Michaelmas 1487, as a result of which new rents of some 25s appear on the accounts of 1490–1. These apart, rents were £39, farms £16 per annum. Decays were also more or less static at about £10 a year.[78] Outgoing rents, which at £9 a year were a large item, also remained unchanged.[79] Thus, once

[72] The boundaries of its seven fields are instructively described in the 1478 terrier: SRO, HA 30/50/22/27/7(1).

[73] For 1469–70, 1477–8, 1478–9, 1481–2, 1490–1: SRO, HA 30/314/10, 30/22/11/3 (bis), 30/369/39, 30/312/424.

[74] The minute manor of Cleves had been owned by the Codon family of Dunwich in the later fourteenth century: BL, Add Charter 17632: a rental of Cleves, then held by Peter Codon, of 1374–5. It kept its identity in the rentals but not in the accounts of the fifteenth century. The Codons remained substantial tenants in Westleton into the sixteenth century; they were bailiffs of Dunwich and sat for the borough in the Commons: Thomas Gardner, *An Historical Account of Dunwich* (1754), pp77ff, 88ff; Wedgwood, p201. The purchase of the estate perhaps took place c.1400, as in May 1403 Sir Roger Swillington undertook, under a surety of £100, to do no harm to Peter Codon of Dunwich: *CCR 1402–5*, p168.

[75] The Darsham lands probably comprised a small manor called Austins: Copinger II, p58. A rental of the time of Sir Roger Swillington has rents from Darsham of nearly £11, another of 1424–5 has Darsham rents of nearly £9: HA 30/312/399, HA 30/50/22/11/10/1.

[76] Perhaps Thorington Hall manor: see Copinger II, p167. The rentals mentioned in the last note include rents of just over £2 from Thorington.

[77] Rents and farms at Claydons were less than £4, at Risings less than £6.

[78] As at Blythburgh, there were reviews every ten years, i.e. 1460 and 1470, but these made very little difference.

[79] These outgoing rents are bewildering in their complexity, involving as they do payments between the manors: Westleton paid 16s 4d to Lembaldes,

decays and outgoing rents have been allowed for, potential receipts from rents and farms amounted to £36.

There were, however, changes with regard to the leasing of the demesne. By an indenture of 10 September 1457 the farm of the demesne was granted to the abbot of Sibton for eighty years at a rent of 7 marks yearly. The lease included the manorial buildings and the great wood, some 16 acres in extent.[80] The abbot and convent of Sibton, who were substantial farmers in their own right in north east Suffolk, who had a grange at Westleton and owned the church there,[81] were in possession in the 1470s but in 1481–2 had ceased farming the whole demesne; this was now leased out in parcels. They continued to hold 8 acres of land by the mill mound, and a meadow called Loppings, at a rent of a £1 a year. The rents of the remaining eleven parcels, leased to various men, amounted to £3 8s 8d. The wood, and two closes containing 55 acres were in the lord's hands: their leased value was said to have been £2 10s 0d. In 1490–1, and apparently since 1487, all the demesne was once more at farm and to various men for a total rent of £7 1s 7d. It would appear therefore that Sibton Abbey had had a good bargain in 1457, and one which they enjoyed for some twenty years. The termination of their lease, long before it was due to fall in, resulted in an increased rent from the demesne of nearly £3 for George and Arthur Hopton, but the break with Sibton had been made by Sir William Hopton, very soon after he had inherited the estate in autumn 1478.

The remaining sources of income at Westleton were unimportant. Works sold raised just over 6s each year and the profits of courts were between £1 and 30s, save in 1490–1 when they were over £5. As at Blythburgh that year, the new young lord's

Lembaldes paid something over 5s to Westleton, for example. Risings, out of a total income from rents and farms of £5 16s 8d, had outgoing rents of £3 9s 8½d, including £2 5s 0d to Lembaldes and nearly £1 to Westleton. Some of the rents paid outside the estate went to the heirs of various people, demonstrating (as in the case of the manor of Cleves) how the estate had been put together through the purchase of small properties.

80 SRO, HA 30/369/325.
81 A. H. Denney, *The Sibton Abbey Estates*, Suffolk Record Society, II (1960), *passim*, and especially p23. They ran a small dairy farm at Westleton in the early sixteenth century: *ibid.*, p34.

councillors and friends had initiated a sweeping judicial campaign: there were in fact two fines of £2 apiece on Adam Harvey and Thomas Leverich for prosecuting suits in courts other than that of Westleton. The profits of the manor were a most variable item; in 1469–70, 1478–9 and 1490–1 there were none. In 1477–8 nearly 30s was received from the sale of reeds, and in 1481–2 William Reynolds paid 10s for an acre of underwood. With the demesne and the manorial buildings at farm for most of this time there can have been no other resources, the reedbeds apart, from which to derive any additional profits. Such then were the items of receipt at Westleton: the rents and farms of the tenants were the most important, the farm of the demesne came a long way second, and other sources were small beer.

In total, bearing in mind that we have already subtracted decays and outgoing rents, potential receipts were about £42 per annum, save in 1490–1 when the new rents, the increased demesne farm, and the large profits of the courts make the total nearer £50. This figure is in fact very close to that of a valor of the estate made in 1505–6.[82] There the 'holl sumne of valor' is reckoned to be £50 11s 8d, before certain deductions are made. This sum was arrived at, however, rather differently to ours. The rents and farms – including probably that of the demesne – were valued at £46 11s 8d per annum, while the sale of wood and underwood was put at £2 a year, as were the profits of the courts. The hopeful estimate of wood sales apart,[83] it is the high figure for rents which is immediately most startling, though it is perhaps less so in the light of our last account of 1490–1, for in that year rents, including the demesne farm, amounted to over £44. Some fifteen years later a figure of £46, based as it was on a new rental,[84] was probably an accurate evaluation of the situation. It was however probably less accurate where it dealt with necessary expenditure, as we shall see.

What do our accounts reveal of expenditure at Westleton?

<hr/>

82 SRO, HA 30/312/400.
83 The phrase was 'may be sold'.
84 That is what SRO, HA 30/312/400 actually is. It is titled: a rental in this 21st year of Henry VII. The brief valor comes almost as an afterthought at the end.

There was, first, the annual pension paid to the heirs of Bartholo-mew Bacon. This perhaps has its origin in a purchase of property within Westleton, and, like other such payments among outgoing rents, was presumably paid in lieu of certain rights, judicial and otherwise, now exercised by the Hoptons. In this case the property concerned may have been the former manor of Minsmere, appar-ently once held by the Bacon family.[85] The fees of the bailiff (for some time Robert Payn, the Blythburgh sheep reeve in 1477–8), and of the auditor of the Norfolk and Suffolk estates, Walter Fulbourne, were also a stable item. The remaining items on the discharge side of the account, in contrast to those we have hitherto discussed, varied both in amount and in type from year to year. In sum, maintenance costs, other local expenses, rents allowed and amercements remitted were £13 in 1469–70, and £14 in 1477–8. In 1478–9 and 1481–2, however, there were only neces-sary expenses and they amounted to only just over £1 in 1478–9 and less than £2 in 1481–2. In 1490–1 merely 13s 8d was spent. These total figures warn us that, with only five accounts to work from, generalizations about expenditure at Westleton are bound to be speculative. Nor is expenditure at all the right word to employ, as an examination of the 1469–70 items will show. For of that £13 just over £11 was for an allowance on the arrears of rent and the relief owed by Peter Codon; the allowance was made in virtue of an agreement that Peter should pay £4 over the following accounting year, a £1 at a time at Christmas, Easter, the Nativity of John the Baptist, and Michaelmas. The bailiff duly recorded this £4 among the arrears at the close of the account. Other rents allowed amounted to 8s and condoned amercements to 3s. Thus the actual costs of the bailiff this year came to only a little over £2, of which the greater part was for the repair of the walls, and for the thatching of the roof, of the hall; the expenses of the steward and the other officers at the courts were just 3s 3d.

In 1477–8, on the other hand, actual expenditure was high and allowances did not count for much: arrears of rent of just over £1 were allowed to John Alned because of his poverty, a fine of £1 for entry into a tenement was cut by half, pardoned amercements

[85] Copinger II, p197.

came to 11d, and that was all. The chief expense this year was of
£5 6s 8d for land purchased by John Hopton from the executors
of a servile tenant, Walter Grimbell: here, as at Blythburgh, the
demesne was being extended and the increased demesne leases of
the 1480s are perhaps accounted for. Hopton was also renting
land this year: 5 acres in Darsham field for 10d, and a close in
Bramfield leased from the owners of that manor, the college of
Mettingham, for £1 6s 8d. This was specifically for the pasture
of his animals. It is our only glimpse, and a tantalising one, of
Hopton's own farming. Other costs of this year were connected
with the making of the terrier, which still survives.[86] John Grickis
spent five weeks during the summer at Westleton and Yoxford
drawing up this detailed survey of the manors in Westleton,
receiving £1 13s 4d as his salary. Food and drink for him, his
servant, for Robert Payn, and for Robert Vincent (bailiff that
year), who worked together for three weeks in the fields checking
the boundaries of lands and tenements, the expense of the tenants
helping them in this task, and the price of paper and ink came to
almost another £1. Grickis, now termed the auditor, also received
a fee of £1 for his labours on the accounts of the farmers and
bailiffs of the Suffolk estates,[87] and another 3s 4d for travelling to
London on the lord's business. Whether the other extraordinary
payments of this year were connected with the making of the
terrier we cannot tell; they may well not be connected with
Westleton at all: Robert Cooper received a fee of 6s 8d, the clerk
of the under-sheriff had a 'reward' of 1s 8d and at Easter 1478
Roger Townshend's clerk got a similar sum, while the under-
steward of the honour of Eye was paid 3s 4d for his favour.
Routine costs were for the cutting, preparation and carriage of
reeds and rushes, some of which went for Hopton's household use,
and for the purchase of wood and nails at Bramfield, destined for
use at Cockfield Hall. Expenses at the courts came to 6s 3d.
Thus 1477–8 was a year of relatively heavy and certainly diverse
expenditure. In comparison 1478–9, 1481–2, and 1490–1 were
years of little activity in this respect. Reeds and rushes were cut

[86] SRO, HA 30/50/22/27/7/1.
[87] Actually for 'making' the accounts: SRO, HA 30/22/11/3.

and carried, the pinfold was repaired in 1478–9 and again in 1490–1, the old barn in 1481–2, and there were the expenses of the courts.

Liveries, the last item of the discharge, also show variation, not so much in their totals as in the manner of their payment. In 1469–70 liveries were largely in the form of straightforward cash deliveries out of current revenues and arrears, two in June and two, after the account had closed, in November, amounting to £30. Another £1 from the arrears of John Wainfleet was also handed over in cash, and a further £2 in cash was delivered as late as December 1470. In addition £1 8s 4d went to Elis Lumhals, the bailiff of Yoxford, as his fee for the preceding year: this money had come from William Jenny, Hopton's neighbour at Knodishall, who had at one sweep paid up four years' arrears of rent. Thus in all liveries amounted to £34 8s 4d.

In 1477–8 – that year of high 'real' expenditure – liveries were only £24 11s 2d, but they were in a very different form to those of eight years previously. Cash deliveries came to no more than £10 12s 11d, of which £3 12s 11d was from arrears; there were then payments to a variety of people, including 6s to Edward Dutchman, no doubt the Edward 'Tutonicus' who also received a robe this year, charged on the Blythburgh accounts,[88] 3s 4d to the parker at Wissett, and 12s 6d to John Bishop, Hopton's attorney.[89] These small payments amounted to just over a pound. Also 3s 4d was given to the vicar of Westleton for singing for the souls of the parents, friends and benefactors of the lord, and John West received £6 for singing at Blythburgh church for the same souls throughout the year. Robert Pilgrim, his fellow chaplain at Blythburgh, also received £6 this year, but this was out of the Blythburgh revenues; as we shall see, however, both were soon to be paid out of the revenues of Westleton. The most interesting liveries in 1477–8 concerned Robert, John Hopton's son: the

[88] SRO, HA 30/314/18 m5.
[89] It looks as though some of the costs of the lord's business affairs were charged on the Westleton account. As we have already noticed at Blythburgh (and will notice again at Yoxford) the charging of central expenses on the accounts of various estates – as convenience dictated – is common practice.

bailiff paid £2 to Thomasin on 10 June for his commons at Snettisham in Norfolk, where he had lately been at school, and on 18 October he paid her £5 for the young man's commons at London. These then were the liveries of 1477-8.

In the following year there was also variety. Of a total of nearly £32 discharged under the heading of liveries, John West received £6 (as in 1477-8) and Robert Pilgrim £4 10s for three-quarters of a year; John Hoo, the Blythburgh bailiff, was paid £7 13s 4d for herrings purchased from him for the lord's house-hold; nearly £3 was handed over to the lord in cash; and Robert Hopton, the new lord's brother, he who had been at school the year before, received a pension of £10. By 1481-2 Robert's annuity came under a separate heading of annual pensions, where it was accompanied by the £5 paid to the heirs of Bartholomew Bacon; if however we add it to the liveries proper we shall have a clearer comparison with earlier years. Among the liveries of 1481-2 appears the £12 paid to the priests John West and Robert Pilgrim for their mass singing; the remaining £10 or so was delivered in cash to the lord. Thus the total this year was just short of £32.

By 1490-1 the movement towards the use of Westleton revenues for pensions and annuities had been completed. This year the Westwood parker's fee of £3 was charged at Westleton under the heading of fees. Under annual pensions featured the £12 paid to the two priests at Blythburgh, Robert Pilgrim and George Hawes (who had replaced John West); this was now termed a life annuity and the priests were stated specifically to be singing for the souls of John Hopton, Sir Roger Swillington, and their friends. George Hawes in addition received 30s for the following quarter year. There was also a new heading of annuities: under this Roger and William Hopton, sons of John Hopton, received £10 apiece; these annuities had been granted them by Sir George Hopton, their nephew, in his will. Altogether these pensions and annuities amounted to over £36. It is therefore not surprising that nothing is recorded under the heading of liveries to Robert Clere, one of the guardians of the new lord, the child Arthur Hopton. Westleton's available revenues were now entirely diverted to the payment of fees, pensions and annuities, and what we have termed central costs. This, it should be noted, was largely a change that came after John Hopton's death in 1478.

None of these payments was taken into account in the valor of 1505–6. Either they were no longer being made or they were not considered as essential charges on the estate. In fact the valor counts as deductions from the 'holl sumne of valor' of £50 11s 8d only a few outgoing rents (adding up to 4s 2d), the ward and suit of court payment to Eye, and an annual pension of £5 to Christopher Calthorp, probably an heir of Bartholomew Bacon. It makes no mention of maintenance costs or other expenses. The final 'valor of the manner of Westleton...by yere clere' is therefore put at £44 13s 4d.[90] Evidently the compilers of the valor had a different understanding of clear value to that of modern scholars. In this instance perhaps liveries at around £30 a year,[91] good indications at least of a minimum figure, are our safest guide to Westleton's clear annual value to John Hopton.

When we turn to examine arrears, however, we cannot manufacture such simple solutions. At the opening of the 1469–70 account arrears totalled £32, a third of the total charge of £93. At the close of the year the sum of arrears was £16. The main deduction had been effected in the allowance made to Peter Codon in the arrears of his rent and relief: in return for the wiping out of £7 Peter agreed to pay the balance of £4 over the succeeding accounting year. The remaining reduction of £9 was, so far as we can tell, effected through payments made in the course of 1469–70.[92] Of the £16 which stood unpaid at Michaelmas 1470, little was of recent origin. Much had been owed, or had been accumulating for years; some debts had had their origin twenty-five years previously. Before we attempt any judgment on this situation, let us see what the fate of these old debts was; in fact many of them were to continue on the books, some until

[90] SRO, HA 30/312/400.
[91] Counting the pensions, annuities, and fees of 1490–1 as 'liveries' the average of our five accounts is £31.
[92] Under the heading of liveries the bailiff accounted for £1 out of the arrears of John Wainfleet and £1 8s 4d, the full arrears of four years' rent paid up by William Jenny, while other liveries he recorded as being from both current revenues and arrears.

1490–1, despite the bold heading of no arrears at the opening of the account of 1478–9. One small item of rent arrears was finally remitted in 1477–8 because of the tenant's poverty, one small fine for respite of suit of court was paid that year, and the debts of former bailiffs (amounting to £6) had disappeared by the early 1480s. Peter Codon may have paid off his £4 in 1470–1, but he was in arrears to the sum of £2 13s 4d at the beginning of 1477–8, and £2 at the end of that year. By 1481–2, however, he too has disappeared. Almost all the other longstanding debts of 1469–70 went on and on.[93] They were still owing in 1481–2: by then they amounted to £4, out of total arrears at the end of the year of £6.

The piecemeal information on arrears is more confusing than otherwise. It poses too many questions. For example, how unusual was Peter Codon's large debt of £11 in 1469–70? Was the administration's method of dealing with it – allowing the greater part of the sum in an attempt to secure the smaller part[94] – normal practice in such circumstances? Why were certain small rents unpaid for nearly forty years? Were they in fact properly arrears? If there was no hope of collecting them why were they carefully recorded each year on the accounts? Why did the extent of 1463[95] or the grand new terrier of 1478 make no difference here? If these questions bear upon the efficiency of estate management at Westleton, or at any rate upon the realism of the documents it concocted, we must retain a sense of perspective, at least in terms of the money involved. For presuming Peter Codon's £11 to have been exceptional, which I think it is fair to do, the long term rent arrears, presumably uncollectable, came to less than £5 after thirty-eight years; their annual value was no more than 2s 6d out of a total rent charge, *after* decays and outgoing rents have been subtracted, of £36 per annum.

In the end we have possibly arrived at a more favourable estimate of the administration at Westleton than that which we

---

[93] The one exception was William Jenny's twenty-five year debt of 4d for respite of suit of court, overlooked rather than paid in 1471; it was seven years behindhand in 1478.

[94] It was of course a common enough procedure; even Sir John Fastolf had to be content with such a compromise: Davis II, pp191–2.

[95] SRO, HA 30/372/2.

had at the beginning of our enquiry into arrears.[96] Perhaps arrears were more of a problem here than at Blythburgh: Peter Codon's large debt should not be dismissed, nor the fact that the greater part of it was eventually written off unpaid. Nevertheless our suggestion that Hopton's clear income from the estate was at least £30 per annum would appear to survive this examination of arrears. There were a large number, and a great diversity of rents to be collected at Westleton, from a wide variety of people, not all of them resident, and some of them rather grand.[97] The administration seems to have gathered in the great majority of them safely each year.

Yoxford, although at no great distance from them, was not at all like Blythburgh and Westleton. It lay inland: there were no marshes and sandy heaths here. In a well-watered valley on the edge of upland Suffolk its rich meadows and fertile clay fields stretched up the shallow slopes to the boundaries with Bramfield, Sibton, and Kelsale. One bailiff administered the four manors of Yoxford, Meriells, Brendfen and Cockfield Hall. Only four accounts survive, two for the 1440s, one (in English instead of the usual Latin) for 1483–4, and the other for 1492–3.[98] With such slight and widely scattered evidence we cannot attempt much. What is possible, nonetheless, is a tentative comparison between the situation of the mid-1440s and that of some 40 or 50 years later, after the death of John Hopton. First let us examine Yoxford in the middle years of the 1440s.

Yoxford itself was the most substantial of the four manors, with

[96] The arrears lists of 1435 and 1479 give some support to this conclusion. In 1435 only two items amounting to 10s were recorded, and the bailiff was stated to owe nothing: SRO, HA 30/50/22/8/3. In 1479 there was but a single entry for Westleton; Elis Lumhals oved £4 for two years' rent of the tenement, the earlier manor, of Cleves: SRO, HA 30/369/31.

[97] For example the priors of Butley and Snape, the abbot of Sibton and the prioress of Campsey, the Duke of Suffolk, the Bedingfield family, dame Matilda Morris, the hospital of St James and the churchwardens of All Saints, Dunwich, and John Tropenall of Kelsale: SRO, HA 30/372/2, 312/399, 369/38, 50/22/11/10/1. Nor obviously were the Codon family of Dunwich easy to deal with.

[98] SRO, HA 30/314/14, for 1443–4; 30/369/393, for 1445–6; 30/369/391, for 1483–4; 30/312/117, for 1492–3: the heading and first entries (arrears and Yoxford charge) are missing.

its farms (including those of demesne) charged at just over £24, and its rents at nearly £15. Brendfen's farms and rents totalled just short of £16, Cockfield Hall's just over £13, and Meriells' between £3 and £4. The farms were all of small parcels, save for demesne meadow at Yoxford for £4 and Middleton meadow in Brendfen for £3, and at Cockfield Hall where Robert Flemming leased the demesne land, meadow, pasture, and woods for £9. His farm of the manor, as it was described, was for twelve years; he had been in possession since 1441–2. The total charge of rents and farms was therefore £61. Various small outgoing rents and payments amounted to 30s, and decays and respited rents came to £6 10s 0d. Thus in the years 1443–4 and 1445–6 the anticipated revenue from rents and farms was £53 per annum. Profits of the courts added £1 2s 5d to this figure in 1443–4, and £2 6s 0d in 1445–6. The odd customary payment of a goose, chickens or capons, and money received for works sold amounted only to a few shillings, but the sale of wood fetched £10 in 1443–4; no wood sales, however, were recorded in 1445–6. So much then for what the estate might be expected to yield in the mid-1440s.

What of necessary expenses? On an estate wholly rented out they were negligible. The heaviest of them was the bailiff's fee of £3. In 1443–4 William Bondes, Hopton's attorney, also received his fee of 13s 4d from this source, though it was the Blythburgh bailiff who paid it to him in the following year.[99] Other 'local' expenses, including the price of hay sent to Westwood and of winter supplies of meat for the household at Blythburgh, totalled not much over £1 in both years. It would seem therefore that between about £50 and £60 a year might have been available to Hopton in the mid-1440s, and that what made the difference were sales of wood, which at £10 in 1443–4 made a considerable addition to his income. In fact he did not receive such sums. In 1443–4 liveries amounted to nearly £55, in 1445–6 they totalled just less than £43. Arrears were the problem, in particular those of Robert Flemming, the demesne lessee of Cockfield Hall.

99 SRO, HA 30/369/46, account book f10v. The fee of Reginald Rene (or Reve), the steward of the East Anglian manors, was not paid out of the issue of Meriells in 1443–4, as it had been paid by Hopton himself: 'quia per dominum': SRO, HA 30/314/14 m2d.

Problem is too strong a word; after all, two accounts hardly give us ground for being so categorical. All we can say is that in those two years Hopton did not get the profits he should have had from Yoxford, largely because Flemming was not paying his farm on time. Flemming apart, however, arrears still appear to have been running high. In an arrears list of Michaelmas 1435 the bailiff John Wolsey had arrears of £13, there was an unpaid amercement of 6s 8d, and Clement Rollesby, the vicar of Yoxford and sometime collector of rents there, owed £1.[100] At the outset of the 1443-4 account, besides Flemming's debt of £14, arrears of £21 were recorded, £3 of this being owed by the previous collectors of rent at Meriells, John Noble and Clement Rollesby. At the close of the account John Noble had 9s 3d outstanding, Clement Rollesby had finally dispatched his debt, and another £1 had also been cleared. A year later, at Michaelmas 1445, Flemming continued to owe £14 and other arrears were £22. By Michaelmas 1446 Flemming owed £21; other arrears were still less than £23. Thus in eleven years between 1435 and 1446 arrears, other than those of Flemming's demesne lease, had increased by £9 which, at less than £1 a year on an annual rent charge of over £60, does not appear quite as desperate a situation as at first sight.

The real problem, if real it was, was presented by Robert Flemming. As we have seen, at Michaelmas 1443 he was £14 in arrears. He had been farming Cockfield Hall at £9 6s 8d per annum, for two years; he had therefore only paid £4 13s 4d out of a required total of £18 13s 4d. In the course of 1443-4 he did better: he paid £11 6s 8d, so reducing his arrears by Michaelmas 1444 to exactly £12. As by the following Michaelmas he owed £13 12s 8½d, he had paid £7 13s 11½d during 1444-5, a year for which we have no accounts. This steadier record was not maintained. In 1445-6 he paid only £2, and therefore at Michaelmas 1446 his debt stood at £20 19s 4½d. Put another way, after five years of his twelve-year lease had run, he was a little over two years behindhand on his annual payments. We do not know how he fared in future years, and we cannot predict how he might

[100] SRO, HA 30/50/22/8/3.

have fared; the situation does not look wholly good in 1446, but it does not look wholly bad either. That he had the capacity to pay and to clear his arrears is evident from the accounts of 1443–4. Nevertheless his dilatoriness meant that in 1445–6 the bailiff, John Wolsey, handed over to John Hopton rather less than Hopton, if he minded these matters, would have looked for. That year in fact he drew from Yoxford about £10 less than what was stated baldly at the foot of the account to be the clear value for the year: £52 13s 4d.[101]

In the following years the administration of Yoxford, at least in terms of rents, appears to have been overhauled. There was a new rental for Brendfen in 1449–50, and in 1471 both an extent[102] and a carefully written and well produced rental of all the manors were made.[103] In this small, bound book each tenant appears with his scattered holdings in the various manors grouped together, and with the full sum of his rent. At the end of the book are manorial lists of tenants, but simply with names and sums; the holdings are not again described. The novel form of this rental, as earlier existing rentals and lists of farms are manorial ones only,[104] would evidently have made the collection of rents and arrears easier, for it enabled the bailiff to see a tenant's total obligation at a glance.[105]

Also after 1471–2 rents and farms were no longer distinguished. Only a handful of farms were not transformed into rents at that

101 SRO, HA 30/369/393: 'valor ibidem hoc anno de claro £52 13s 4d'. It is in the same hand as the account itself.
102 These two are both to be found in SRO, HA 30/369/2.
103 SRO, HA 30/369/1.
104 Cockfield Hall for 1420–1 (SRO, HA 30/369/306); Yoxford and Meriells from the time of Sir Roger Swillington (SRO, HA 30/369/292); Yoxford and Brendfen, undated, but before 1443 (SRO, HA 30/378/3).
105 Yet, oddly enough, the accounts were drawn up in the old manner. In 1483–4 rents remain under their separate manorial headings as they had done in 1445–6; if therefore the bailiff collected from each tenant his rent for all his holdings, he still had to divide up the monies into manorial sums (if he was to keep any check at all on arrears). This somewhat complex process would surely have involved a deal of paper work, on different scraps of paper, and perhaps a variety of money bags: the bailiff on his rent collecting rounds may have had a cluttered appearance. At least he did not have to keep distinct accounts for each manor, as he had done in 1443–4. When he had had to do that he had the additional burden of debiting himself as one bailiff and crediting himself as another; this would have involved even more calculations on pieces of paper.

time and these were not therefore included in the new rental; they comprised certain parcels of land, meadow and pasture at Yoxford, Middleton meadow at Brendfen, and virtually all the demesne land, meadow and pasture at Cockfield Hall. The explanation for this aspect of the rationalization of 1471 is surely that the greater part of the former demesne at Yoxford, Brendfen and Meriells at last came to be regarded officially as land which the tenants rented, in the same way as they rented their bond or free tenements. Presumably too this was a final recognition that on these three manors direct exploitation of the demesne was a thing of the past, and was not to be something for the future. At Cockfield Hall it was a different matter; there the demesne had been treated differently in the mid-1440s when it was leased en bloc, now it was excluded from the 1471-2 rental, and therefore could be directly farmed again, as we shall see it was.

The chief object of the 1471 rental, however, may have been to take account of decayed and respited rents. The outcome here, as one would expect, was simply that the decays and respites which were allowed in the 1440s (and thereafter) were formally incorporated into the new rents. In other words, the rent charge was merely rationalized by reducing it to the reality of what was collectable. In brief this meant, according to the rental, a charge of £39, excluding Cockfield Hall demesne, Middleton meadow and other parcels at Yoxford, which did not feature in it. This was a drop of about £7. That £7 was now written off. Thus, in the accounts of 1483-4 there was a rent charge of £39, no decays, and a single allowance of 6s 5d. Pretty well all that the 1471 rental represents, therefore, is a bringing of the books up to date: that was the limited nature of administrative renewal.

What besides rents comprised the charge in 1483-4? At Yoxford various pieces of land and meadow were leased for £3. Another 9 acres of meadow were retained by John Hopton's widow Thomasin for hay for her own use. She also retained for the same purpose the 10 acre Middleton meadow in Brendfen and the greater part of Cockfield demesne: land, meadow, pasture (most of it enclosed) and the manor house itself with its gardens and ponds. A good many of these closes and other pieces at Cockfield were in her hands because they were required for the dairy.[106] Close by, at the North Grange on the Sibton Abbey estate of Sibton, there was another dairy farm.[107] Sibton Abbey by the late fifteenth century had also abandoned demesne farming, apart from this new venture, which in the early sixteenth century was evidently an increasingly profitable one.[108] At Cockfield, however, it seems likely that the produce from the dairy was mainly for household use; that was certainly the case in 1492–3 when the dairy was leased out and Thomasin took a good part of the value of the lease in kind. So in 1483–4 most of the demesne at Cockfield was used for this small home dairy;[109] only a few parcels were leased out for £2 10s od in all.[110] The bailiff later added to his charge £2 12s 4d received from the lease of lands, meadow and pasture pertaining to a tenement called Cleves.[111]

In addition to these small sums from farms, £4 11s od was recorded for the sale of faggots from Yoxford wood, £1 12s 11d as the profits of the three courts held during the year, and 2s 7d as the value of rents in capons and chickens – the single goose went straight to Thomasin's kitchen. Thus the total charge in 1483–4 amounted to £54. That this was almost all real revenue we have already mentioned; there were no decays or respites and just one allowance of 6s 5d, which was for Cleves tenement then in Thomasin's hands. Outgoing rents were a few shillings more than in the mid-1440s, at £2. The bailiff, William Audley, received no wages, and his expenses (under the heading of allowances) comprised a single item: 4d for parchment for his account, for the

106 So I take 'deyry': SRO, HA 30/369/91.
107 It first rendered a separate account at the abbey audit in 1507: Denney, 37–9, 141–2.
108 Ibid., pp12, 39. They also had a small dairy at Westleton at this time, ibid., p34.
109 Is it worth the remark that it may represent Thomasin's concern for a wholesome diet? In a broader context the dairy farm at Cockfield Hall is more evidence of a better standard of living in late medieval England.
110 In a marginal note Thomas Carter was allowed his 4d farm for Pyntlesacre, as he had already been charged for it under the heading of rents.
111 The tenement itself was in the lady's hands 'being of the purchase and gift of the lord'. This may be another instance of Hopton extending his landed resources by purchase.

account of Thomasin's properties in Surrey and Sussex, for a rental for those properties, and for an arrears account of bailiffs and other officers. Audley ought therefore to have been able to hand over to Thomasin, in one form or another, a little over £51 from current revenues. This is pretty well what he did. He delivered to her in cash £47 8s 5¾d and five bullocks valued at £2 10s 0d. The situation compares favourably with that of the mid-1440s. In the intervening forty years Yoxford has not necessarily become a more profitable estate, but it appears to be better and more adequately run in the mid-1480s than it was in the mid-1440s. This is borne out too by the nature of the arrears of 1483–4.

At the beginning of the year they stood at £24. In the course of 1483–4 the former bailiff John Fountains fully discharged his arrears of £12 by liveries of cash to Thomasin.[112] William Audley's arrears at the close of the account amounted to £13, but £12 of this was desperate debt, the individual sums of which it was composed being so described in an arrears list of Michaelmas 1479.[113] Desperate it clearly was. A tenement called Gouthers in Sternfield (its tenants unnamed in the 1471 rental[114]), for which 5s a year was due to the manor of Yoxford, had rendered nothing since Michaelmas 1471; the tenants of a tenement called Patras in Heveningham (in 1471 Sir John Heveningham and the abbot of Sibton)[115] had paid nothing of their rent of 4s 6d per annum since the same date; the tenement called Burches in Middleton (its tenants also unknown in 1471),[116] had not produced a penny of its annual rent of 4s since 1458; and William Jenny had not paid his annual 4d fine for respite of suit of court since 1461. It would seem that from these outlying holdings, situated in nearby estates

112 John Fountains would appear to have been bailiff during the immediately previous year, for it was he who delivered the half-yearly rents to Thomasin during 1483–4; perhaps therefore he was active until Easter 1484, as rents were due at Christmas, Easter, Midsummer and Michaelmas. He was recorded, under the heading of wages of the bailiff, as gathering part of the rents and farms but, like Audley, who was also recorded here as gathering the residue of the rents and farms, he did not receive anything. Probably it had not yet been worked out how they should divide the fee for the year.   113 SRO, HA 30/369/31.
114 And therefore presumably unknown: SRO, HA 30/369/1 f13.
115 *Ibid.*, f2v.   116 *Ibid.*, f23v.

owned by other lords,[117] rent was virtually impossible to collect in any usual way – probably it was not collectable at all, possibly Hopton had no wish to collect it. Jenny's fine, one presumes, was something to be forgotten within the context of other considerations. Thus of William Audley's undischarged arrears of £13 at Michaelmas 1484, only a £1 was what we might call normally realizable revenue. Undoubtedly then all was well at Yoxford in the mid-1480s.

How was it some ten years later in 1492–3? It is not easy to tell, for the accounts of that year are not complete. Moreover they are extremely complicated in form: under the heading of allowances appear not only allowances of a varied kind, but also largely undetailed expenses discharged by the bailiff; there are important marginal additions at the end of the account; and there are two farmers at Cockfield Hall with their own separate accounts. It is the Yoxford charge which is missing. It is unlikely that much would have changed since 1483–4, at least in terms of rents, as the rents of Brendfen, Meriells, and Cockfield Hall were still the same. Four acres of Middleton meadow in Brendfen, however, were now leased out at 4s an acre, two of the lessees being members of the family, Nicholas Sidney, Thomasin's son, and Robert Knevet, probably her grandson. Wood sales fetched 28s, and the profits of the courts were £2 9s 5d. Outgoing rents were much as in 1483–4, though allowances on rent were somewhat higher, chiefly in favour of Richard Butler (on Thomasin's express command) and Edward Jenny, all the latter's annual rent of 10s 8½d being remitted. Ordinary estate expenses were also rather higher: the cost of cutting faggots for the household kitchen and for hedging around Yoxford wood came to 35s.

The real change was at Cockfield Hall. It was now leased out but in a most complicated manner. Various parcels were leased under the bailiff's charge for about £3. The lady's yard ('yard domine') was leased to Ralph Lunneys; this holding, comprising mainly enclosed land, was farmed by Lunneys for £6, and he accounted for it separately. Finally Thomas Walpole farmed the

---

[117] Sternfield was a de la Pole estate, Heveningham was held by the family of that name, Middleton was owned by the Audleys.

site of the manor, with various unnamed parcels of land, for around £4; he too rendered his own account. Thus Cockfield Hall farms now amounted in all to some £13. If we recall Robert Flemming's lease of Cockfield Hall in the 1440s, at £9 6s 8d, we are justified in remarking upon the increased yield of some fifty years later. While the extent of the demesne may have been greater,[118] the establishment of the dairy farm was one reason for that increase, for Lunney's husbandry included dairying in 1492–3. In fact he and Thomas Walpole ran between them what amounted to a home farm, supplying Thomasin's household with many of its needs. About half of their leases were rendered in kind. Lunneys delivered cheese, butter, milk, eggs, chickens and geese, as well as oats and malt; he carted wood, some for the house of Richard Butler, he provided three yards of russet cloth for one of Thomasin's servants, he was allowed 4d 'pro le Shredyng de Bricheslow', and he pastured three bullocks belonging to the lady. In cash he paid her £3 12s 4d and so fully discharged his farm. Walpole delivered fish and geese, carted faggots, ground corn, and pastured[119] three of Thomasin's cows for the whole year; he paid her £1 in cash and thus, to within one penny, also balanced his account for the year.

The bailiff too only paid part of the Yoxford revenues to Thomasin in cash, a mere £4 in fact. By far the greater part of the monies that became available to him he spent: on fish, wine and other provisions for the household, for cloth, a 'marbilston' and other things, the details of which were in three bills examined by Thomasin, and in one case explained by William Eyre, and duly allowed by her.[120] These expenses totalled £41. In addition in a marginal note he was allowed £12 for corn and malt, presumably purchased for household use. Finally he accounted for £4, which was the price of grain given to the guilds of Peasenhall

---

118 See p70 above for the purchase of Cleves tenement, in Thomasin's hands in 1483–4.
119 The term 'jestyng' is presumably agistment.
120 The bills have not survived. They might have been the cost of the funeral of John Hopton's great-grandson John Hopton who died in January 1490, aged 2. William Eyre, as one of the guardians of the child, would naturally have been involved.

and Laxfield for the making of malt.[121] Clearly, in 1492–3 the
role of the Yoxford bailiff was a more active one than that of his
predecessor had been in 1483–4. Whereas in the former year
William Audley was barely more than a rent collector, handing
on what he had collected to Thomasin in cash, in 1492–3 the bailiff
was also acting as her cofferer, spending the Yoxford revenues on
the household resident there. Like the Blythburgh bailiff of the
1460s he was, at one and the same time, a local and a central
official, or so we would describe him in our tidy but anachronistic
fashion.

The reason for this probably stems from the great changes
which had occurred within the family itself between 1483–4 and
1492–3. In 1483 Thomasin's stepson, Sir William Hopton, had
been the head of the family. He lived at Westwood; she, the
dowager, lived at Yoxford, no doubt quietly enough managing
both her household and her dairy farm. But in 1484 Sir William
died, in 1489 his son Sir George died, and the following year
Sir George's son John also died; this left Sir George's second son
Arthur, who at under two years old certainly could not take
control of the interests of the family. It is likely then that by
1492–3 Thomasin found herself unexpectedly committed to family
affairs again, and thus her household at Yoxford became the
important one. Probably there with her was the young Arthur
Hopton, for when he came to maturity he rebuilt the house at
Cockfield Hall and made it his home. Thomasin was too busy for
her dairy at any rate: it now was leased out. Equally the role of
the bailiff as cofferer indicates not only that household matters
were perhaps of greater importance, but also demonstrates that
Thomasin had to hand over to him at least the more routine
aspects of them.

Yoxford was a valuable property; its fertile soils ensured that.
It was worth £50 a year or more to the Hoptons, perhaps considerably more than that by the 1480s. About £40 of this came
from rents; the most profitable land was demesne meadow and

[121] Two shillings was allowed for faggots delivered simply to the guild ('ad
Gildam'). This was presumably a Yoxford guild. Evidently plenty of
brewing was going on.

pasture, most of it enclosed; whether leased out or used for the home dairy farm it clearly brought a good return. Nor should we forget, in this country of hedges and copses, the value of wood sales; just as we would wish to know more about the dairy farm, so would we about those too. As always too many questions go unanswered; it is the same when we turn to Westhall.

Westhall also lies on the well-wooded clays of upland Suffolk, a few miles north of the small market town of Halesworth. We have no accounts for it from the time of John Hopton; there survive no rentals or extents. What we do have are two accounts from the fourteenth century, for 1376–7 and for 1394–5, one from 1428–9 (in a badly damaged condition), and another for 1481–2.[122]

The early accounts at least reveal what a tiny estate Westhall was. There wood sales were probably the most important item of income; they were worth more than £5 in 1376–7, over £6 in 1394–5, and about £3 in 1428–9. Rents and farms together were a mere £5. The profits of the courts were a little over £2 in 1376–7 and in 1394–5, just 29s in 1428–9. So much for the revenues of Westhall. Decayed and outgoing rents had increased from 1s 3d in 1376–7 to 8s 4d in 1428–9. Ordinary expenses, mainly for the cutting and carting of wood, and of the courts were about £1 in all three years. The bailiff's fee was also £1. The few pounds then remaining were delivered in cash to the receiver, Geoffrey Darsham in 1376–7, the long serving Richard Daniel in 1394–5 and 1428–9. An uncomplicated estate it would seem, which was worth £10 or less a year when John Hopton obtained it in 1430. Evidently what mattered most from year to year were sales of wood. They would make the difference between £10 and less.[123]

Less is certainly what the account of 1481–2 appears to offer. That year the bailiff was Robert Payn, whom we have encountered as sheep reeve at Blythburgh and bailiff at Westleton, which

[122] SRO, HA 30/50/22/20/9(10), 9(11), 9(12), 9(13).
[123] There are no traces of demesne farming at Westhall by 1394–5, but there is the briefest of stock accounts on the dorse of the account of 1376: it concerns 1 bullock which was sold, and 1 sheep which went to the household at Westwood.

he was this same year. This year too he was bailiff of Thorington, and he accounted for Westhall and Thorington together. Moreover he evidently supervised the farmer and bailiff of the two equally tiny Norfolk estates, just across the Waveney, of Pirnhow and Ellingham, as their accounts follow his for Westhall and Thorington and their liveries were made by him.[124] As Robert was a household officer as well he must have been a busy, not to say indispensable, man. At Westhall he himself leased the manor house, and its adjoining closes of arable and pasture, comprising 32 acres in all, for 30s. His farm was included under the heading of rents which, there being no longer any separately distinguished farms, were only a few shillings less than the total of £5 of fifty years before. Decayed and outgoing rents, respites and allowances were however a few shillings more, at 15s. Wood sales only fetched just over £2, and the profits of the courts were down to 13s 5d. On the other hand expenses were up to £2. However, these are hardly local expenses; most of them were for the cutting and carriage to Westwood of faggots over a period of two years, the making of hurdles for the lord's fold course at Blythburgh, and the preparation of planks and other timber for the repair of the house at Westwood and their conveyance there. Robert Payn used the word foreign to describe them in his marginal heading. Clearly, Westhall's woods were of considerable importance not only, perhaps not principally, as a source of revenue, but also as a source of supply of household fuel and timber. That always has to be remembered in terms of Westhall's productivity.

Thorington was at a little distance from Westhall. It lay to the south and in fact adjoined Blythburgh on the west. It too was small. Rents were under £10 in 1481–2; these included demesne arable and pasture and what must have been a large holding in neighbouring Wenhaston, called Wangfords. Decays, allowances, respites and outgoing rents totalled £2. There was no court that year and there were no expenses. Robert Payn's liveries from Westhall *and* Thorington were a little over £10, nearly £9 in cash and 26s 8d paid to John Reynold, as the final instalment of

[124] Viz: all of SRO, HA 30/50/22/20/9(13).

10 marks, the cost of a messuage adjoining the cemetery at Blythburgh church, purchased from him by Sir William Hopton.[125]
The largest item on the account was arrears, all were longstanding, Katherine Love's were outstanding. She had arrears of
£2 3s 4d which were static, but her arrears of 8s 8d annual rent
were accumulating each year: at Michaelmas 1482 she had not
paid a penny since 1453 and in all owed £12 11s 4d. At Michaelmas 1482 arrears totalled £16. None looks as if it could be
collected.[126]

The brief accounts of Philip Bosard, farmer of Pirnhow, and
Henry Cobbe, bailiff of Ellingham, follow Payn's. Bosard's lease
was £11 13s 4d per annum. He was exactly a year behindhand in
paying it. Cobbe accounted for rents and farms at Ellingham of
£6 0s 5d and the single court produced 3s. He paid his arrears of
11s. 5d to John Hoo, the Blythburgh bailiff, handed over 14s 9d
to Sir William Hopton, and on Sir William's command delivered
£5 to Thomasin. His own fee was 6s 8d, expenses were 2s, and
thus he balanced his account.[127] Together Thorington, Pirnhow
and Ellingham may have been worth about £20 to John
Hopton.[128]

For Wissett we have no accounts at all on which to base such
guesswork. The parish is on fine farming soils immediately to the
north west of Halesworth, separated from Westhall only by
Spexhall. All we know is first that in 1463–4 John Keswick the
bailiff delivered to John Hoo, the Blythburgh bailiff, some £25,[129]
and second that Keswick's arrears, standing at £30 in 1473, were
over £60 in 1479 when, *in addition*, desperate debt at both the
manors of Wissett and Wissett Roos totalled £70.[130] Two things

125 Here again is evidence for demesne expansion by purchase as at Yoxford
and Westleton.
126 Compare the situation at Michaelmas 1479: SRO, HA 30/369/31.
127 Oddly enough there had been no arrears in 1435 when a Henry Cobbe
was also bailiff of Ellingham: SRO, HA 30/50/22/8/3.
128 The previous year when the Blythburgh bailiff was acting as receiver for
the East Anglian estates he had £5 from Thorington, £8 from Pirnhow,
and £5 from Ellingham.
129 SRO, HA 30/314/18 m1.
130 SRO, HA 30/369/294; HA 30/369/31. John Keswick came from a local
family which had a tradition of service to their landlord. One John was

seem evident: Wissett with Wissett Roos was a valuable estate and arrears were a big problem.[131]

Easton Bavents was not a Swillington property; John Hopton acquired the reversion to it from Ela Shardlow in 1435 for 400 marks, and she granted it to him outright in return for an annual pension of 20 marks in 1451. A coastal estate just north of Walberswick, and separated from it only by the town of Southwold, Easton, like Dunwich to the south, was being steadily eroded by the sea. Now nothing remains but a narrow strip of deserted seashore; in the fifteenth century it was still a substantial estate. A number of accounts survive from the fourteenth as well as from the fifteenth century. We are not concerned here with an attempt to study Easton Bavents over a long period; whether it was as profitable to its lord in 1430 as it had been in 1330 is none of our business. It would not have preoccupied John Hopton either. It is however worth our while examining the estate just before its purchase by Hopton; this we can do from the two surviving accounts for 1429–30 and 1431–2. By 1436–7 (the next account to have been preserved) Hopton was farming the estate from Ela for £20 per annum; the situation at that point is also worth our study. We can then move on to the series of accounts, beginning in 1459–60 and ending in 1480–1, which come from the period of John's, and briefly his younger son Thomas', ownership.

important enough in Sir Roger Swillington's administration to travel to London on his behalf (Leeds City Archives, Swillington account 1408–9) and well enough liked by Sir Roger to be left 5 marks in his will of 1416. Another John was bailiff at Wissett in 1435 (SRO, HA 30/50/22/8/3). The John of 1479 must be the third of these, as the John of 1435 was termed junior.

131 Two items comprised £52 of the desperate debt of 1479. Christopher Willoughby of Parham owed for a relief £27 10s 0d, and a tenement called Hoodmans in Hintlesham, a very long way off, beyond Ipswich, had paid no rent since 1430, that is never since John Hopton had been lord: total arrears were £24 10s 0d. Another of these outlying tenements, Checkering Hall in not so distant Walpole, was 47 years in arrears, but these only amounted to £2 7s 0d, and in this instance the tenant was known, being the master of the college at Wingfield. Other important neighbours who owed rent or amercements were Sir John Heveningham, John Jermy the elder esquire, William Micklefield esquire, the prior of Blythburgh, and the prior of Rumburgh: SRO, HA 30/369/31.

The contrast between the 1430s and the later years is in fact a considerable one, for in 1429–30 Easton was being directly farmed for the benefit of the household, whereas in the 1460s and 1470s, apart from a brief time of experimentation, the demesne was leased out. It is evident that in 1429–30 there was a flourishing, though small, home farm which met many, perhaps most, of the ordinary provisioning needs of Ela Shardlow's resident household.[132] What was the estate worth that year? The accounts are remarkably straightforward so that this question is for once not too difficult to answer. The bailiff's charge, including arrears of £5 17s 8d, was £55 8s 2d. Half of this sum, £27 7s 4d, was the value of provisions supplied to the household from the farm,[133] and a further £5 2s 0d was for 34 stones of wool sold at 3s the stone.[134] Apart from the wool, and rabbits sold locally for £2, no agricultural produce of the farm was sold, it was all for household use. The bailiff discharged in all £55 1s 6d, leaving himself owing just 6s 8d, an unpaid amercement of two years' standing. There were no decayed, or remitted rents, and only 10s 1d in outgoing rents. Expenses were all local, for stock and seed purchased, wages at harvest time, the ploughmen's stipends, repairs to carts and ploughs, harness and other equipment, the costs of shearing and treating the sheep, the wages of a ratcatcher and so on. Repairs at the manor house cost 11s 5d, and repairs to a house in the village, obviously extensive, cost another £3. In all they totalled £10 4s 3d. There remain liveries. These comprised the provisions supplied to the household, which totalled (as we saw in the charge) £27 7s 4d, cash out of the current charge amounting to £11 8s 10d, and cash from arrears of £5 11s 0d, being the price of wool sold to John Dunche of Stowmarket and Thomas Good of

---

132 SRO, V5/19/1/12. The grange account reveals that 8½ acres were sown with corn at 2 bushels per acre, 10½ acres with rye at 2 bushels per acre, 37½ acres with barley at 2 bushels per acre, and 7 acres with peas at 2 bushels per acre. There were at Michaelmas 1430 8 stotts, 2 plough oxen, one bull, 4 cows, 22 pigs (including a boar and a sow), and 359 sheep, a further 100 sheep having been sent to pasture on another manor during the year. In the course of the year the household consumed 200 pairs of rabbits, 327 pigeons, and 900 hens' eggs.

133 The cost of carting firewood and other unspecified things from other places to Easton – 61 cartloads at 1s the cart – was included in this sum.

134 Nine stones remained in Ela's custody.

Colchester. We can confidently assume that Easton Bavents in 1430 was an efficiently run, ably managed, productive and profitable property. Bearing in mind that this was a good year when maintenance and running costs were low,[135] the estate's clear annual yield in cash and provisions was around £38.

Within a year, however, there were radical changes which stemmed from the departure of the household; Ela moved to Cotton in central Suffolk and the home farm was run down. During 1430–1 all the animals except the sheep were moved to Cotton, and by 1431–2 only a few acres were being sown with barley and peas.[136] The household was not being supplied at all from Easton by that time. A good part of the demesne was leased, and the rabbit warren and dovecot were also farmed out. The flourishing home farm of two years previously was no more, and the bailiff's burdens were very different. He was chiefly occupied with paying off the debts of Sir John Shardlow, Ela's son; they were mainly small sums owed to local men, Richard Nunne of Covehithe, Robert Sparrow of Beccles, the prior of Wangford for example – but in all they came to nearly £16. He was also busy buying fish, wine and other things for dispatch to Cotton and paying for the fulling of cloth at Reydon which also was for Ela's use. And he may have had trouble with the tenants.[137]

There was nonetheless one great event. At Christmas 1431 Sir John Shardlow entertained the Earl of Suffolk at Easton. They feasted on curlew and other wildfowl. Perhaps too they discussed matters which might be raised at the forthcoming parliament, duly summoned on 25 February 1432, in which Sir John sat as knight of the shire for Suffolk. What might have become a useful connection[138] was not to be: Sir John died in 1433. He left no

---

[135] There was not much replacement of stock or capital equipment, nor does the bailiff seem to have received his fee. On the other hand a village house presumably did not have to be rebuilt every year.

[136] SRO, V5/19/1/13: 13 acres of barley, 7 acres of peas. The demesne ploughs had also been sent to Cotton; the ploughing of these acres was done by men with their own ploughs.

[137] The arrears of £8 16s 8d from the previous year were 'super...[MS damaged]...tenentes per liberam cartam habendos etc.': SRO, V5/19/1/13.

[138] It was a close connection: Staffs RO, D641/3, packet 5, Costessey Accounts, 1431/2.

children, and he appears to have been yet another local man who was last in the direct male line. No doubt as a consequence of Sir John's death, Ela sold the reversion of the Easton estate to John Hopton in 1435; moreover, having moved to Cotton, she also leased the estate to him. He was the lessee in 1436–7 when we have our next surviving account.[139]

Having seen the home farm in dissolution in 1431–2 we are surprised to see it resurrected in 1436–7. Whatever Hopton's intentions in purchasing the reversion and taking the estate on lease, it is altogether unexpected to discover him running a farm there. Was he impressed by what he had seen before 1431? Yet John Hopton had no household at Easton; he therefore can only have intended to farm either for his own household needs at Blythburgh or for the market. What was he up to in 1436–7? In that year he had 11 acres sown with rye, 35 acres sown with barley, and 5 acres with peas. At Michaelmas 1437 he had four stotts, a cow, which was leased to the bailiff, a sow, and some two hundred sheep. It was a smaller farm than Ela Shardlow's had been, but John may have been building it up, particularly where the livestock were concerned, though in the course of the year 1436–7 he had not acquired any animals, and had in fact sold his four pigs. How much was this venture costing him? Compared with the expenses of 1429–30 a startling amount. The stipends of ploughmen, shepherds and the bailiff alone amounted to nearly £9, harvest and threshing costs were £4, and other agricultural expenses, including the purchase of seed, the repair of ploughs and carts, weeding and carrying, and the dipping and shearing of the sheep, were £2. In all then, agricultural expenses were about £15, 50% more than those of 1429–30, when both arable and animal husbandry had been on a larger scale. Nor did John even cover his costs. Nothing at all was supplied to his household, and only grain, mostly barley, was sold for £9. The 187 wool fleeces remained unsold, but even if we take them into account at the 1429–30 selling price of 3s a stone, at 20 stone 7lbs[140] they would only fetch about £3. In 1436–7 at any rate

139 SRO, V5/19/1/14.
140 Thus estimated in the grange account, that is at 9 fleeces to the stone;

Hopton's farm at Easton does not appear to have been a paying proposition. The contrast with 1429–30 is stark. Smaller production at a higher cost was hardly good husbandry. When John and the experienced Richard Daniel arrived during the year to take a look at things they cannot have been pleased.[141] Nor can they have been at the audit of the bailiff's accounts for the year: of a charge of £25 in which there were no arrears, he had discharged over £16 in expenses, had delivered nothing to Hopton, and had paid only £5 to Ela Shardlow of the annual farm of £20.

Plainly this was an unhappy state of affairs. The cost of bringing in the harvest had more than doubled since 1429–30, the demesne ploughmen were now paid a wage of 6d a week in addition to their stipends, and they no longer did the threshing. Moreover, the customary services of the unfree tenants were exacted: 11 weeding works, 11 harvest works, as well as a few ploughing services.[142] There was also trouble with Nicholas, the shepherd who fled in August 1437; thirty sheep were held to have been lost owing to his negligence. We have not got the full story even of the cost of the Easton farm in 1429–30 as neither bailiff's nor shepherd's fees are recorded, yet there is sufficient evidence to suggest that Hopton had to pay more to get his work done: workers, living in or hired by the day, struck better bargains with him than they had with Ela Shardlow, at least in cash terms. What lay behind that? We cannot tell, but it is worth remarking that one difference may have been in the nature of the relations of employer and workers: on the one hand Ela, a widow since 1399 living on a family property, on the other John, the young Yorkshireman, an outsider and an absentee. At that point, alas, we have to let his perhaps over-ambitious venture be.

---

see K. J. Allison, 'Flock management in the 16th and 17th centuries', *EcHR* xi (1958), p105. The 1431–2 selling price however had been 2s 4d for a stone of 10 lbs and at 6 fleeces to the stone: 'recepta de 332 velleribus lane pondere 56 petri lane petrus ad 10 libras sic venditis Edmund Wulman de Hawley John Dunche et Thomas Couper de Stowemarket hoc anno precio petri 2s 4d.' SRO, V5/19/1/13.

[141] They did not stay long: the bailiff was allowed a mere 10d for their entertainment.

[142] Ploughmen and harvesters had 2d worth of victuals, weeders only a pennyworth.

Our next accounts are over twenty years later, for 1459–60. By then, apart from the sheep, the home farm was no more. By then too Ela was dead and Hopton had become the owner of Easton Bavents. As we turn to examine the good series of accounts for the 1460s and 1470s,[143] we might bear in mind whether Hopton's 400 marks had secured for him an estate which was worth what its purchase price so clearly represented: twenty times its annual value, 20 marks a year.

During the period 1459–1481 there were important developments: another, limited attempt at arable husbandry in the later 1460s, a review of the whole situation in 1470–1, which resulted in a new bailiff and a new regime of a single farmer who also had charge of the demesne sheep flock, and after Hopton's death in 1478 further changes which are largely hidden from us by the last two brief and uncommunicative accounts.

In the midst of change rents in total remained almost static. They had been around £5 in 1429, so they still were in 1481. The profits of the courts, on the other hand, varied, but they were not great and they averaged 17s a year. On the discharge side of the account only outgoing rents at 10s were untouched by the changes in the way the estate was run. We might here deal also with decays, allowances and respites of rent, though they varied slightly, for their variations were not related to those changes either. There were only a handful of rents which raised more than passing difficulties for the bailiff; none of these was of great consequence. They arose through coastal erosion. The first example was in 1475–6 when he was allowed 2d on the rent of John Wiseman because part of John's tenement had fallen into the sea.[144] Of this damage done by the sea we hear more in the following year's accounts. The bailiff was then allowed 3s 8¼d of a rent of 7s for a 14 acre tenement, as 7½ acres were in the sea, and

---

143 SRO, V5/19/1/16 is a bundle of 14 membranes comprising 14 accounts between 1461–2 and 1481–2; the 1465–6 account is a detached survivor and is numbered V5/19/1/17.

144 He was not allowed another 4d, claimed on the same grounds on the part of Thomas Palmer's messuage. His claim continued to be disallowed until 1478 when he ceased to make it. The new rental of that year may have eased matters. This rental does not survive, we only have references to its subsequent use.

is 2¼d of a rent of 2s for a holding of 4 acres 3 roods, as 2 acres 3 roods and 16 perches had disappeared in a similar fashion. He was allowed these sums again in 1477–8. Claim and allowance then disappeared. A new rental of 1478 may have taken them into account. Demesne land was also slowly disappearing into the sea, a few perches here, an acre there, and demesne leases were accordingly adjusted downwards.[145] Changes other than of the natural order were also affecting the demesne, however. To these works of the man John Hopton we now must turn.

Until 1471–2 the demesne was farmed out in small parcels, in 1459–60 and 1461–2 for £4 12s 8d a year, according to arrangements, not detailed in the accounts, made by the supervisor, John Ulveston. By 1464–5 there had been readjustments: leases then totalled just £4. The most important was held by Thomas Crowe, the rector, and John Martin, and included the site of the manor house and a field of 14 acres called Longfurlong; their lease, arranged by the supervisor, by then John Tasburgh, was for eight years, of which 1464–5 was the second. In the following year, however, various properties were taken over for the lord's husbandry, one of them being Longfurlong: farms were therefore reduced to £3. By 1467–8 more demesne land, including the site of the manor house, was in the lord's hands and farms were further reduced to a little over £2. They remained at about this figure until the reversal of policy in 1471.

Why had John taken over more than half the demesne in the second half of the 1460s? Most of the parcels were stated in 1470–1 to be for the use of the lord's sheep, and formed part of the fold course in operation at Easton. Some, however, were used for arable farming, as we would expect where a fold course was involved. Longfurlong, for example, was ploughed in 1465–6 and Adam Cottingham, a demesne servant, did the ploughing with the lord's plough and horses. In 1467–8 barley and rye were harvested. The first grange account dates from 1468–9: 8 acres of Longfurlong were sown with rye that year, and another 20 acres in various parcels were sown with barley. The greater part of

[145] For example in 1464–5: one piece of land, then of 4½ acres, which lay between Churchway and the sea had lost an acre by erosion.

the grain from the harvest of 1468 was delivered to the lord's household, though a little was sold. This is the only grange account which survives. In 1470–1, when the administration of the estate was being carefully examined and overhauled, apparently only 11 acres of barley were harvested, although 18 acres had been ploughed and sown. Summer 1471 saw the last demesne harvest and the end of this brief renewal of a home arable farm. By the autumn the demesne was once more entirely leased out. What prompted Hopton to begin, and after six years to halt this enterprise we cannot really say, though it is easier to think of why he stopped than why he began. It was after all a very small arable farm, seemingly of not more than 30 acres, hardly farming on an entrepreneurial scale. Also, supervising the tenants' services at harvest[146] may have been too much of a chore for a bailiff who was not perhaps dependable: John Grymel, bailiff since 1461, was replaced in 1470. Moreover it may have been a decision of 1470–1 that the demesne sheep were to play a larger role in the manorial economy.

In 1459–60 and throughout the 1460s Hopton had his own demesne flock. There was a shepherd who received regular wages: William Drane until 1465–6, Adam Shepherd in 1467–9 and John Deynes, of whom much more later, in 1470–1. The flock presumably grazed on demesne pasture as well as on the sandy heaths in the early 1460s, for in 1461–2 fences were erected between the demesne and common arable fields and the demesne pasture,[147] but it seems likely that a fold course was also in operation, considering the costs of maintaining hurdles, the sums received from tenants for the manuring of their holdings by the lord's folded sheep,[148] and the information given in 1470–1 that demesne arable was 'in cursu bidencium domini'.[149] Equally suggestive is the fact that when demesne land was taken into the lord's hands from 1465–6 onwards the sums received for agistment

146 Their customary labours were used in 1468–9 and 1470–1, for example.
147 'inter terras domini ac communam ac pasturam domini'.
148 For example in 1459–60 (8s), 1465–6 (9s 6d for 9½ acres) and 1467–8 (7s for 7 acres).
149 There is also the mention of cullet sheep. In 1464–5 the bailiff was paid 2d 'pro bidencibus providendis de coliettione pro pastura domini pro anno sequente'.

went up dramatically. I interpret this to mean that more sheep could now be grazed on the demesne pasture, that tenants' sheep could pasture there with the lord's sheep, which would fold also on the now available demesne arable as well as on the tenants' arable in the open fields.

Unfortunately there is no indication of how large Hopton's flock was at this time, just as there are no details of how profitable that flock was; as at Blythburgh, sheep accounts and accounts of wool sales were presumably kept separately. We do learn from the manorial documents, however, how many sheep owned by others were being grazed on the demesne pasture. Whereas there were only eighteen in 1459–60 and thirty in 1464–5, in 1465–6 there were 280; accordingly the sum received went up from a few shillings to £2 13s 4d. Most of this was paid by a Nicholas Nel for his 220 sheep. He paid over £2 again in 1467–8 and just £2 in 1468–9. By 1470–1 Nicholas was the sole payer of agistment dues: he was grazing 400 sheep at a charge of £4. That year too the lord's new shepherd, John Deynes, who took over from Adam Shepherd at Christmas 1470, received wages for three-quarters of a year which amounted to considerably more than a demesne shepherd had received in the past, even for a full year. This, we will recall, was the last year of demesne arable farming at Easton, the year in which the redoubtable Robert Payn visited the estate on numerous occasions to sort out the affairs of the dismissed bailiff John Grymel. All this indicates that a major decision was taken in 1470–1:[150] to concentrate on sheep and to discontinue the direct exploitation of the demesne arable was a major part of that decision.

The other part was to lease virtually all the demesne to the shepherd, John Deynes: 1471–2 was the first year of his ten-year farm. For an annual payment of £7 he held the manor house, 40 acres of arable, all the sheep pasture, the heath (with its valuable furze and brushwood), the customary services of the tenants, and the rabbit warren.[151] In this arrangement the demesne

[150] A year of decision elsewhere too, for instance the influential new rental at Yoxford and the recovery of the throne by Edward IV.
[151] In addition he held a close of 10 acres and an odd ½ acre for a farm of

sheep flock under Deynes' control was to have an important place, Deynes received £3 a year for pasturing 300 sheep of the lord's: in other words Hopton paid him what were agistment dues. How large the demesne flock had been in the 1460s we were unable to tell; it was certainly augmented in 1471–2; Nicholas Nel died in the course of that year and sheep to the value of £2 10s 0d were purchased from his executors, while in January 1472 Robert Hopton (John's brother), John Hoo of Blythburgh, and others were at Easton overseeing the marking of these sheep. All in all the decisions taken in 1470–1 simplified quite drastically the administration of the estate.[152]

Before we turn to this simpler situation of the 1470s we should briefly examine the other profits of the manor, some of which John Deynes absorbed in his lease in 1471–2, but the most important of which he did not: Easton Bavents mere. In 1459–60 John Northyn and John Stodham were in the third of a seven-year lease; for an annual £2 6s 8d they had the fowling and fishing rights; they did not have use of the lord's boat, nor did they have charge of the swannery. In fact that year five swans were delivered to the household and a cygnet was sold for 2s. It cost 6s for their upkeep, including two bushels of oats to feed them in winter. In 1464–5 as many as thirty-five swans were delivered to the household, priced at 1s apiece. But it was a hard winter that year: on the mere the ice had to be broken and ninety-five swans had to be fed on oats and rye during the harsh weather. The boat was also repaired. The expenses of the swannery totalled 16s. It was also the last year of Northyn and Stodham's lease. The new lease of 1465–6 included the swannery and the use of the

10s 5d. The demesne lands were newly measured this year by one Peter Candelar and Hopton's officers.
152 John Deynes is not specifically stated to be leasing the fold course, as the two demesne farmers at Blythburgh in 1490–1 were said to be leasing the two fold courses there. Throughout the 1470s there were no other agistment dues than those paid by Hopton himself, nor were there payments from tenants for the manuring of their holdings by the lord's sheep. The latter might have been paid to Deynes, but one presumes that he, if a sensible man, would fold the sheep on the demesne arable, as was the normal practice with any fold course: Alan Simpson, 'The East Anglian Fold Course: some queries', *Agricultural History Review*, VI (1958), p89.

lord's boat as well as the fowling and fishing. John Hoo and John Grymel, the bailiff, had to deliver six swans to the lord each year, keep the boat in repair, and dredge the harbour when necessary: all the earlier accounts record payments for this labour and in 1464–5 it had cost 8s 10d. As at Dunwich, keeping the harbour clear was an unceasing task; the sea was not kind on that coast, eroding on the one hand, silting on the other. Grymel and Hoo's lease was for no set term; they paid £3 6s 8d for it a year, and seem therefore to have had a hard bargain. Still they held it for over ten years, giving it up in 1476–7. That year the mere was in the lord's hands and was worth, according to the ubiquitous Robert Payn, £2 15s 4d per annum. It remained in the lord's hands in 1477–8 and was again valued by Robert Payn, though on this occasion his valuation was not recorded. By 1479–80, however, Henry Brown of Covehithe and John Wene farmed it almost on the same terms as the lease of twenty years before, and at the same annual rent of £2 6s 8d. The only difference was that unlike Northyn and Stodham, they had the use of Hopton's boat. Thus where the mere was concerned there was also experimentation on the part of the administration.

Other profits of the manor which John Deynes did not farm from 1471–2 were less important than those of the mere. First, there was the customary due of 4d paid by each boat which was drawn up on the shore in the winter; no doubt these were the fishing boats of Easton men, for their number did not fluctuate greatly. There were between a dozen and sixteen boats that paid dues in any one year, and there had been about the same number in the 1430s. Second, there was what was known as petty custom: each horse carrying fish (presumably away to market) paid $\frac{1}{4}$d, every cart 2d.[153] In 1436–7 this had produced 3s. By 1459–60 the carts have disappeared never to return; the charge on the horses produced 2s $9\frac{1}{2}$d. It was never more than 1s in subsequent years, until 1480–1 when it was 2s. Can the yearly variation of between 16 and 134 horse loads of fish really reflect variations between seasonal catches? It seems unlikely. There is certainly no correlation between horses and boats laid up in the winter: the greatest

[153] See the 1429–30 account: SRO, V5/19/1/12.

number of horses was in the year that there were the least number of boats, 1459–60, the greatest number of boats when there were the least number of horses, 1471–2. How many loaded horses never got counted, how many farthings never got collected?

There were also other profits to be had in virtue of Easton's seaside position: the odd fine paid by boats from other places which put into shore there, the sale of wood from wrecked ships. These amounted to only a few shillings in the occasional year, although from time to time a wreck might produce more than that. In 1431–2, for instance, there had been a pipe of red wine, valued at £2 and consumed by the household. Hopton was never so lucky,[154] at least not in the years for which we have evidence, but in 1464–5 a wrecked ship was sold to a William Berebrewer for £2, and in 1472–3 a wrecked boat (or a boat from a wreck) was in a good enough condition to be taken for the lord's use. Finally there were reeds from the marshes, usually cut for the lord's use (thatching the manor house in 1464–5 when it was under repair, for example), but from time to time some were sold for a few shillings. So much for items which were not incorporated into John Deynes' farm in 1471–2.

Of the manorial profits which he did farm only two had previously been of any importance, the rabbits and the furze and brushwood of the heaths. Sales of furze and brushwood were a regular item on the accounts, ranging from 10s to nearly £3 a year in the years between 1459 and 1469 for which we have the accounts.[155] Sales of rabbits, on the other hand, were infrequent. 1465–6 was the only year in which they were at all remarkable. A London poulterer was entertained in November 1465, though entertained is altogether too grand a word for what the 2d spent on him can have provided. Whether it was he or (after such entertainment) someone else who eventually bought 200 rabbits we cannot discover, but they were disposed of in London for 36s. Another sixty were sold to Robert Blomville for 9s, and other

---

154 An empty pipe and two empty barrels turned up in 1470–1; the pipe fetched 8d, the barrels were taken for household use.
155 The furze (bruar') was by far the most profitable; it was sold by the day, that is, I assume, what could be cut in a day.

small sales brought the total to £2 11s 0d. The warren, however, was probably not being properly maintained, as the large sales of 1465–6 were the result of a catching operation which entailed an unusual expenditure on nets, and there is never any note of rabbits dispatched to the household. Perhaps John Deynes took more care of the warren after 1471–2.

The comprehensive ten-year lease which he took on then continued until our accounts come to an end in 1481. We have noticed that it included the manor house and its farm buildings; these were extensively repaired at the lord's cost in 1470–1 and 1471–2, and the barn in 1474–5; over £2 was spent in each of these accounting years. Apart from the house itself and the barn, the stables and the bakehouse received attention. It would seem that all was made shipshape for the new tenant. Only a very few parcels of the demesne were not farmed by him; these amounted in all to about 25 acres and were leased for just over £1 in 1471–2. As the years went by even these farms were reduced or extinguished: John Deynes took on a little more in 1473–4, a little more fell into the sea, some properties were taken into the lord's hands. By the time John Hopton died in 1478 these additional farms totalled no more than 15s 8d. As for Deynes' activities at Easton we are largely ignorant. He was regularly paid £3 each year for pasturing the lord's 300 sheep; after 1471–2 the expenses of shearing the sheep no longer appear on the accounts, and after 1472–3 the costs of marking them also disappear; presumably these tasks came under Deynes' control and were laid to his charge; possibly he presented a separate account and was reimbursed directly for what he had spent in this way; possibly the £3 covered such expenditure. During 1476–7 the flock was reduced: Deynes was paid for the custody of 200 sheep throughout the whole year, of 80 for three-quarters of a year, and of 40 for a quarter of a year. Thus of the 320 sheep at Michaelmas 1476, there were only 200 a year later, and by May 1478 Deynes' custody of those 200 had also ceased. In November John Hopton died. Although John Deynes' farm continued, the two remaining accounts mention no payments to him for grazing sheep, indeed for that matter they do not mention sheep at all. In all probability the 200 sheep had been transferred to Blythburgh in the late spring of 1478.

We have not discussed liveries. They are of course part of a larger problem, a problem we cannot solve without knowing what John Hopton's sheep flock produced for him, and that knowledge we do not have. We ran into similar difficulties at Blythburgh. How profitable an estate Easton was is therefore not a question which we can answer accurately. For the moment we will defer discussion of the profitability of Hopton's sheep farming at both Easton and Blythburgh. Here we need to know what Hopton might have expected to receive from the other sources of income at Easton, and how much he actually did receive in liveries. This too is where arrears come in.

By taking the charge and subtracting from it arrears, outgoing rents and local expenses, and cutting the more complicated arithmetic short at that point, we find that in the early 1460s John might have anticipated an average of £11 a year to be available to him from Easton in cash; that in the later 1460s, when the home farm was in being, he might have looked for £6 or £7; and that in the 1470s, when Deynes was in control he probably could have expected about £11 once again.[156] What was the value of the home farm during its short life? We have only the accounts of 1468–9 to guide us. That year grain worth 9s 3d was sold, and grain delivered to the household was worth, using the prices at which it was sold that year, £4 7s 8d.[157] In other words demesne arable husbandry at Easton, in monetary terms at least, broke about even. So much for what John Hopton might have hoped for. What did he in fact get?

Apart from the few years after 1465 when the demesne arable farm was in being and produce from it presumably was sent to the household (as it was in 1468–9), John on average got about £10 a year. The greater proportion of this in most years was in cash, but

156 The £3 paid each year to John Deynes for looking after the demesne flock counted for the bailiff as a livery; for our purpose here I have taken it as a local expense.

157 Three quarters of barley were sold for 7s 6d. The 31 quarters delivered to the household were therefore worth £3 17s 6d. The 3 bushels of rye were sold at 7d a bushel. Thus the 2 quarters 2 bushels delivered to the household were worth 10s 2d.

the bailiff also made payments to other persons on the lord's warrant, and spent on household provisions – usually fish, and mainly herrings, but in 1468–9 also a porpoise and a turbot. His disbursements included the salary of the Hopton boys' schoolmaster in the 1460s, William Yarmouth, vicar of Covehithe, and the purchase price of a tenement, paid to Thomas and Agnes Helm, and subsequently her executors in the 1470s.[158] On one occasion he paid John's brother Robert's annuity of £6 13s 4d, and on others he saw to the needs of the young scholars at William Yarmouth's school.

Liveries were of course made from arrears as well as from current revenues; and in so far as Hopton was receiving on average £1 less each year in the 1460s and 1470s than he might have expected, this was because arrears denied it him. Arrears at Easton are and were complicated. Some of the complications and perhaps all of the inconsistencies in the accounts of the 1460s should be laid at the bailiff's door. John Grymel's dismissal in 1470–1 was connected with his mishandling of arrears, for during that year Robert Payn came specifically to examine arrears of rent and it was Robert who seems to have put the arrears situation into shape for the new bailiff, William Botild.[159] At Michaelmas 1471, after Payn had made his review, William Botild's total arrears were set at £11, some £4 of which comprised old arrears, chiefly of rent unpaid since John Grymel became bailiff in 1461–2. Robert Payn's review, however, cut their advance to a slower pace, if it had not halted them in their tracks. At Michaelmas 1475 they had not yet reached £5. During 1475–6 he was at Easton again, and once more enquiring into rents; perhaps too there was concern about John Deynes' farm: he was by then £4 in arrears.

[158] This might seem at first to be another example of Hopton's extension of demesne by piecemeal purchase; in this case, however, he promptly resold the tenement.
[159] Let two examples suffice. The tenants of land lately John Nottingham's were recorded in 1459–60 as being two years in arrears on an annual rent of 11d; in 1467–8 they were said to be three years in arrears; but in 1470–1 they were recorded as owing 11s 11d, that is for the 13 years since 1458–9. John Childerous was stated in 1464–5 to be four years in arrears with his rent of 1s 7d per annum; in 1470–1 he was said to owe 29s in rent from the time John Grymel was bailiff: this is of course much more than 1s 7d a year over ten years.

By Michaelmas 1478 he owed £5 13s 10d. At that date the other accumulated arrears stood at £5 8s 0d, and there were also amercements of 6s 8d which had not been paid. Yet this was hardly a situation to cause anxiety. Nor, so far as we can tell, did it. At Michaelmas 1479, a year after John Hopton's death in November 1478, an arrears list was drawn up for Thomasin.[160] It is fortunate it survives for it shows that John Deynes had paid off £3 of his arrears in the course of 1478–9; he was therefore left owing £2 13s 10d, and we may presume that he also discharged this sum, as there is no mention of it or any other arrears of his on the accounts of 1479–80 and 1480–1. As for the other arrears, they were wiped off on John Hopton's death.

That, however, the unpaid rents among them were uncollectable is apparent from the accounts of 1479–80; for there they all are dutifully recorded as unpaid since 1478–9. If they were uncollectable in the form under which they appear on the accounts, why had there not been measures taken to alter that form? It is odd (in our eyes) that, despite the marking out of boundaries between Easton and Covehithe in 1465–6,[161] the new extent and rental of 1472–3,[162] the new rental of 1478–9, and all Robert Payn's enquiries at various times,[163] these particular items remain fossilized among the arrears of every account. All this activity also bore small result so far as the total rent charge was concerned: it remained virtually unchanged over twenty years. That is a much more damning indictment of the administration of Easton Bavents. Getting rid of an incompetent bailiff after ten years is one thing, a static rent roll for twenty is another.

What also is clear from our survey of Easton is that in this period it was never worth to John Hopton the £20 a year he paid

160 SRO, HA 30/369/31.
161 William Hopton, John's eldest son, John Tasburgh, the supervisor, and Walter Fulbourne, the auditor, were busy on this task that year.
162 In 1467–8 also William Grimbald had been paid 2s 2d for renewing an extent. The writing of the extent ('le dragge') in 1472–3 cost 13s 4d.
163 Besides Payn's visits, Hopton and his council were at Covehithe, probably staying with William Yarmouth, the vicar, for two days in May 1468, meeting the tenants, examining rents and looking into the demesne situation. There seems to have been no lack of attention paid to the management of Easton.

for leasing it from Ela Shardlow in 1436–7. We have to guess at the reasons for his readiness to pay that much; perhaps one of them was that £20 a year was necessary to secure the reversion of the estate, which Ela had sold to him for 400 marks. If John wanted to make sure of Easton, he may have had to pay more than it was worth. The 20 marks annual pension which he paid Ela from 1451 until her death in 1457, in return for her grant of the estate outright, was much closer to its financial worth to him. Twenty marks also looks like the annual value on which the reversionary purchase price was based. We cannot tell with any accuracy what profits his 300 sheep brought him, but if there was rather over £4 a year from the sale of wool,[164] then the estate yielded him about £14 a year clear. Although this is the roughest of rough calculations it indicates that £13 6s 8d is a pretty good estimate of Easton's clear value. It probably took Hopton all of twenty years to recover his 400 marks, though I think we may assume that at his death in 1478, twenty-one years after he had begun to take its profits solely to himself, he can have had the satisfaction of knowing that Easton had paid for its purchase.

Of course he may never have had that satisfaction; for he may never have thought in such terms. We possibly go wildly astray in foisting our preoccupations, indeed our compulsions, upon him. His satisfactions may have been of a different kind altogether.

A last point might be made, obvious as it is. Because we have such a good series of accounts for Easton we can see how rapid were the changes which took place there. If there had been a gap of no more than eight years in that series, between 1464–5 and 1471–2, we should never have known of the demesne farm. For Blythburgh there are no accounts between 1466–7 and 1477–8, for Westleton none between 1469–70 and 1477–8, at Yoxford none between 1445–6 and 1483–4. What happenings at those places are hidden from us?

It is those awesome gaps in our evidence which stay in the mind

164 Calculated at 9 fleeces to the stone, and at 3s the stone (the 1429–30 price and see Davis II, no. 731, dating from c.1470), 270 fleeces, viz. 300 less tithe, would fetch 90s. But I take it there would not be 300 fleeces each year from 300 sheep.

94

after all that we have endeavoured to do with what comes between them. We hesitate, therefore, to give any estimate of what income John Hopton drew from his East Anglian properties. Yet we must offer some indication, if only so that he may be placed, albeit in no hard and fast way, among his fellow gentlemen. Social position was not solely determined by income, especially landed income. John Hopton's origins, the way in which he came into his property, his seeming lack of ambition once established, and his relative detachment from any political interest, local or national, these may have weighed more with his contemporaries than how much money he had to spend. How he spent what he had was no doubt also important. That is a matter we must come to shortly.

How much then did his East Anglian estates produce for him? Our earlier statement[165] that they provided him with a clear annual income of at least £200 appears to have stood the strain of our examination. Blythburgh is, apart from Wissett, the property which we have least confidence about: £40 however seems safe enough; Westleton at £30, Yoxford at £50, Westhall at £10, Thorington, Pirnhow and Ellingham at £20 together, seem reasonable; Wissett at £30 is not much more than a guess; Easton Bavents at £10 will have to do. To these sums would have to be added the profits of sheep farming[166] (about £4 a year at Easton, but how much at Blythburgh?) and probably of cattle raising, of which something in a moment.

There are also the Yorkshire estates to bear in mind. How much the large and valuable estate of Swillington was worth in John's time we do not know. It may have been as much as £300 per annum; and it is unlikely to have been less than £100.

John was therefore, and at the lowest estimate, in receipt of a clear income of £300 a year. He was a well-to-do gentleman, more than merely well-off, just less than very rich; wealthy is probably the best word that can be used of him. Yet (and to anticipate) wealth is not my impression of him. Is extravagance inseparable from wealth? Certainly it is not. Yet that style of life

---

[165] See p24 above.
[166] Many of the expenses of which, we ought perhaps to remember, have been calculated in the ordinary charges of estates discussed above.

one associates with a man of some wealth seems not to have been John Hopton's style. That is a rash statement no doubt, for it may be argued that we do not have any full details of his expenses, merely a few Blythburgh accounts and the rough book of Nicholas Greenhagh. His possible lavishness is not likely to be revealed by those sources: what opportunity was there? And yet the life he lived seems (and there are some hints which we will have to discuss later) at a lower key, of a different pace, less expansive, even more thrifty than one would expect of a gentleman of £300 a year. Was it the style of a country gentleman pure and simple?[167]

Does the fact he had no receiver indicate that he was in essence a country man, a gentleman who lived on his estates and was never far from them for any length of time? Probably not. Besides, Richard Daniel, whom Hopton inherited along with the Swillington estates, was his receiver-general in 1435.[168] Daniel, in Swillington employment by 1394–5,[169] was rector of Swillington from 1411 until his death in 1458.[170] He was the Gras' receiver in Norfolk and Suffolk in 1428–9.[171] We hear no more of him in Suffolk after 1436–7.[172] He had no successor as receiver. Hopton

[167] My reluctance to admit he was a rich man is apparent. Yet, if the surviving income tax returns of 1436 are to be believed, he was. There were richer commoners, men of more than £400 per annum, but not many; one of them, for example, was Sir John Fastolf with over £600 per annum. It is this handful of very rich knights, most of them of political importance, who so impressed K. B. McFarlane nearly forty years ago, and whom I have in mind when describing John Hopton as 'just less than very rich'. We should, however, remember that income tax returns always underestimate income, and we should, moreover, note that in the returns for Essex there are two knights and two esquires with over £300 per annum; in other words, in wealthy East Anglia John may not have been as rich as an examination of the 1436 figures makes him appear. See H. L. Gray, 'Incomes from land in England in 1436', EHR, xlix (1934), especially pp620–3, and 633; K. B. McFarlane, 'Parliament and Bastard Feudalism', Transactions of the Royal Historical Society, xxvi (1944), reprinted in Essays in Medieval History, ed. R. W. Southern (1968), especially pp253–63, and the tables.
[168] SRO, HA 30/50/22/8/3: arrears list.
[169] When he was called supervisor: SRO, HA 30/50/22/20/9(11).
[170] T. D. Whitaker, Loidis et Elmete (1816), p260: instituted 9 March 1411; his successor was William Friston, instituted 19 November 1458, John Hopton being the patron.
[171] SRO, HA 30/50/22/20/9(12). He was present at Hopton's first court at Westwood, 22 February 1430: SRO, HA 30/312/194.
[172] When he was busy at Easton Bavents: SRO, V5/19/1/14.

did, however, have a supervisor: John Ulveston in the 1440s and 1450s, and John Tasburgh in the 1460s. And of course he had his steward,[173] and his auditor. Walter Fulbourne was his auditor for thirty-five years. In the later years one man stands out: Robert Payn. He was bailiff of Westleton in 1469–70 and already a household official. He was busy at Easton Bavents throughout the 1470s, was by 1477–8 provisioning clerk of the household *and* sheep reeve at Blythburgh, and in 1478–9 was again bailiff of Westleton. In 1481–2 he was not only bailiff of Westleton, but also bailiff of Westhall and Thorington. No doubt his various offices stemmed from his all-round ability; he obviously was a key member of staff in John's declining years.

John himself played an active part in the affairs of his estates, perhaps as active a part as his steward (and stepson-in-law), Sir Roger Townshend, played in the affairs of his. Sir Roger's notes on his sheep and arable husbandry, with their tone of exasperation common to employers of all ages, could perhaps as well be those of John Hopton.[174] Other members of his family too were active; his brother Robert, his eldest son William, and his wife Thomasin. Thomasin, thrust into a central role after the early deaths of her stepson William and his son Arthur, had long before then taken a leading part: in 1473 she was in charge of the revenues of Yoxford and Wissett, which were assigned for the expenses of the household.[175] One would dearly like to know the reasons behind that arrangement.

---

[173] Reginald Rene (or Reve), also probably inherited with the estates, conducted Hopton's first court at Westwood, 22 February 1430: SRO, HA 30/312/194, *sub* expenses. He was still steward in 1443–4: SRO, HA 30/314/14. By 1470 Roger Townshend was steward: SRO, HA 30/312/198, Westwood courts of Easter, 1470, Christmas 1471.

[174] For example on his ploughmen:
'Item neither horses nor harneys conveniently purveied in tyme ner well kept when ther have it, and long of ther coming to ther werk and than do it so lecherly and untreuly that it were better oftyn tymes undon because of the gret losse. Wherfore we must se these thynges amended or lef all ouste.' These notes, dated 13 August 1486 and in his own hand, are on the last folio of his sheep accounts covering the accounting year 22 Edward IV–1 Richard III: NRO, Townshend MS 1475 (1F). John bought malt from Sir Roger: arrears list drawn up on 2 February 1479; in the margin is the annotation that the money owing for the malt, 36s 8d, has been paid: NRO, Bradfer-Lawrence MS V, no. X.45.

[175] SRO, HA 30/369/294.

One aspect of the management of the Suffolk estates requires additional comment. What more can we say concerning Hopton's sheep farming? Too little I fear is the answer. He was not a large-scale sheep farmer. Only at Blythburgh and Easton Bavents do we have any evidence of sheep. Yoxford, Westhall and Wissett were not in sheep country, but Blythburgh and Easton, on the sandlings, had plentiful marsh and heath: there were Hopton's fold courses. We have seen how his approach varied at both estates. Did he have a flock even when the demesne was leased out? Certainly he did at Easton in the early 1460s, and again under the custody of John Deynes, the demesne farmer, in the 1470s. At Blythburgh we know that he had a flock of 700 sheep in 1435,[176] at least 586 in 1454–5, and 721 in December 1478. What of the years between? When the demesne there was leased out in the 1460s there are no references (however incidental) to sheep in the accounts, but that means very little, for the references to numbers of sheep at Blythburgh which we do have are not in two instances from accounts at all, and from a very unusual set of accounts in 1478: an arrears list gives us the size of the flock in 1435, the bailiff's rough notebook supplies the figure of 1454–5 (it is a jotting of a delivery to the shepherd), and the accounts of 1477–8 were drawn up at a time of necessary stocktaking, John Hopton having died in November 1478. The accounts which we could do with would be those of the sheep reeve at Blythburgh (in 1477–8 Robert Payn), and of John Deynes, the demesne farmer and shepherd at Easton Bavents in the 1470s.

Without such accounts we cannot proceed much further. To attempt at all to assess John Hopton's sheep farming and his profits from it would be vain indeed. We would need the sort of sheep accounts which survive for Sir Roger Townshend's farming to have a more complete idea of John's. Townshend had, in the later 1470s and early 1480s, between 6000 and 8000 sheep in ten or twelve flocks on as many Norfolk estates.[177] Sir William

176 In 1429 Roger Borhed was presented by the Blythburgh jury for over-stocking ('superonerat') the commons and fields with 400 sheep: SRO, HA 30/312/194, court of December 1429. The estate could carry plenty of sheep.
177 See the Townshend and Bradfer-Lawrence collections in the Norfolk

Calthorp had at least 1400, for that many he bequeathed in his will, though as he mentions the residue of his sheep, there obviously were more.[178] John undoubtedly was closer to his friend and feoffee Calthorp than to his steward Townshend in the scale of his operations. Small as his profits may have been, there must have been some,[179] and they have to be emphasized. They have to be, if only because they have not been taken into account in the valuation of his estates, or if they have, as at Easton Bavents, only in passing.

We should also bear in mind cattle as well as sheep. In 1448 the Blythburgh bailiff bought sixty bullocks at Harleston.[180] Were these for fattening in the marshes and then for sale in the market? It seems more than likely, for in November 1482 we discover the steward of John, lord Howard travelling to Blythburgh to buy twenty great oxen from William Hopton at £1 a head.[181] As the sixty bullocks of 1448 cost only £20 8s 6d, fattening beef may have been a profitable business, more financially rewarding than keeping sheep. It is fitting that we should close this chapter on that tentative and hesitant note, for such has been the necessary mode throughout. It is fitting too that we should end with fat bullocks, which may have provided a large part of Hopton's income yet about which we know only incidentally, indeed almost accidentally.

Record Office and K. J. Allison 'Flock management in the 16th and 17th centuries', *EcHR*, xi (1958), p100.

[178] PRO, PCC 23 Vox, dated 31 May 1494, proved 23 May 1495. The Earl of Suffolk had over 750 sheep in his fold courses at Costessey in the early 1430s; their wool was sold in Norwich: Staffs RO D641/3, packet 5, Costessey Accounts 10–11, 14–15 Henry VI.

[179] One rough calculation might be for the 1470s: 700 sheep at Blythburgh, 300 at Easton, at 9 fleeces to the stone, selling at 3s the stone, less 100 fleeces for tithe, £15. How much did the 139 bundles of wool from the clips of 1477 and 1478, which lay in the Blythburgh woolhouse on 8 December 1478, fetch?

[180] SRO, HA 30/369/46 f39v.

[181] *The Household Books of John, Duke of Norfolk, and Thomas, Earl of Surrey, 1481–1490*, ed. J. Payne Collier (Roxburghe Club, 1844), p329.

JOHN HOPTON'S

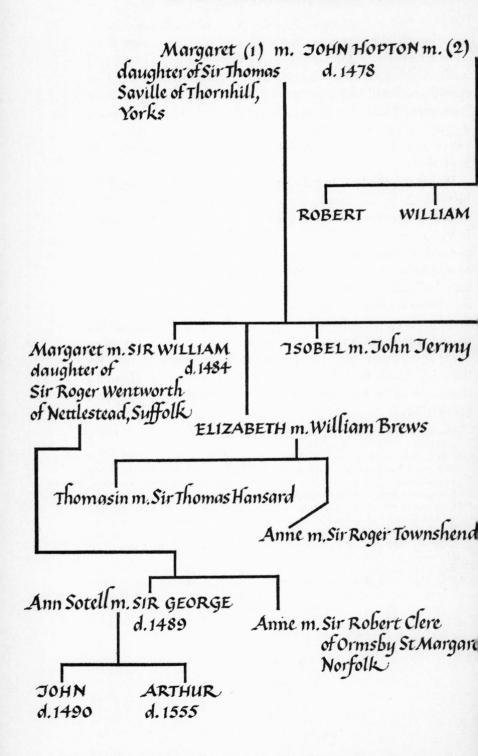

Margaret (1) m. JOHN HOPTON m. (2)
daughter of Sir Thomas   d. 1478
Saville of Thornhill,
Yorks

ROBERT   WILLIAM

Margaret m. SIR WILLIAM   ISOBEL m. John Jermy
daughter of   d. 1484
Sir Roger Wentworth
of Nettlestead, Suffolk

ELIZABETH m. William Brews

Thomasin m. Sir Thomas Hansard

Anne m. Sir Roger Townshend

Ann Sotell m. SIR GEORGE   Anne m. Sir Robert Clere
        d. 1489   of Ormsby St Margaret
                              Norfolk

JOHN   ARTHUR
d. 1490   d. 1555

FAMILY

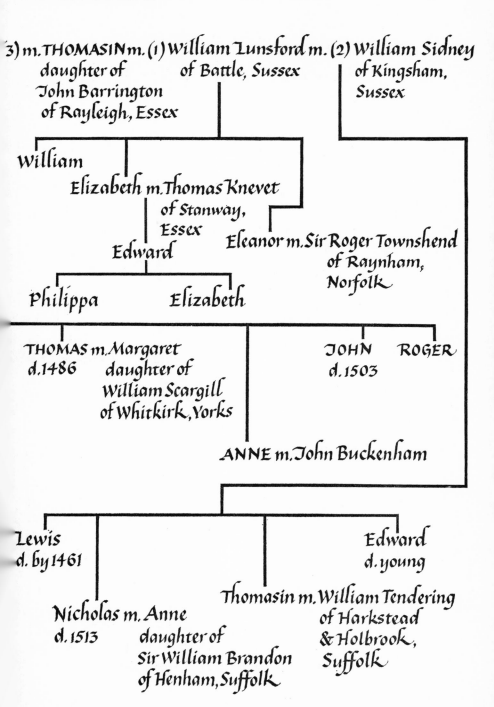

3) m. THOMASIN m. (1) William Lunsford m. (2) William Sidney
    daughter of   of Battle, Sussex   of Kingsham,
    John Barrington   Sussex
    of Rayleigh, Essex

William

    Elizabeth m. Thomas Knevet
             of Stanway,
             Essex
      Edward   Eleanor m. Sir Roger Townshend
                           of Raynham,
 Philippa   Elizabeth   Norfolk

THOMAS m. Margaret   JOHN   ROGER
d. 1486   daughter of   d. 1503
      William Scargill
      of Whitkirk, Yorks

        ANNE m. John Buckenham

Lewis   Edward
d. by 1461   d. young

               Thomasin m. William Tendering
                      of Harkstead
  Nicholas m. Anne   & Holbrook,
  d. 1513   daughter of   Suffolk
      Sir William Brandon
      of Henham, Suffolk

3
JOHN HOPTON AND HIS FAMILY

There ar aboughte and in Suffolk but fewe men as of gentilmen and
men of substance but if it be in Blithing hundre, were Hopton is
grete...'

John Bocking to John Paston 8 May 1456
Davis 1, p142

Who knows whether the best of men be known? or whether there be
not more remarkable persons forgot, than any that stand remembred
in the known account of time?

Sir Thomas Browne, 'Urne-Burial' in *Works*,
ed. Geoffrey Keynes, vol. 1 (new ed., 1964), p167

Already we have an impression of John Hopton the man, however
hazy it might be. He is beginning to emerge from his background. We will never get him clear; he will never stand out in
the foreground; he will always be a figure in a landscape. It is
his landscape certainly, but he does not dominate it with
his individuality as say Gainsborough's Mr and Mrs Andrews
do theirs. Or, more to our point, as the Pastons blaze forth,
dazzling us with their personalities. They, and their part of the
landscape, come before us so brilliantly that other characters in
other places, obscure in comparison (we peer closely to try to
perceive them), appear not merely dull but also so ill-suited as to
be not at all fitting. The Pastons, their friends, enemies, and
neighbours are larger than life; or at least, so marvellously well-
drawn are they (by themselves and by each other), that that is
what they have become. They seem so real, indeed they are so real
in contrast to their dim contemporaries, that theirs is taken for
the only reality. Yet, for all that we have difficulty in discerning
him, John Hopton esq. was as real as John Paston esq.

He did of course know John Paston: they were witnesses to
charters together,[1] and we have no doubt they ran across each

[1] For example, *CCR 1461–68*, pp208; 227–8.

other in matters of business, local government or possibly recreation and pleasure. It would have been infrequently, I think, for their worlds were different, coincident rather than convergent. Hopton was not of Sir John Fastolf's circle, for example, though he and Fastolf were involved in each other's land dealings in the 1430s: Hopton very indirectly in Fastolf's acquisition of Titchwell in 1431, Fastolf more importantly in Hopton's purchase of Cockfield Hall in 1440.[2] Hopton undoubtedly had the better, that is the cheaper and easier bargain.[3] In fact the two men by the later 1440s had fallen out, if indeed they had ever been 'in'. It was the wardship of Thomas Fastolf of Cowhaugh, Nacton, Suffolk, which set them apart. Sir John Fastolf set great store by having the custody of his distant relative's lands; but there were others who sought to control the young man and his property too, and they were far better placed politically than Sir John. Sir Philip Wentworth, de la Pole retainer[4] and royal household servant, was Fastolf's principal antagonist in this affair. He, like Sir John, worked through agents and one of these, his brother-in-law Robert Constable, was granted the keeping of Thomas Fastolf's lands in November 1447. John Hopton was one of his two mainpernors (or sureties); the other was John Ulveston, at this time an influential East Anglian lawyer associated very closely with the de la Pole interest and Hopton's steward.[5] In 1447 therefore Hopton was, however loosely, connected with that group of men, the followers of the Duke of Suffolk, whom Fastolf saw as his persecutors as well as his opponents; they, not he, were fattening themselves on the good things of the land which political favour put abundantly in their way. Sir John was one of the thin kine. No wonder that as with Joseph's brothers, the iniquity of it all began to prey on his mind. No doubt he soon placed John Hopton squarely among the number of his enemies, for by 1451

---

[2] Magd. Coll., Titchwell 6; SRO, HA 30/369/180.

[3] For Fastolf's manor, see P. S. Lewis, 'Sir John Fastolf's lawsuit over Titchwell, 1448–55', *Historical Journal*, 1 (1958) pp1–20, for Hopton's, see chapter 1.

[4] In 1453–4 he was receiving an annuity of 20 marks from the dowager Duchess Alice: BL, Egerton Charter 8779. For a too brief biography of him, see Wedgwood, pp934–5.

[5] *CFR 1445–52*, p79.

John's eldest son William was married to Sir Philip Wentworth's sister and (a few years later) we catch a glimpse of William maintaining his brother-in-law's quarrel at Cowhaugh.[6]

Hopton and John Paston may have encountered each other during this long drawn out dispute, as Paston and Thomas Howes were Sir John Fastolf's agents.[7] Any such encounter does not, however, appear to have bred ill-will between them or their families: not long after John Paston's death in May 1466 Hopton was ready to witness documents which sought to strengthen the Paston hold on those estates they claimed Sir John Fastolf had bequeathed to them.[8] This, nonetheless, was not commitment to their cause; commitment (in general) was not perhaps Hopton's strong suit. Besides, he and John Paston were neither near neighbours nor had they in temperament and interest a great deal in common. Probably it would be true to say that they knew of each other far better than they actually knew each other.

On one occasion Paston was given an estimate of Hopton's social standing: John Bocking wrote to him in 1456

There ar aboughte and in Suffolk but fewe men as of gentilmen and men of substance but if it be in Blithing hundre, were Hopton is grete.[9]

Whatever John Paston made of this, we are grateful for Bocking's opinion that John Hopton was a substantial gentleman, even if he is not absolutely sure of himself. No more are we. We have, as Bocking may have had, an idea of what such a man should be, how he should behave, what, in his position, with his wealth, he should do. What possibly gave Bocking pause, and what perhaps makes us hesitate, is just that discrepancy between what Hopton had and what he did. Of such a man of substance much was expected, particularly by the government, especially by his fellows:

[6] Gairdner II, p235; Davis II, p104.
[7] For the instructive story, see Mandy Kuijvenhoven, 'Sir John Fastolf: the rights of wardship', unpublished Keele BA dissertation, 1972. Paston indeed was more than Fastolf's agent in this matter; as a marriage for his daughter Margery was in prospect, if young Thomas Fastolf's wardship could be secured, he was an interested and energetic party: Davis II, pp104–6.
[8] Magd. Coll., Norfolk and Suffolk 47: 28 August 1467.
[9] Davis, I, p142.

both looked to a man of his sort to undertake or to share those tasks of administration, those responsibilities and duties which (we almost catch ourselves saying) were the lot of every well-to-do gentleman in every English shire. If that is how we think, then we must make some sort of exception for John Hopton, as in this way of things he did very little. A description of his activity in local affairs will therefore not take us long.

We should not altogether dismiss what he did; he was after all twice sheriff (in 1436–7 and in 1444–5), and he was on the commission of the peace from 1444 to July 1458 and again from July 1461 to December 1468.[10] That he was not on the commission in 1459–60 suggests he was considered untrustworthy by the government of those years. This is really one of our very few indications, perhaps our only one, that Hopton cared about politics; or rather that anyone else took any notice that he might care, *if*, that is, the government was taking notice, for the later 1450s were the very time in which he was most active as a casual commissioner (of enquiry, of arrest, of array). Between January 1436, when he was first a local commissioner, and December 1455, a period of precisely 20 years, he was only six times on such commissions.[11] One of these commissions was for Yorkshire, that of February 1438 for the arrest of Alfred Manston, the only occasion when the government made use of him outside East Anglia. An average of one commission every three years or so does not amount to much. He certainly was not one of those workhorses upon whom governments could always rely; if anything he seems to have been workshy. Yet between December 1455 and February 1460 he was on ten commissions, including that of array of December 1459, and that to resist the Earl of Warwick of February 1460.[12] It would be foolhardy to attempt any sort of political interpretation of what ultimately seem to be routine matters. Perhaps, just perhaps, the government removed him from the commission of the peace in

---

[10] *CFR 1430–37*, p303; *CFR 1437–45*, p303; *CPR 1441–6*, p479; *CPR 1446–52*, p595; *CPR 1452–61*, p678; *CPR 1461–7*, p572; *CPR 1467–76*, p631.
[11] *CPR 1429–36*, pp523, 524; *CPR 1436–41*, p148; *CPR 1441–6*, p463; *CFR 1445–52*, p171; *CPR 1446–52*, p479.
[12] *CPR 1452–61*, pp300, 301, 302, 344, 402, 409, 488, 490, 517, 560, 606.

1459 because they were suspicious of his connection with the Earl of Salisbury and his family. It can hardly have been a close connection, and probably connection is altogether too weighty (and weighted) a word to describe what may have been the most tenuous, the most distant of relationships. Dare we even call what may only have been a nodding acquaintanceship a relationship? What do we know? Merely that in November 1429 Hopton and William Routh put their dispute concerning Swillington to the award of Richard Nevill, earl of Salisbury,[13] and that Hopton, who maintained his links with Yorkshire,[14] was a witness to a charter, the beneficiary of which was Salisbury's son, Sir John Nevill (later Lord Montagu) in July 1455.[15] We cannot really make any sort of a brick from straw like this.

East Anglia was where (if only for a few years) he found a patron. John's lands were bordered by the estates of ecclesiastical foundations – Bruisyard nunnery, Sibton and Leiston abbeys, Mettingham College, Thetford priory – but none of these was of more than local importance. Beyond their manors lay those of the Duke of Suffolk: he if anyone was Hopton's natural lord. Thus in the mid-1440s, when William de la Pole, duke of Suffolk had become the king's principal councillor, it is no surprise to discover John Hopton deriving some benefit from his local lord's success: he became an esquire of the king's household. He entered the household between autumn 1444 and autumn 1446, probably nearer the later date, when preparations were being made for the parliament which eventually was held in February 1447 at Bury St Edmunds. His stay at the centre of things was short; he left the household between autumn 1449 and autumn 1450. His eldest son William, who had become an esquire of the household in 1447–8, lasted a little longer into the 1450s, until after 1452, though probably not long after.[16]

13 BL, Lansdowne MS 255 f237,.
14 For example his commission of 1438: *CPR 1436–41*, p148. And see also *Yorkshire Deeds*, III, ed. William Brown, Yorkshire Archaeological Society, Record Series, 63 (1922), p37; *CCR 1435–41*, p439. By November 1458, however, he is styled 'late of Swillington' in what appears to be a Yorkshire transaction: *CCR 1454–61*, p348. And see *CCR 1461–8*, p144.
15 *CCR 1454–61*, p62.
16 In the surviving books of the Keeper of the Wardrobe of the Household or

In the circumstances of the later 1440s, and bearing in mind the local origin of the connection between John and the duke, his membership of the royal household is not as significant as it would have been at some other time. He got in only during the final period of the duke's ascendency, when the household, particularly the esquires, rose to exceptionally high numbers, when probably even those on the margins of the duke's local affinity were being drafted in to augment his central following. His membership promptly ceased on the fall of the duke in 1450. In this extra-ordinary situation John's appearance in the king's household does not give us cause for supposing his association with the duke was close. Quite the contrary: so tardy a leap upon the bandwagon, or indeed, as may have been the case, his being hauled aboard, suggests that John was on the periphery of the duke's interest. There is no evidence of a closer association; moreover, would not room have been found in parliament for such a substantial Suffolk gentleman if the connection had been close?[17] In 1447, for instance, when Sir Philip Wentworth sat for Suffolk and a place was found for John's steward, John Ulveston, at Yarmouth. Yet John never sat in the Commons, not once in his long life.

He was however an elector, though not, so far as we can tell from the surviving records, until after he himself as sheriff had made the return for the election of the county knights at the shire hall in Ipswich on 7 January 1437.[18] Ten years later at the election of Philip Wentworth and William Tyrell esquires, an

---

the Controller John is not listed among the 'scutiferi aule et camere' for 1438–9, 1441–2, or 1443–4. He is listed for 1446–7 (PRO, E101/409/16, fs33v–36v); again for 1447–8 (E101/410/1, pp58–63), and 1448–9 (E101/410/3, fs30–2). William Hopton appears for the first time in 1448–9, and he, but not his father, is listed for 1450–1 and 1451–2 (E101/410/6, fs39–42; E101/410/9, fs42–4). No books survive after 1452. For this information and its interpretation I am indebted to David Morgan.

17 Particularly as room was found for John's brother Robert in the parliament of 1449–50. Robert, much closer to the de la Poles than John, sat for Wallingford, a crown–de la Pole pocket borough.

18 PRO, C219/15 part 1, no. 72. He troubled to record 68 names of those (presumably) present. Only a dozen were of the rank of gentleman or above.

important event for the Duke of Suffolk's group, John was ranked third on the list of electors present at the shire hall on 24 January 1447.[19] Ahead of him were named Roger Wentworth and Gilbert Debenham, immediately behind him his son William Hopton and Philip Wentworth's brother Henry, who possibly was or became one of Hopton's nearest friends. John Ulveston and William Harleston, the duke's partisans, were also named as were, after the seventeen esquires, seven 'frankleyns': that was the total of electors.[20] At the next election, that for the first parliament of 1449, John was named second on a list of some sixty persons. Philip Wentworth was again chosen, this time with Gilbert Debenham.[21] Just over nine months later on 27 October he was at Ipswich once more for the second election of the year. His name heads the list. Below him were named many esquires who were more closely linked with the Duke of Suffolk than he was: Thomas Brews,[22] William Tyrell, William and John Harleston, John Ulveston, John Andrew, George Wiseman, Andrew Griggs, John Sulyard.[23] Altogether there were between 150 and 160 electors recorded; they chose John Howard and Thomas Cornwallis

19 For Tyrell, retained by the dowager Duchess of Suffolk in 1453–4 with a fee of £10 per annum (BL, Egerton Charter 8779), and executed with the Earl of Oxford and others of East Anglia in 1462, see Wedgwood, p893.

20 PRO, C219/15 part 4, no. 58.

21 PRO, C219/15 part 6, no. 60.

22 Thomas Brews demonstrates the error, so easily slipped into, of assuming that these gentlemen's allegiances were exclusive; sometime, apparently before 1454, Brews was regarded by the Earl of Oxford as being close enough to the Duke of Norfolk to know, or be able to gather, 'th'entent of my Lord of Norffolk': Davis II, p42.

23 All these men appear in the dowager duchess's East Anglian Receiver General's accounts of 1453–4 (BL, Egerton Charter 8779). John Ulveston was her steward in Suffolk, fee £10 per annum, Andrew Griggs was himself the Receiver-General, with the same fee, William Tyrell was feed at that sum also, George Wiseman at £2, and John Andrew at £2 13s 4d. Among those who turned out on her behalf at Eye on 8 August 1454 'pro diversis transactis et transgressionibus per Thomam Cornwaleys armigerum et servientes suos factis communicandis et videndis' were (inter alia) Sir Philip Wentworth, Sir Miles Stapleton, Thomas Tuddenham, Thomas Brews, John Heveningham, John Ulveston, William Harleston, Richard Dogget, John Andrew, Andrew Griggs, and John Sulyard. Hopton (we may note) was not named; he is very unlikely to have been among the unnamed others. For Thomas Cornwallis of Brome near Eye, elected by most of them as their knight of the shire five years before in October 1449, see Wedgwood, p225.

esquires as the county's representatives; neither of them was the Duke's man.[24]

A year later, after the death of the duke, the rising of Jack Cade and the return of the Duke of York from Ireland, when the Suffolk electors met at Ipswich on 23 October 1450 Hopton was not among them, or at any rate was not recorded by the sheriff as being among them.[25] Nor was he stated to have been present when, after much trouble, the delayed election to the 1453 parliament was held at Ipswich on 12 March. His brother Robert Hopton and many old de la Pole hands – if we may term them that – were, however. Henry Wentworth, William Tyrell, John Heveningham, John Ulveston, Richard Dogget, George Wiseman, William Harleston, John Andrew were among the seventy odd recorded electors who chose Sir Philip Wentworth and Gilbert Debenham esquires as knights of the shire for the parliament which had already opened.[26] But John had returned for the next election, that for the parliament which followed the first battle of St Albans in 1455; he was named fourth on a list of over 200.[27] He was present too at the election on 12 November 1459 of Sir Philip Wentworth and William Tyrell to the Coventry parliament, the Lancastrian government's last unarmed political show of strength. Whatever the nature of the commitment of the two knights of the shire to that government – both were killed by its successor – the men who elected them were on any account a mixed bag with an assortment of commitments, allegiances and priorities. They included Sir Roger Chamberlain, John Howard, and John Wingfield[28] (none of whom was a firm friend of the

[24] PRO, C219/15 part 7, no. 52. For a comment on this election, see R. Virgoe, 'Three Suffolk parliamentary elections of the mid-fifteenth century', *BIHR*, xxxix (1966), p187.

[25] PRO, C219/16 part 1, no. 55. For comments, see Virgoe, p187, and K. B. McFarlane, 'The Wars of the Roses', *Proceedings of the British Academy*, L (1964), p90.

[26] PRO, C219/16 part 2, no. 58. Thomas Cornwallis was there too. For the trouble prior to this election, see Virgoe, pp188–91. Robert Hopton was also apparently a de la Pole servant: PRO, KB9/118/2 part 1, no. 17. For him, see below, pp150–1.

[27] PRO, C219/16 part 3, no. 37. This election was disputed; the reasons and circumstances are obscure: Virgoe, pp191–2.

[28] See Wedgewood and Virgoe for these three men.

regime), Henry Wentworth, Thomas Brews, John Heveningham, John Ulveston and Gilbert Debenham (who were still no doubt picking themselves up and sorting themselves out, as was the dowager Duchess of Suffolk, after the fall of their lord in 1450).[29] Some of these, Henry Wentworth for instance, continued to turn up for elections at the shire hall at Ipswich for another seventeen years yet: John Hopton, however, was not one of them.[30]

What are we to make of this? I think we ought not to make much. We could of course jump to any number of conclusions. One only appears to me inescapable: John Hopton was on the fringe of the group of Suffolk gentlemen who had attached themselves to the Duke of Suffolk, among whom were his associates, probably his friends (John Ulveston, the Wentworths, perhaps Thomas Brews, possibly John Heveningham).[31] That too was inescapable in the county in the 1440s. So may have been his membership of the king's household in the second half of the decade: not to have joined the duke's supporters, by then dominant at the political heart of things, would have been foolish, albeit they no doubt wanted him more than he needed them. The disaster of 1450 may therefore have faintly reverberated in Hopton's life. It hardly cut short a blossoming political career, as it did in the case of John Ulveston or Edward Grimston:[32] Hopton cannot by any stretch be said to have had a political career. Disappointed he may have been, but more on behalf of others than on his own account.[33] One fancies that it may have been on their account too that he was omitted from the commission of the peace in 1459 –

29 PRO, C219/16 part 5, no. 30.
30 Returns for parliaments of 1467, 1472, and 1477: PRO, C219/17 part 1, no. 79; part 2, no. 61; part 3, no. 70.
31 At a slightly lower social level there was also Robert Hopton, John's brother, in de la Pole service in 1450.
32 For Grimston, see M. J. Constantine, 'Edward Grimston, the Court Faction and the political crisis of 1450 to 1453', unpublished Keele BA dissertation 1973.
33 Particularly on his son's behalf. William's position in the king's household and his marriage to Sir Philip Wentworth's sister were an admirable start to a 'Lancastrian' career. However, the grant to him of the custody of Dunwich for ten years in June 1450 (CFR 1445–52, p159) turned out to be the only reward which came his way before that career was ended. It had to be restarted in an entirely different direction: see below, p136–9.

the government associated him with the likes of those who still had some commitment to the dowager duchess, and she at this time was busy building bridges across to the Yorkists.[34] This explanation has the merit of seeming less far-fatched than the one (scouted diffidently above) which sees the government leaving him out because of a connection with the Nevills. Its other merit is that it would have the government of 1459 not knowing what it was doing, which is more plausible than an explanation based upon the opposite.[35]

One of the things John did, apparently, feel committed to was parliamentary elections; but as one of the foremost gentlemen of the county (we have Bocking's word for that) probably he considered attending them as much a social obligation as a favour he might do the Suffolk group or the Wentworth family, who had a more evident political interest in their outcome. For he was not a man who did much for his friends; even the part he took in the transactions in land of his neighbours was minimal to the point of being marginal: mainpernor for Sir William Phelip, lord Bardolf

---

[34] Marrying her son to the Duke of York's daughter: *Cal Anc Deeds* IV, A6337–6343.

[35] A study of the commissions of the peace for Suffolk during the second half of the 1450s beautifully demonstrates the Lancastrian government's bewilderment. Hopton (as we have seen) was omitted in January 1459. Thomas Brews was dropped in January and June 1459; he however was included again in August, was dropped again in March 1460, and included once more in May. John Harleston disappeared (for good) in December 1455, Gilbert Debenham in December 1458, only to reappear in May 1460. Reginald Rous, a feed man of the dowager Duchess in 1453–4, was omitted in June 1459, was reappointed in August, and promptly dropped again. Richard Waldgrave, John Howard and Robert Willoughby disappeared in January 1459; they were not to appear again. John Andrew and Sir Philip Wentworth dropped then also, reappeared in June 1459 and remained on the commission thereafter. William Allington and John Wingfield were dropped that June; Allington was never reappointed, Wingfield surfaced briefly in March 1460. As some dropped out others replaced them: William Tyrell, never before a commissioner, first appears in June 1459, so does John Clopton; John, duke (more properly earl) of Suffolk, and John, viscount Beaumont appeared in March 1460 – they made up, presumably, for the omission of the Duke of York. The Duke of Norfolk, the Earl of Oxford and Thomas, lord Scales, like the lawyers William Yelverton, William Jenny and Thomas Billing, were appointed to every commission: *CPR 1452–61*, p678. We ought perhaps to record here that John Ulveston, like Thomas Tuddenham, had disappeared (for good) as long before as October 1450: *CPR 1446–52*, p595.

of Dennington in 1431,[36] witness to a quitclaim of the Abbot of Leiston to John and William Jenny in 1451, and a feoffee of Sir John Heveningham in 1473 is the sum of it.[37] Being but once a feoffee is, I believe, most unusual.

What I also believe is that we have to place him, as it were, outside those groupings of patrons and clients which we have come to regard as the very stuff of which fifteenth century local society was composed. Of these social and necessarily political frameworks, however, Hopton seems to have been independent.[38] Of course there is so much that we do not know about him. Yet however broad and deep our ignorance, there would, I feel, have been much more smoke if the fire had been one worth our rushing to investigate. Hopton, let us repeat, was *not* an active man, on the government's or his friends' behalf; he was not a man of affairs; not only was he apolitical (or as nearly so as the time and place allowed), he was also not very, or perhaps not at all, social, in a sense of playing an accepted role in society, the role that society, as well as we, would have expected of him. Or did it, and should we?

Possibly allowances were made for him because he was not up to it: a man not to be reckoned with, a man without qualities, a man who lacked weight. Perhaps he was one of those bumpkin squires, with whom we are familiar from the eighteenth century, not unlike Sir John Oglander's neighbour Sir John Meux: 'of a homely nature as never having any breeding or good naturals, he was the veriest clown of a gentleman...After his clownish

---

[36] *CFR 1430–37*, p49. Sir William Phelip had had the brief custody of Margaret Gra's Suffolk lands after her death: SRO, HA 30/312/194, court of 1 December 1429 (Margaret died 7 October 1429: John's first court was held 22 February 1430).

[37] *CCR 1447–54*, p288; BL, Harley Charter 51 F3.

[38] My late discovery of him as a member of a jury which in February 1453 indicted Arthur Nowell (one of that group of ruffians, servants of the Duke of Norfolk, whom we might call the Nowell gang), does not upset my view of his independence: it is his *only* appearance in the large collection of documents resulting from the oyer and terminer enquiry of the first half of 1453 into this and other gangs' apparent hooliganism, much of it directed at the de la Poles' servants and property. This seems to be a file recently put together; its material complements that in the Paston letters (e.g. Davis 1, pp58–68); it is numbered KB9/118/2, and is in two parts; Hopton appears in part 1, no. 133.

humour a good honest man'.[39] Good honest men, whether they
are clowns in fact or only in the eyes of the world, are difficult for
society as well as for historians to cope with. Indeed some believe
they are like either the Unicorn or the Dodo. For it is not true
that the good which we do lives after us; the unspectacular, every-
day good that we may do, if remarked at the time, is not recorded
for the future; it disappears, so far as historians are concerned,
without trace. It is therefore possible, because he leaves so little
mark upon the past, that John Hopton was that unusual thing, a
plain honest man.

He was not, we ought to remember, a lawyer; we should
remember it because the gentleman lawyer or the gentleman with
a legal training behind him has very deeply influenced our view of
the fifteenth century gentry. These men of law were important,
more important even than their actual number, large indeed by
that century, suggests; they were men who were pretty well into
everything, and we tend therefore to expect to find them everywhere. But they were neither quite everywhere nor quite into
everything, though it still comes as a shock to discover Sir William
Stonor not knowing (as a Justice of the Peace) how to deal with
regraters and forestallers of grain, and having to turn for advice to
his legal counsellor Richard Page.[40] For gentleman like Stonor it
was wise advice to avoid lawsuits; such wisdom was offered him
by his uncle William Harleston,[41] and Harleston, as an adviser of
the Duke and dowager Duchess of Suffolk,[42] and thus an opponent of the Pastons in the contest over Drayton and Helsdon,[43]
knew all about lawsuits. John Hopton, who knew William

[39] *A Royalist's Notebook*, p160.
[40] *Stonor Letters and Papers* II, p59.
[41] *Ibid*., p98: 'And of certen thynges I wold desire you and pray you in the
name of God, that ye wolle not over wissh yow, ner owyr purches yow,
ner owyr bild you; for these iij thynges wolle plucke a yongman ryth lowe.
Ner medyll not with no gret materis in the lawe.' See Sir John Oglander,
'Be advised by me. Have no suits in law, if possibly thou mayest avoid
them': *A Royalist's Notebook*, p14.
[42] See above, p108 and as a councillor in 1451, see Staffs RO, Jerningham
Papers, D641/3, packet 5, Costessey Accounts, 1450–1. By 1463–4 he had
replaced Richard Dogget as supervisor, Staffs RO, Sulyard Papers
D641/4, unnumbered bundle 3, Haughley Account, 1463–4.
[43] For example, Davis I, pp301, 311; II, p311.

Harleston,[44] also knew about lawsuits, having had his fill of them between 1429 and 1435. Moreover, he appears to have kept clear of them more successfully than Sir William Stonor, whose ambition and pretensions tended to run away with him. Unpretentious, unambitious is how we might think of Hopton, if we cannot bring ourselves to consider him good and honest. An absolute clown or a real country bumpkin we cannot, I think, allow him to have been. Nonentities (as the world judges) could sit on the commission of the peace, could be sheriff, could manage their property efficiently; but incompetent and silly men could not.[45] There is no indication in the estate accounts that others were thinking for him, though such indication would be hard enough to come across; ignorance and incapacity can be as well hidden from the historian as goodness and honesty. Still something somewhere might have made us suspicious. Nothing has. What we have to note, however, is that inactive as he was in his early manhood and middle age, that is until he was about 50 in 1461, thereafter, until his death in 1478, he took virtually no part at all in those matters of local administration and those affairs of county society in which most men of his sort made their mark.

He did, as we have seen, return to the commission of the peace in July 1461 and there he remained until December 1468. He was, in July 1463, an assessor of a parliamentary subsidy; he was, in November 1470, on a commission of arrest.[46] He witnessed a deed or two[47] and he got into legal difficulties over the repayment of a small debt[48] in the 1460s. That, however, is about the extent of it.[49] The last six or so years of his life, so far as the world outside

44 They were feoffees of Sir John Heveningham. The third feoffee was John Heydon. In their company Hopton has every appearance of being a lamb among wolves: BL, Harley Charter 51 F3.
45 John was about thirty-two when he was first a Justice of the Peace; Sir John Oglander was ten years younger, 'I wase putt into ye Commission of ye Peace att ye adge of 22 yeres, when I not well understoode myselve or place, and was aschamed to sitt on ye Bench as not havinge then any hayre on my face, and less witt': *A Royalist's Notebook*, pxiv.
46 *CFR 1461–7*, pp100, 104; *CPR 1467–76*, p249.
47 For the Pastons for instance, see above p104.
48 *CPR 1461–7*, p411.
49 He received a pardon in December 1471, being described as sheriff of Norfolk and Suffolk: PRO, C67/48 m27, a reference I owe to David

his family was concerned, are a blank. We might think it significant
that not only was John not active in local affairs, but that from
around 1470–1 (when he was into his sixties) others of his family
were; that it was Robert, his brother, and William, his son, who
were on the commission of array for Suffolk in May 1472, and
that William, for those dangerous few months of 1473 when the
Earl of Oxford was causing the government some concern, was on
a commission of the peace for Suffolk[50] as well as for the West
Riding. Were they, so to speak, the deputies of the head of the
family, who, because he was unable to carry out even the handful
of duties required of him by the government, performed them for
him? Hazardous as the interpretation of evidence like this is, it
does appear quite likely that in his later years John Hopton retired
pretty well altogether from the conduct of what we might term
public business.

It may be too that he took, in his sixties, a much diminished
part in family and estate matters. In 1473 it was Thomasin, his
wife, who was receiving the revenues assigned for the maintenance
of the household;[51] the conjunction of assignment with the responsibility taken by, or given to, Thomasin strongly suggests that
John was incapable of running things himself. We also find in the
1470s that Thomasin receives direct payments from bailiffs of
manors whose revenues were not in 1473 assigned to household
use, for example, Easton Bavents in 1476–7 and Westleton in
1477–8,[52] while a number of payments from Blythburgh in 1477–
8 were made under her authority, including the expenses of her
husband and Masters Jenny, Townsend, and Sulyard who went
hunting there.[53] It is an entry which stops us in our tracks. If John
could hunt, why could he not manage his household? Or did he
only go along with his friends to watch their sport? Or did he let
Thomasin run things simply because she was better at it than

Morgan. In fact William Knevet esquire had been the Lancastrian sheriff
of November 1470; Sir John Wingfield replaced him in November 1471:
CFR 1461–7, p280; *CFR 1471–85*, p30. John had not been sheriff for
over 25 years.
[50] *CPR 1467–76*, pp353, 631.   [51] SRO, HA 30/369/31.
[52] SRO, V5/19/1/16; HA 30/22/11/3.
[53] SRO, HA 30/314/18 m5.

he and was determined to do so? It is evident that Thomasin and he had agreed an arrangement for her to play a large role in the financing of the household as early as 1464–5, when there is an incidental reference to it on the Blythburgh accounts. The assignment of Yoxford revenues was involved, as it was in 1473, so that Hopton's withdrawal, in this respect, may have begun then, or before then, possibly when they were married in 1457.[54]

In 1465–6 and 1466–7, at any rate, Thomasin was purchasing wine, fish and cloth for household consumption.[55] But let us halt before we get carried away by the perhaps attractive idea that John Hopton was a man dominated by his wife. In the first place such speculation is idle; given the nature and quantity of our evidence, we are, in making conjectures of that kind, building on sand. Secondly, plenty of payments, indeed the majority recorded on those accounts which we have for the 1470s are by the lord's command;[56] moreover we find Hopton himself attending the courts at Easton Bavents in 1476–7.[57] And finally, with regard to that ostensibly strange hunt at Blythburgh in the course of 1477–8 – even odder when we reflect that Hopton was in his late sixties and about to die – we must be most cautious: Thomasin's authorization of the expenses of that day (hardly longer as they amounted to less than 5s), and of other payments made during that accounting year may simply themselves reflect the fact that when the accounts were drawn up Hopton was dying or dead (for he died 10 November 1478), and therefore her warrant was necessary for certain costs, as yet unauthorized. This explanation is supported by her authorization of the expenses of Robert Hopton and John

54 SRO, HA 30/314/18 m2 dorse: Elis Lumhals, the Yoxford bailiff, delivered cash to Thomasin for household expenses, according to an agreement between the lord and the lady. In 1473 it was the revenues of Yoxford and Wissett which were assigned for household use; these were the principal estates in which she had a life interest by grant of her husband, that is they were her dower lands after her death: *CIPM Henry VII* vol I, pp131–2. Could there have been two households after 1457, his at Westwood, hers at Yoxford?
55 SRO, HA 30/314/18 ms3, 4.
56 For example, Westleton and Blythburgh in 1477–8: SRO, HA 30/22/11/2; HA 30/314/18 m5.
57 SRO, V5/19/1/16.

Tendering at Blythburgh, incurred under the lord's instruction during the previous accounting year but only now allowed.[58]

What then we know, or appear to know, is that John, never at any time in his life a very active man in the wider world of county affairs, and never so far as we are aware active at all in the affairs of the country at large, did less and less as he grew older. Moreover Thomasin his wife, probably from the mid-1460s, certainly by the early 1470s, took on a large measure of responsibility for the management of the household. So far I think we may go, but no further, in that direction at any rate. That admirable lady, Thomasin Hopton, however, we are surely committed to pursue before we return to Hopton himself. After all the woman a man chooses for his wife reveals something of that man.[59] John's first wife Margaret Saville we can assume, given the circumstances of the marriage, was not his choice. They were married in April 1427. Margaret had died by December 1451, as in that month John obtained licence to found a chantry (to be called Hopton chantry) in Blythburgh parish church, the priest of which was to celebrate mass daily for the good estate of John himself, all his benefactors, and for the soul of his late wife Margaret.[60] We know nothing of Margaret save that she bore John numerous children. Of his second wife Thomasin Barrington we know more.

They were married in 1457. Before they were, they entered into an agreement by indenture at London on 18 February 1457. Its terms were these. First, Thomasin was to enjoy her independent income of £30 per annum from lands settled on her by her feoffees, without any interference from John. These lands certainly included those she held in dower in Sussex and Surrey from

---

[58] Compare the same account (SRO, HA 30/314/18 m5): by her testimony Henry Haven was allowed 3s 6d for ploughing done two years before; and Easton Bavents in 1477–8, where money was delivered after John's death, the delivery being warranted by Robert Payn and confirmed by Thomasin: SRO, V5/19/1/16.

[59] 'The themes for which a man retains an affinity are as infallible a guide to his sensibilities as the women for whom he retains an affection': Benny Green on Count Basie.

[60] *CPR 1446–52*, p567: she cannot have been long dead in December 1451; she was alive in the accounting year 1449–50: SRO, HA 30/369/46 f53v.

her last husband William Sidney.[61] Secondly, she was to have for
herself all her own moveable property. Thirdly, and out of her
£30 a year, she was to provide for the maintenance of her children
by her previous marriages. John was not to be involved in this
expense: any of the £30 not so laid out was to be put by, at her
discretion, to advance them in marriage. Fourthly, a trust (if that
word may be used) was to be established for the further benefit of
those children: in order that they should be able to make good
marriages – in the words of the indenture, that they might be
reasonably advanced and preferred after their degree – an
annuity of 20 marks out of Thomasin's inheritance was to be
granted to trustees to accumulate until the time of her death, at
which time it could be used to the advantage of any children still
unmarried. Lastly, a bequest of 100 marks by Thomasin's last
husband, William Sidney, to their daughter Thomasin was to be
none of John's concern, and was to be employed by Thomasin the
mother for Thomasin the daughter's marriage, or so the rather
ambiguous wording suggests. Such then was the arrangement
they put their seals to a little after St Valentine's day 1457.[62]

It was a businesslike transaction undertaken by the two parties
with the advice of their councils. Neither was young, nor could
they have rushed into marriage even if they had desired to, for
each had responsibilities, commitments and interests which had to
be asserted, protected and maintained. That they should come to
a formal accord about these before they got married was typical

61 For arrangements of these properties between her and William Sidney
their son, he granting her estates in Surrey on 20 December 1452, and
between her and her feoffees, they undertaking to pay her a pension of
£8 from certain Sussex and Surrey lands on 16 October 1456, see BL,
Harley Charters 56 B25, 26, 27. I believe I owe these references to David
Morgan.
62 BL, Harley Charter 51 G12. Thomasin soon set about the business of
securing the 20 marks annuity. On 10 March 1457 she granted her mother
Elianor, her brother Thomas, and John Michelgrove the custody and
marriage of her son by her first husband, William Lunsford, during his
minority: this seems to have been a necessary first step. The next was a
grant made by her on 9 April of 20 marks of rent out of her manor of
Lambourn Hall in Essex to her trustees. Once that had been done
Thomasin granted, two days later, Lambourn Hall to her mother for her
life. The estate duly fell in to her in 1462 on the death of Elianor: BL,
Harley Charters 56 B28, 29, 30, 31 and Charter 46 143.

of the age they lived in, probably typical of them and undoubtedly extremely sensible. What however is unusual is their marriage not the agreement which preceded it. They were both middle-aged: John was in his late forties, Thomasin was probably well into her thirties.[63] He was a widower with a large family, she was in her second widowhood and she had children by both her previous husbands, very young ones by her second husband, hence her need to take precautions on their behalf before embarking on matrimony for the third time. Although she was encumbered in this way Thomasin not only had property in her own right, she enjoyed lands in dower from two marriages. She could, one feels, have married a younger man than John Hopton, if she had wanted to, and as most women in her position not only wanted to but did. Equally there is little doubt that John could have found a younger woman for his second wife, as most men in his position would have done, and did. As it was, however, this mature couple found each other attractive enough, children and all, to marry. The pre-marriage agreement of 1457 shows their maturity, and, if we may go so far, their equality. Thomasin was no Jane Copperfield: John therefore, although not a likely-looking Mr Murdstone, had no chance of behaving like him. From this marriage no Davy was to suffer; indeed young Nicholas Sidney (the candidate for such a role) appears only to have benefited from what we have to account as his mother's wise decision.

We learn most of Thomasin from her will. The formality of the estate accounts is such that they reveal virtually nothing of her ability let alone of her character. All they do show is that she was an active woman; of her activities, however, we are granted but a few glimpses, and even these are allowed to us only because from time to time household expenditure appears on the accounts. Moreover, whatever the exact nature of the arrangement whereby she became responsible for the revenues assigned for household use, the odd glimpses we do have of her as the mistress of a household

---

[63] Thomasin's age is uncertain. Her father John Barrington of Rayleigh, Essex, died in 1418 (according to his brass: Pevsner, *Essex*, p322), or a little later (according to *VCH Essex* IV, p27: c.1426). As she died in 1498 she lived to a good age: into her seventies, perhaps her eighties or even nineties.

are routine enough: Margaret Paston or Elizabeth Stonor did no less. Nor, so far as we can see, did Margaret, Hopton's first wife. She received money from the Blythburgh bailiff (also we must remember, the lord's cofferer), had cloth from him and was involved in the provisioning of the household.[64] We find Thomasin playing a similar part; she too sees to the clothing of children and servants, is concerned in the purchase of foodstuffs and wine, and infrequently receives money from manorial bailiffs.[65] At Blythburgh she appears to have held things together immediately after the death of Sir William Hopton early in 1484.[66] And as a widow at Yoxford we have seen her running what seems to us an efficient dairy farm. Efficiency and responsibility are very much what one associates with her, for it was on her behalf that a list of arrears was drawn up at Michaelmas 1479, that is at the first real opportunity since her husband's death in November of the previous year. The list[67] comprises not merely her dower estates but other Suffolk manors as well; she was, therefore, taking the initiative in sorting things out, not just in her own interest but for the benefit of her stepson William, now head of the family.[68] It was his business she was seeing to here. Such shrewd attention to the family's affairs is rather what we have come to expect, having always before us Margaret Paston, who, whatever her husband in his more critical and vexed moods may have believed, saw to matters in his absence in a most resourceful fashion. Yet, before we come to reckon all women to have been the paragons the Goodman of Paris would have approved of, we should recollect Elizabeth Stonor's apparent inability to keep within (in household matters at least) Mr Micawber's formula for happiness. In other words Thomasin's application to, and capacity for, the proper ordering of the affairs of the family should receive their due. Thomasin, as surrounded by children as that other old lady who lived in a shoe,

[64] See Nicholas Greenhagh's rough account book: SRO, HA 30/369/46 fs30, 46, 53, 53v, covering the years 1446–50.

[65] SRO, HA 30/314/18 ms3, 4, 5; V5/19/1/16, 1461–2.

[66] Liveries were directed to her from June 1484 until Michaelmas 1485: SRO, HA 30/314/18 ms8 and 9.

[67] SRO, HA 30/369/31.

[68] And also (as Easton Bavents is included) to the advantage of another of her stepsons, Thomas, who had this estate after his father's death.

was unlike her in that she did know what to do, and, we can feel
sure, did it.

The multitude of children and grandchildren and the purpose-
fulness are the impressions one is left with after reading her will.[69]
It is a careful document, not particularly devout; nor does it
contain many bequests to others than her own children or grandchildren. Friends do not feature very much at all, but then at her
great age most of her old friends would have been dead, most of
her old servants too,[70] though a number of servants are left pairs
of sheets, including Faith of Mylne and Richard the Gardener.
An old servant who quite clearly had become an old friend was
Richard Coppeshurst. As early as 1463-4 we come across him
riding about the lord's business; a dozen years later in March
1476 he acted as Thomasin's attorney in a settlement of Brendfen
manor at Yoxford, and in 1477-8 he was paid for work on the
park fence at Westwood.[71] In her will Thomasin forgave him all
the money which he owed her, gave to him two mill stones for a
horse mill, and left him and his wife Anne her tenement in Yoxford called Kethill, which should pass to their heirs, on condition
that they should find a priest to pray for her soul for a year at
Yoxford. To Idony Coppeshurst Thomasin bequeathed her best
kirtell, a gown lined with black, and a black fur. Possibly another
friend was William Woodbridge, canon of Leiston Abbey, to
whom her executors were to pay £2 each year for three years.
William Clopton (left a gold ring with two diamonds and a
sapphire in it) was as well as being a rather distant relation perhaps
also a friend,[72] like Jane Blakeney and Margery Calthorp (each
left a mantle), and Thomasin Jenny, a nun at Barking, who was
given 10s. Thomasin Rookwood, who, like her daughter Thomasin
and *her* daughter Elizabeth,[73] was left a pair of amber beads, was

---

[69] PRO, Probate 11/11, dated 4 November 1497, proved 10 February 1498.
[70] As was perhaps Joan, Thomasin's maid in 1463-4, who boarded with the
bailiff's family for three weeks: SRO, HA 30/314/18 m1.
[71] SRO, HA 30/314/18 ms1, 5; BL, Harley Charter 51 G13.
[72] He was the husband of her granddaughter Thomasin Knevet (*CIPM
Henry VII* vol III, pp276-7); to their son, Francis, Thomasin left a gilt
spoon.
[73] It is not entirely clear whether Thomasin Rookwood had two daughters,

probably a friend rather than a relation. Everyone else who received a bequest was certainly a relative of Thomasin's; two things about them are at first glance remarkable: that only one was a Hopton, and how many of the women were named Thomasin.

Some of John's children by Margaret Saville were dead by 1497: Sir William, Thomas of Easton Bavents, and Elizabeth who had married William Brews. John, the priest, was alive, and to him Thomasin left a 'table' belonging to an altar which had been his mother's. John was vicar of nearby Reydon and perpetual curate of Southwold and there was, therefore, every reason why he should be left a devotional image associated with his mother. There were not necessarily, however, any such compelling reasons why Thomasin should remember his brothers and sisters or their children; some at least were grown up, even married, before she had become their stepmother. They and she need not have been at all close. Besides, she had so many children and grandchildren of her own to remember. Undoubtedly it was not hostility or indifference to her last husband and his family which she felt, for she desired to be buried in the tomb where John Hopton's body lay in Blythburgh church, while to the altar in that church where Hopton's chantry priest celebrated she bequeathed vestments of purple velvet. And she did after all remember Jane Wentworth, a member of the family into which Sir William Hopton had married more than forty years before; to her she left 10 marks to enable her to make her profession at Bruisyard nunnery. Nevertheless, it is (and one can hardly expect it to be otherwise) her own children and their children whom she had most in mind when she drew up her will in November 1497.

Reading it we cannot help but have the impression of a grand old lady who was the respected, indeed at 80 or more perhaps the venerated, matriarch of a family which extended into half a dozen counties and through four generations. Her long life and her three marriages entitled her to that position, one, we might think, of considerable social significance; but it can only have been

Thomasin and Elizabeth, or whether she had, as I have inferred, a daughter Thomasin and a granddaughter Elizabeth.

her personality that called forth the respect which so many Thomasins reflect. Including her own daughter, dead by 1497, and the Thomasins we have mentioned already (Thomasin Jenny, Thomasin Rookwood and her daughter Thomasin), there were in all six Thomasins named in her will. The other two were Thomasin Woodhouse, the married daughter of Eleanor Townshend, a daughter of our Thomasin by her first husband William Lunsford of Battle, Sussex, and Thomasin, a daughter of Nicholas Sidney, our Thomasin's only surviving son, indeed only surviving child, by her second husband William Sidney of Kingsham, Sussex. This is confusing: there are in fact fewer Thomasins than at first sight there appear to be. However that may be, to her family Thomasin was a dominating figure; and to her, as her will makes abundantly clear, that family was a dominant concern.

It would have been unusual if it had not been; on the one hand her children had to be taken care of, and that consideration, as the 1457 agreement witnesses, included the provision for them of advantageous marriages; on the other hand she had property not only to administer but also ultimately to dispose of. Her eldest son William by her first husband William Lunsford, still a minor in 1457, by 1498 was dead, and it was his son William who was Thomasin's heir at law; he was said to be more than 30 years old. He was ultimately to inherit the bulk of her estates in Essex, but not until 200 marks were taken from them for the benefit of Edward Knevet, further sums levied on them for the performance of her will, and a priest, Friar Ralph Harleston, had been maintained for fifteen years to pray for the soul of her grandfather Totham, her soul and for the souls of others. Even then Nicholas Sidney, her most favoured son, was to receive a life annuity of 10 marks out of these lands.[74] William was bequeathed only a

---

[74] *CIPM Henry VII* vol II, pp99–100, and the will. The friar's fifteen years of prayers were in lieu of 'xv yere, the whiche be behinde for my Graundfader Totham'. Thomasin's behaviour is in stark contrast to that of John Paston and his two sons, who let Judge William Paston's soul, despite his expressed wish for the foundation of a perpetual chantry, struggle through purgatory unaided for at least 43 years and probably until purgatory itself disappeared in the sixteenth century: Davis I, pp44–5; II, p609. A study of chantries which were not founded would be valuable.

bed with its hangings; his sisters Jane and Emeline received £4 and Dame Elizabeth Lunsford, who was a nun, a pair of black beads set in gold and 6s. 8d.

Thomasin's eldest daughter by her first husband was also dead by 1498, but her children (or grandchildren) were more handsomely treated than were the Lunsfords. This daughter Elizabeth was married in the early 1460s: in 1463–4 John Hoo, the Blythburgh bailiff, rode to Stanway in Essex to pay John Knevet esquire, 50 marks, and his son Thomas and Thomas' wife Elizabeth 5½ marks.[75] The payments, particularly that to John Knevet of Stanway, no doubt related to his settlement upon Thomas his son and Elizabeth Lunsford of the manor of Wheatley in Rayleigh, Essex, made in November 1462.[76] Within a year or two we find their son in John Hopton's household: along with Hopton's own younger children, Edward Knevet in 1465–6 was provided with clothing.[77] He was then only a baby, for he was still a minor in 1480, when after his father's death his lands and marriage

---

[75] SRO, HA 30/314/18 m1.

[76] BL, Harley Charter 52 F45, printed in *Collectanea Topographia et Genealogica*, IV (1837), p156. The Knevets have taken some sorting out. David Morgan has once again been helpful. Robert Knevet of Downhall in Rayleigh died in 1419 (his will, dated 1 January, proved 18 January 1419, is BL, Harley Charter 52 F34). Thomas his son and heir held, besides Downhall, Wheatley in Rayleigh, Ramsden Belhous, and Stanway, all in Essex; he was called 'of Stanway', and it was in the chancel of All Saints' church, Stanway that he desired to be buried (his father had been buried in St Mary's, Ramsden Belhous); for Thomas, see particularly BL, Harley Charters 52 F36, 37, 39, 40, 41, 43. He died in 1459 (his will is PRO, Probate 11/4, dated 4 October 1458, proved 21 July 1459), leaving three sons, of whom John Knevet of Stanway was the oldest. John married in 1443 (BL, Harley Charter 52 F39); he made a settlement of Ramsden Belhous on 3 August 1460 to a group of feoffees who read like a roll-call of recently victorious East Anglian Yorkists: Henry, viscount Bourgchier, Sir William Bourgchier, Thomas Bourgchier, Sir John Marney, Sir Roger Chamberlain, John Howard, John Doreward, Thomas Waldegrave, William Doreward, Richard Doreward, Clement Spice, Walter Writtle and half a dozen others: BL, Harley Charter 52 F44. He made his will (PRO, Probate 11/7 f186) on 10 February 1477; he also desired to be buried at Stanway, and he left £2 towards an alabaster table for the high altar there. Thomas, his son and heir, who had clearly received Wheatley on his marriage to Elizabeth Lunsford, was not to have Downhall; that was to go for life to John of Buckenham Castle, already more notable than his elder brother, and founder of the more distinguished branch of the family.

[77] SRO, HA 30/314/18 m3.

were granted to Sir Thomas Montgomery of Faulkbourn, Essex, and he did not have seisin of his property until seven years later.[78] His mother had died long before, on 5 July 1471.[79] Thomasin made him her chief executor. As we have seen, he was treated by her with generosity: he was to have 200 marks from her Essex lands, having already had as much during her lifetime.[80] She also gave him her 'table' so that it might remain with her blood, though exactly why she singled out the Knevets as the representatives of her blood we cannot now know. To Edward's daughter Phillipa she left a gilt cup to drink sweet wine out of; to Elizabeth Knevet, another daughter and Edward's eventual heir,[81] she left a silver salt which her father then had, and her book of 'legenda sanctorum', and to Robert Knevet she left a seler with a tester of blue hangings, and a covering of green and white flowers lined with linen, a feather bed, a transom, sheets and blankets. Robert was renting pasture from her at Yoxford in 1492–3, but what his relationship to Edward and Elizabeth was we do not know.[82] There is also a mystery attached to Stanway itself. It ought to have been in Edward's possession in 1497, having descended to him from his father. Yet in her will Thomasin treats Stanway as being in her own hands, desiring that £40 be levied from it towards the carrying out of her last wishes. Stanway church too she greatly favoured in her will, bequeathing to it her 'portrous', an altar cloth of velvet and gold embroidered with garters, 26s 8d towards the purchase of a cope, and £2 for repairs where they

[78] *CPR 1476–85*, p238; *CCR 1485–1500*, p65. He was in possession of Wheatley in 1488: BL, Harley Charter 51 G14.

[79] Inscription on her tomb at Yoxford, now lost: J. Weever, *Ancient Funerall Monuments* (1631), p783. For the explanation of why tombs at Yoxford church were for so long attributed to Walberswick, see Parr, II, p12; III, p74.

[80] The money was for his own use, *not* for the performance of the will; the *IPM* says that the original enfeoffment to this use was for 400 marks; probably by 1497 he had received half the sum: *CIPM Henry VII* vol II, p99.

[81] She was said to be eleven at her father's death in 1501, and to have been abducted by John Rainsford, who within two years had married her. She died in 1508 without children: *CIPM Henry VII* vol II, pp257–8; III, pp276–7, 319; *CCR 1500–9*, p29; *CPR 1494–1509*, p321.

[82] SRO, HA 30/312/117. In Edward's will of 1501 he was left £3 6s 8d, a gown and a doublet; to a Richard Knevet Edward left simply £3 6s 8d: PRO, Probate 11/16. Were they illegitimate?

were most needed. Edward, however, certainly lived there for he termed himself of Stanway in his will of 1501, which was drawn up there, and he desired to be buried in Stanway church beside his first wife Anne.[83]

This marriage of her daughter into the Essex branch of the Knevet family clearly was due to Thomasin's own connections with that county, especially with her first home, Rayleigh, from where the Knevets themselves also originally came. These connections she maintained until the end. She desired to be buried at Rayleigh, if it fell out that she should die in Essex, and to the church there she left 5 marks for the glazing of a window with the life of St Thomas. Another benefactor of that church, and his work still survives, was one of her executors: William Allen of Rayleigh, yeoman, was responsible for the building of the south chapel, where he lies buried.[84]

It was not, however, Thomasin's connections but those of John Hopton which led to the marriage of her second daughter by William Lunsford, Eleanor. It seems likely that it was this Eleanor for whom Thomasin was purchasing cloth in 1465–6,[85] for although called 'filia domini' there is is no other reference to an Eleanor Hopton. She married, probably not long after this, Sir Roger Townshend of Raynham, Norfolk, a successful lawyer who founded his family's fortune.[86] He did so a generation after William Paston (like Townshend a justice of common pleas) had founded his family's fortunes out of the practice of the law, and it may be that the Pastons' own troubles of the 1460s and 1470s, when Townshend gave them legal advice and lent them money on mortgage, were what helped him prosper. Townshend was steward, feoffee and executor of John Hopton, and he was retained for life with a fee of £2 by Sir William Hopton, being his chief steward and of his council; Thomasin continued to retain him as a

[83] PRO, Probate 11/16.
[84] Norman Scarfe, *The Shell Guide to Essex* (1968), and Nikolaus Pevsner, *Essex, sub* Rayleigh. The date of the chapel is said to be *c.*1517. William is described as a yeoman in Thomasin's will.
[85] SRO, HA 30/314/18 m3.
[86] Wedgwood, p864 has him married to his son's wife, an incestuous blunder made worse by the fact that she was a granddaughter of John Hopton.

member of her council after Sir William's death, and it was therefore on her order that in 1484–5 he received his fee.[87] When he
made his will in 1493 it was his mother-in-law whom he first
remembered after making his lengthy and extremely hard-headed
religious bequests: 'to my moder Hopton' he left £2. He gave
similar sums to his married daughter Thomasin Woodhouse and
to his young daughter-in-law Anne. To Eleanor his widow he left
all his cash, plate and other goods, and the responsibility for the
maintenance and marriage of his children. She was his sole
executrix.[88] The confidence this businesslike man placed in her
suggests that she took after her mother.[89] Was it for this reason
that mother and daughter might not have got on? All that
Thomasin bequeathed to Eleanor in 1497 were her beads of gold,
but she was to pay for them as much as they were worth according to the discretion of the executors. If she bought them she did
not enjoy them for long. She died in September 1500.[90]

Another connection made by Thomasin as a result of her
marriage to Hopton might also have been of advantage to her

---

[87] *CPR 1476–85*, pp142–4; SRO, HA 30/314/18 ms7, 8, 9.

[88] PRO, Probate 11/10. He left £200 each for the marriages of his daughters
Anne and Elizabeth so long as they married with the advice and agreement of their mother.

[89] Like her mother, and at the same time, she had a dairy farm; not only
that, it was at a place where Townshend and Hopton properties coincided,
Wissett. In 'the abstractions oute of the accomptes of the arrerages of
dyverse Bayles Fermours and othir Officers of Dame Alyenore Towneshend
late the wyfe of Syr Roger Towneshend knyth at the Feaste of Seynt
Mighell Tharghaungell the ix yere of the reyne of Kyng Henry the vij',
under the heading 'Wysett' Robert Odyerne of Spexhall, 'fermour of the
newe deyary of the ladyes ther', was a little over half a year behindhand
with his money. During Sir Roger's lifetime this taking stock of arrears
was, it seems, a yearly exercise: three such lists, varying however in
content and form, survive from the later part of Edward IV's reign.
This list for Michaelmas 1493 must have been drawn up well after the
date to which it applies for Sir Roger did not die until 9 November that
year: NRO, Bradfer Lawrence V, no. X 13. For Thomasin's dairy at
Yoxford in 1492–3, see chapter 2, p70. Eleanor also had swans. On the
inside of the back parchment cover of a terrier of East Raynham dating
from Edward's reign (NRO, Townshend MS 1476) there are numerous
random jottings; they include the drawing ⌒ with beneath it 'This
is the marke of Dame Alinor Touneshend Swanse.'

[90] *CIPM, Henry VII* vol II, p302. Blomefield VII, pp131–2 makes use of her
now lost will: she desired as a memorial to herself and her husband the
building of an Easter sepulchre at East Raynham church. It still survives.

family, in this instance to her brother Thomas Barrington of
Rayleigh. The manor adjoining Blythburgh to the north west,
Blyford, was owned by the Micklefields.[91] In 1464–5, on John
Hopton's command, 10 marks was delivered to William Micklefield esquire by the Blythburgh bailiff, for what purpose is not
stated.[92] It was to this William that Thomas Barrington's daughter
Elizabeth was married; he acquired Blyford in 1471 on the death
of Robert his father; Thomas Barrington had died two years
before; Elizabeth was already dead.[93] However, it was Thomasin's
children by her second husband, William Sidney of Kingsham,
Sussex, who were to benefit most from the connections opened up
to her by her marriage with John Hopton.

Her first husband, William Lunsford, died between April and
August 1445. All their four children were under age at the time
of his death; in his will he directed that Thomasin was to have
custody of them.[94] In the next four years she added to their
number three or four more children, born to her during her brief
marriage with William Sidney, who died 8 October 1449.[95] So
many children in so short a space is not unusual in the later Middle
Ages,[96] nor is the fact, unsurprising in these circumstances, that
one of them died in infancy and another was dead by 1461.[97]
Twice widowed within half a dozen years, Thomasin with her
clutch of small children turned, as we have seen, to John Hopton;
in marrying in 1457 they brought together into one household
(for even if the indenture of 1457 envisaged for Thomasin's
children a distinct financial arrangement, one household they

[91] Copinger II, p19.
[92] SRO, HA 30/314/18 m3.
[93] In Thomas Barrington's will (dated at Hatfield Regis, Essex, 17 September, proved 24 October 1469: PRO, 6 Wattys) Elizabeth is referred to as
William's late wife. Thomas left to Robert their son £10, and to Anne
their daughter £20 towards her marriage.
[94] They are not named in his will (PRO, PCC 31 Luffenham) but were
William, Elizabeth, Eleanor, all of whom we have discussed, and John, for
whom see *Coll Top et Gen* IV, p156.
[95] According to a now lost inscription on his brass at Cranleigh, Surrey:
VCH Surrey III, p91, see Wedgwood, pp768–9.
[96] McFarlane, *Lancastrian Kings*, p17. The dire consequences of such frequent pregnancies suggested there did not overtake Thomasin though they
probably did *her* daughter Thomasin, see p129 note 99 below.
[97] HMC, *De L'Isle and Dudley MSS*, I, ppix–x, 4–6.

seem to have made) as many as seven or eight children. One of the children of her second marriage, called Thomasin after her, had been provided for by her father, so far as marriage was concerned, by a bequest of 100 marks.

When that money was used, however, it was to marry her to a Suffolk gentleman, William Tendering esquire, of Harkstead and Holbrook, and it comprised no more than a quarter of what Thomasin had to raise to get such a husband: on 20 November 1481 William Tendering acknowledged at Yoxford the receipt of 50 marks, final instalment of a marriage portion of 400 marks with which she purchased him as a husband for her daughter.[98] Thomasin bore him one daughter who survived, two sons and other daughters who died young.[99] She herself died in 1485,[100] many years before her husband's death in 1499. She was buried in Yoxford church and perhaps it was for her tomb that her mother purchased a 'marbilston' and had it brought to Yoxford in 1492–3.[101] It is striking that not only Thomasin Tendering but also her stepsister Elizabeth Knevet should have been buried at Yoxford. Why were they not buried where they lived? They were not old when they died: did both die in childbirth while at their mother's house, where they used to go to have their children? Yet even if that speculation were true, to be buried where they died was not necessary. Whatever the truth, it seems clear that the links between mother and daughters were strong ones. That they appear to have been no less strong between mother and son

[98] BL, Harley Charter 56 H39.
[99] The two boys were William and John; they were buried at Yoxford: Parr III, p11 records a now missing inscription from the church there to William and John Tendering, the sons of William Tendering esquire. I presume it was this John Tendering, Thomasin Hopton's grandson, whose expenses, with those of her own son Robert Hopton, at Blythburgh in 1476–7, she authorized in the accounts of the following year: SRO, HA 30/314/18 m5. Of other children who died young Thomasin's surviving brass at Yoxford is suggestive: she is depicted naked in a shroud surrounded by seven children, five of whom are also shewn in shrouds. Her fate may therefore have been similar to that of Mary Bohun, Henry Bolingbroke's first wife, who died in childbirth aged 25, having produced seven children in eight years. Thomasin Tendering did not have her mother's stamina.
[100] On 20 October according to the inscription on her brass at Yoxford.
[101] SRO, HA 30/312/117.

(as we shall shortly see) suggests not only that Thomasin Hopton was a woman of character, but that she had a personality which, among her children at any rate, encouraged affection as well as commanded respect. Moreover, Thomasin could love as well as be loved. In her will she made provision for her Tendering grand-daughter, Dorothy, who by that time was of marriageable age; £30 was set aside for her marriage; but if she should die before marriage then the same sum was to be expended on the singing of a thousand masses for the soul of her mother Thomasin Tendering. Dorothy did not die before she married. By the time of her father's death only a little over a year later in March 1499, she was married to Francis Southwell esquire, a member of another important gentle family of East Anglia.[102] She and Francis no doubt found useful the bed, hangings, counterpane, pillow and sheets that Thomasin bequeathed to Dorothy in her will.

It was nonetheless her only surviving son by William Sidney whom she appears to have favoured most. Certainly she trusted him: by 1479 Nicholas was in charge of her Sussex and Surrey estates.[103] Brought up in the Hopton household,[104] in 1468–9 he was at school at Covehithe with Roger Hopton and William Haliday; at hardly less than 20 he must have been rather long in the tooth for schooling.[105] He continued to live with his mother in her widowhood at Yoxford where he had property; firewood was freely delivered to him from the early 1480s, he rented pasture in Middleton meadow in the early 1490s.[106] And at Yoxford he, like his sister, chose to be buried;[107] that was in 1513, some years after his mother's death. Evidently he still lived there, even though he had inherited the Sidney lands in Sussex and Surrey and Thomasin had left to him and his heirs male her lands

[102] *CIPM Henry VII* vol II, pp168–9.
[103] SRO, HA 30/369/31: arrears list of 1479. The arrears of the tenants and farmers were written in a book which was in his keeping. He was also one of her feoffees: BL, Harley Charter 51 G13.
[104] Clothes were bought for him in 1466–7: SRO, HA 30/314/18 m4.
[105] SRO, V5/19/1/16.
[106] SRO, HA 30/369/391; HA 30/312/117.
[107] His tomb (pictured in Parr II, p11, from Davy's MSS in the BL), in fragments in Munro Cautley's time (*Suffolk Churches* (3rd edition, 1954), p354), has now entirely disappeared.

in Sussex too. She also left him an annuity of 10 marks out of her Essex properties, on condition that he did all in his power to help her executors. She made a similar stipulation in leaving £20 for the marriage of his daughter Thomasin. To father and daughter she was also generous with her moveable goods. To Thomasin she bequeathed her sheets and a pillow, her crystal and coral beads enamelled with blue and set in silver and gilt, and her book of Our Lady's life. Nicholas was bequeathed books too: her mass book, her psalter and her Hoccleve, 'my book of Englissh callid Ocliff'.[108] Also he was to have a bed of silk cloth (called bawdekin), cushions and a counterpane of the same stuff, another counterpane of arras with an image of St George, all her brass and pewter, two great andirons, and a large bowl of silver with a lid precious enough to have a name, 'Revell', a piece which Nicholas in turn was to bequeath some fifteen years afterwards: a 'gret boll pece called Rewell with the brode arowe hede in the bottom'.[109] To each of Nicholas' children Thomasin left £1, and Francis Sidney, called 'my child', was granted 26s 8d towards his healing. Anne Sidney (presumably, though she is not termed dame, Nicholas' wife) was left a pair of 'poyntells' of gold ('that cost me £2'), whichever of Thomasin's best gowns she would choose to have, and another gown furred with fox. Anne was a daughter of Sir William Brandon; here was yet another and advantageous alliance with a new neighbour, for Sir William, one of the most influential of Thomas Mowbray, duke of Norfolk's councillors, had a house at Henham.[110]

Despite inheriting, through the death of his brothers without issue, the Sidney lands in Sussex and Surrey, and thus becoming, as the editor of their manuscripts has it, 'ancestor of the famous Sidneys',[111] Nicholas remained a Suffolk man. So he termed himself in his will: Nicholas Sidney of the county of Suffolk,

---

[108] Could this have been Bodleian Library, Oxford, MS Digby 185?
[109] His will, dated 1 February 1513, proved 11 February 1513: PRO, 10 Fettiplace.
[110] *CIPM Henry VII* vol II, p27. They were not married in 1475, when Sir William made a will; Anne was the second of six unmarried daughters he then made provision for: PRO Probate 11/8. For an inadequate sketch of Brandon, see Wedgwood, pp102–3.
[111] *HMC De L'Isle and Dudley MSS*, I, p. ix.

esquire. He had lands in Bramfield, Darsham and Thorington as well as in Yoxford; in the chancel of St Peter's, Yoxford, his body was duly laid.[112] His affection for this place, where his mother had lived, must have been great.

The picture of Thomasin towards the close of her long life we cannot pretend has been at all sharply drawn: she does not come out plainly. Still, Thomasin has every appearance of being the grand old lady, admired by her family, loved by some, maybe no more than respected by others. Not a markedly pious old lady, yet as ample prayers for her soul were to be sung and devout works were to be done, one who evidently knew the value of things, religious as well as secular.[113] Good things she certainly liked to have about her, good clothes, good linen, good jewels, good plate, even good books. But not luxurious things. Excess, whether it be of piety or of the things of this world, was apparently alien to her. Moderation, orderliness, perhaps even correctness is what one would expect of her. Perhaps Sir John Oglander's vivid description of his wife goes some way towards an idea of John Hopton's:

... a most careful wife who was no spender, never wore silk gown but for her credit when she went abroad, and never to please herself. She was up every day before me and oversaw all the outhouses: she would not trust her maid with directions but would wet her shoes to see it done herself.[114]

Thomasin, however, was grander than that: undoubtedly she wore silk gowns to please herself. There was more to her than an

112 PRO, 10 Fettiplace. Apart from Sir William, his heir, he left three sons, Robert, Francis and Thomas. Thomasin his daughter had married and she had a son, Nicholas Ganell.

113 A thousand masses were to be performed, 500 immediately after her death, a further 500 as soon as possible. A priest was to celebrate at Blythburgh, or wherever she was buried, for a year, and John Everard, a priest who received 6 yards of cloth on Thomasin's order in 1477–8 (SRO, HA 30/314/18 m5), was also to pray for her soul for a year. Her bequests to Stanway and Rayleigh churches we have already noted. She left 10 marks to Yoxford church towards the making of a new aisle, presumably the south aisle and brick south chapel (for which see Parr, III, p16), and 6s 8d to the high altar there, £1 to Wissett church, and £1 to the nuns at Bruisyard. She also left sums for the repair of roads at Yoxford and Stanway and of the road leading from Canewdon church to her own Lambourn Hall, the hall itself being of c.1500 according to Pevsner. I would suggest that this represents rather a restrained piety.

114 *A Royalist's Notebook*, p241.

efficient housewife, more to her perhaps than the stately matriarch, more to her quite probably than there was to John Hopton.
But we are too dogmatic. We do not know enough of John to
dismiss him in this casual fashion. If we had his will we might
have to change our opinion. We are in danger, I think, of making
the wife more intelligent than her husband, a favourite device of
romance. To laud one we do not have to disparage the other.
If we sense that Thomasin had her wits about her there is every
reason to suppose that John had too.

One matter we should so much like to know more about is the
education which Thomasin and John gave their children. We have
only some tantalizing glimpses of the boys going to school. John
Hopton, who became a priest, we know most about. In 1452–3
the Blythburgh bailiff paid 33s 4d to the parson of nearby
Brampton for John's board for a year; in 1455–6 the same bailiff
recorded his expenses in going to Norwich to see his master
John.[115] Had John been sent away to learn? We can only guess
how old he was, but from what follows he can only have been very
young; that, however, was in keeping with the age. We do not
hear of him again until the early 1460s when he and other
children of the lord and lady[116] were at school at Covehithe.
In 1463–4 the Blythburgh bailiff purchased for them all manner
of gear (shoes, pattens, caps, hats and candles) at a cost of nearly
35s. Perhaps too the robes the tailor John Abbot made for the
lord's sons that year were in the nature of what Miss Janet Becker
called (she was writing in the 1930s) 'school outfits'.[117] Also in
1463–4 the Blythburgh bailiff paid the expenses of the young
John Hopton and others at Wissett for two days killing deer for
the vicar at Covehithe. This looks like a school holiday, a holiday
which gave the boys some exercise and filled their teacher's larder.
For undoubtedly this schoolmaster John and Thomasin had such

---

[115] SRO, HA 30/369/46 fs11, 101v. A Robert Iverich was vicar of Brampton
at this time, instituted 24 February 1436. The next institution (without
reference to the name of his predecessor) was of Thomas Payn on
27 March 1469.

[116] The phrase surely indicates that Thomasin's as well as John's children
were concerned: SRO, HA 30/314/18 m1, under liveries.

[117] M. J. Becker, *Blythburgh: an essay on the village and its church* (Halesworth, 1935), p59.

133

confidence in during the 1460s, was the vicar of Covehithe. The following year, 1464–5, he received on the lord's instruction 25s 3d from the bailiff at Easton Bavents. No reason for the payment was given, nor was it in the next accounting year when out of the Easton revenues he received £2. It seems safe to assume nonetheless that he was being paid for the board of the Hopton boys under his charge. John Hopton may have finished his schooling that year; early in June 1466 the bailiff at Easton gave him 6s 8d, and sometime during 1465–6 the Blythburgh bailiff gave him 4s, the price of a haircut for him and his brothers: 'pro rasura pro eo et fratribus'.[118] If John left the Covehithe school in 1466 and went up to Cambridge,[119] other young members of the family continued there, or soon afterwards arrived. In 1467–8 the vicar received the very considerable sum of £4 10s; the following year he only had 35s, but Roger Hopton, William Haliday and Nicholas Sidney had another 11s 8d while they were at school at Covehithe. William Haliday, otherwise unknown to us, was still there in 1470–1, when the vicar was paid 12s 6d for his board.[120] We might note here that John Hopton's care for education comprehended the schooling not only of a stepson but also of a boy who was apparently none of his kin.

Who was this schoolkeeping vicar of Covehithe? He was William Yarmouth, a Cambridge Master of Arts, who had been at the University in the 1450s, and who had been appointed to Covehithe in 1459.[121] He was a feoffee of John Hopton and of Thomasin,[122] and an executor in 1470 of his fellow Cambridge graduate and near neighbour, Dr Robert Scoles, vicar of Reydon with Southwold since 1444. Dr Scoles was a man of parts: a doctor of theology who owned books of astronomy and an astrolabe, who bequeathed to the town of Southwold for its defence his arms and armour. In Southwold church, to which he also made many bequests, he desired to be buried.[123] Thomas Crowe, the rector of Easton Bavents, was also one of his executors. Was there, therefore, in this small corner of Suffolk, a group of

[118] SRO, HA 30/314/18 m3.   [119] Emden, *Biog Reg Camb*, p313.
[120] SRO, V5/19/1/16, 17.   [121] Emden, *Biog Reg Camb*, p665.
[122] *CPR 1476–85*, pp142–4; *CIPM Henry VII* vol II, p131.
[123] Emden, *Biog Reg Camb*, p512.

clever men who enjoyed each other's company? Robert Scoles died in 1470. William Yarmouth, although of a younger generation, probably died not many years afterwards. However, he lived long enough to see a former pupil succeed his old friend, and possibly patron, at Southwold: John Hopton, now also a Cambridge man, was admitted vicar of Reydon with Southwold within a week of Dr Scoles' death in June 1470.[124] William Yarmouth was alas no longer at Covehithe by the late 1470s for young Robert Hopton was sent to school elsewhere.

Robert can only have been John's son by Thomasin, and it was Thomasin who in June 1478 received from the Westleton bailiff £2 to pay for Robert's keep at Snettisham, Norfolk, where he had lately been at school. It looks as though his schooling there had been concluded, for on 18 October Thomasin had a further £5 from the Westleton bailiff to pay for Robert's board in London.[125] Why Robert should have to go so far as Snettisham to school – was the priest there a particularly skilled teacher, his reputation widely known?[126] – must for the time being at least remain a mystery; the reason for his being in London need not. He had entered Lincoln's Inn at Michaelmas 1477.[127] He was still there in autumn 1482, when he was fined 1s 8d for playing cards outside the Inn,[128] but thereafter we lose all trace of him. Possibly like the unfortunate Walter Paston, who died in the summer he took his first degree at Oxford, Robert died before he could make use of his education.[129]

---

[124] Scoles' will is dated 6 June; it was proved on 19 June (NRO, Norwich Cons. Court, Reg. Bettyns, f83); John was instituted on 13 June. What part, if any, did these two long-lived vicars Robert Scoles, 1444–70, and John Hopton, 1470–1503, play in the building and furnishing of Southwold church? Could the two figures carved on the ends of the stalls in the chancel be representations of one or other or both of them?

[125] SRO, HA 30/22/11/3.

[126] William Grey was instituted to Snettisham on 28 April 1477 on the death of Richard Castleacre, who had held the benefice since 1443. The Snettisham churchwardens' accounts covering the later 1470s were, however, supervised by John Damshyll priest: NRO, PD 24/1, fs62v–68v.

[127] *Lincoln's Inn Admission Register* 1 (1896), p20. He was admitted at the same time as Edward Sulyard, the son of John Sulyard, Thomasin's nephew.

[128] *Black Book of Lincoln's Inn* 1 (1897), p76.

[129] He was not the only one of the family to have gone to Lincoln's Inn.

Like the Pastons John and Thomasin Hopton cared about education; they were concerned that a number of their boys (John, Roger and Robert Hopton, and Nicholas Sidney) should undergo a schooling in grammar, in Latin grammar that is. John and Thomasin were in no way unusual in wanting such schooling for their sons; we need to make no particular point of that: it is what we would expect of gentlefolk.[130] The point worth stressing, however, is that the schooling was informal. In other words at Covehithe in the 1460s there was a man who could and would teach boys; to him therefore boys went. We tend to be mesmerized by the endowed educational establishments of the late Middle Ages, indeed of the modern age also, so that on them our attention is concentrated. It should not be. They were un-important. Most boys who had an education had it at the hands (very much at the hands, one imagines)[131] of teachers like the vicar of Covehithe, William Yarmouth.

There is no record of the education given to the other Hopton boys (for example the eldest, Sir William), or the girls, for Thomasin would not have neglected them. That John Hopton was ambitious for his children we cannot however doubt. His ambitions for himself may have been satisfied all at once in 1430 when he came into the Swillington estates, but of his children he surely had high hopes. The career of his eldest son shows he wanted the family to go further.

Apart from William's membership of the king's household, from 1447–8 until sometime after 1452, and his marriage into the Wentworth family c. 1450, which show his father's ambition for him, he is an entirely anonymous figure until the 1460s. This, so far as family affairs are concerned, is a result of the lack of

His stepbrother Nicholas Sidney had been admitted in March 1474: *Admission Register*, I, p19. Nicholas was there in 1476–7, when he was assigned a chamber (*Black Book*, I, p62), so they may have been there together for a little while.

130 Just as we should expect them to send a boy to finish his education at university or at the Inns of Court. Thus John went to Cambridge, Robert, and Nicholas Sidney to Lincoln's Inn.

131 Agnes Paston wished her son Clement to be beaten by his London tutor if he was not up to scratch, 'And so ded the last mayster, and the best that ever he had, att Caumbrege': Davis I, p41.

accounts before that decade;[132] how far he was in fact a negligible figure in a wider context we cannot say, but that so little is to be found about him during the 1450s suggests that he had not yet made his mark. If he had attached himself to the Duke of Suffolk's interest in the late 1440s, and to that interest and to no other, it could be that in the decade after 1450, when that interest was virtually extinguished so far as national politics was concerned, he was no more involved in the political rough and tumble of that testing time than was his father. He comes alive for us only in 1465.

In the accounting years 1464–5 and 1465–6 he was busy on his father's behalf: with John Tasburgh the supervisor assessing the damage done to tenants' crops at Blythburgh by the lord's rabbits, at Easton Bavents with Tasburgh again, and with others of his father's officers supervising a court which met to adjudicate on the seaside boundary between Easton and Covehithe, and at Dunwich and Westwood with his father, William Jenny and William Pickenham to discuss the matter of the harbour, that old controversy which had cropped up again to exercise Hopton on the one hand and the Dunwich authorities on the other.[133] No doubt he had been active after this fashion for some time before the mid-1460s. He does not appear to have been so active again; there are no further references to him at all in the surviving accounts. He had, one suspects, too much to occupy him elsewhere. In November 1465 he became sheriff of Norfolk and Suffolk for the first time,[134] and in January 1466 he was appointed to the commission of the peace for the West Riding; on that commission he continued until November 1470.[135] His omission at that time is

---

[132] William features only once in Nicholas Greenhagh's rough notebook (SRO, HA 30/369/46 f101v): in 1455–6 Nicholas recorded the cost of meat and drink for William and Thomas his brother and of oats for their horses.

[133] SRO, HA 30/314/18 ms2, 3; V5/19/1/17.

[134] Sir John Howard gave him (as sheriff) £1 on 12 April 1466, possibly for some official service connected with Howard's agreement, reached that day, with Henry Wentworth, William's close friend, over land: *Manners and Household Expenses of England in the Thirteenth and Fifteenth Centuries*, ed. Beriah Botfield (Roxburghe Club, 1841), p341.

[135] *CFR 1461–71*, p168; *CPR 1461–7*, p577; *CPR 1467–77*, p638.

significant for it demonstrates that William was not trusted by the
Earl of Warwick and those others who held power during the
Readeption; in their judgment he was a committed Yorkist.
He duly returned to the commission of the peace in June 1473,
and was on other commissions in the West Riding during the
1470s.[136] Called 'of Swillington',[137] he was primarily involved
on the government's behalf on West Riding matters; probably
also he looked after his father's estates there. He maintained his
Suffolk contacts, particularly with the Wentworths,[138] and was
briefly a commissioner there in 1472–3.[139] On his father's death
he went to live in Suffolk again, for from that time until his own
death he was on commissions, including that of the peace, only for
that county. Five days before his father died on 10 November
1478, he had been appointed for his second term as sheriff of
Norfolk and Suffolk.[140]

It was nonetheless a Yorkshire connection that was the making
of him. By 1476, and no doubt from before this, he was attached
to Richard, duke of Gloucester, and acted on his patron's behalf
as feoffee and mainpernor.[141] Later he probably became one of

136 Including the commission of array of 2 March 1470: *CPR 1467–77*,
pp199, 408, 490, 572, 638.
137 For example, in his pardon of 28 November 1471 (PRO, C67/48 m34),
and in a Yorkshire deed which he witnessed: *Yorkshire Deeds* 1, ed.
William Brown, Yorks. Arch. Soc., Record Series, 39 (1909), p65.
138 HMC, 11th Report, appendix VII, p93, letter 1 – these 'Calthorpe' letters
are now in the Norfolk Record Office, Le Strange Collection P20. To have
the king write on your behalf a letter like this was what made being of
his household so worthwhile: in this respect the 1470s in East Anglia
were not unlike the 1440s. Sir John Wingfield was the influential man in
this instance, the arrangement of a marriage for a daughter of his with
Sir William Calthorpe's son's son and heir the matter on which the king
wrote to urge the dilatory Sir William along. Yet, from the fact that the
marriage did not come off we may conclude that Edward IV was no more
able to overawe this particular country gentleman than was his father
over twenty years before: K. B. McFarlane, 'Parliament and Bastard
Feudalism', *Transactions of the Royal Historical Society* 4th series, XXVI
(1944), p57, f2.
139 *CPR 1467–77*, pp353, 631; Walter Rye, *Suffolk Feet of Fines* (1900),
p309. He married his daughter Ann to Sir Robert Clere of Ormsby St
Margaret, Norfolk; she died 23 January 1506, many years before her
husband: Blomefield v, p1574, from a memorial inscription at Ormsby.
140 *CPR 1476–85*, pp317, 397, 466; *CFR 1471–85*, p153.
141 *Yorkshire Deeds* VI, ed. C. T. Clay, Yorks. Arch. Soc., Record Series, 76
(1930) p20; *CPR 1476–85*, p34; *CCR 1476–85*, pp189, 346–7; *CFR*

Richard's councillors,[142] for his closeness to the Duke is made abundantly clear in the summer of 1483. William was knighted at Richard's coronation, and a few days later on 4 July was appointed Treasurer of the Household.[143] He had shared in the success of his master, but he was spared the ignominy of sharing in his failure by his death, while still in office, on 7 February 1484. Coming as it did, when he and Richard were at the highest point in their fortunes, William's death must have seemed most untimely. For his family, however, it was a happy stroke. Sir William did not live to fight for Richard at Bosworth, as he most probably would have done, and that, whether he had survived or been killed in the field, could only have brought distress upon the Hoptons. As it was they escaped such misfortune. Sir William's son George was a young man with none of his father's thoroughgoing commitments; and, like so many others in the summer of 1485, he avoided making any.[144] In fact when it came to a choice he made the right one; he fought at Stoke for Henry VII and was knighted.[145] Sir George's enthusiasm for the new monarch, which has every appearance of a son looking to atone for the sins of his father, and which went so far as the naming of his second son Arthur, came to nought: Sir George died in July 1489. Within six months his eldest son John was also dead; it was therefore (and not inappropriately) Arthur who, after a long minority, was to carry the family further forward in the first half of the sixteenth century.[146]

What of John Hopton's other sons? They are alas really no

1471–85, pp162–3; HMC, *Various Collections* VII (1914), p32; BL, Cotton MSS, Julius BXII, f241v.

[142] He was not among the feed councillors listed in 1476–7: PRO, DL 29/637/10360A. He was farming the estate of Blaxhall, Suffolk, from the duke, that year: *ibid.* He seems only to have had small pickings out of the attainder of George, duke of Clarence: *CPR 1476–85*, p124.

[143] W. A. Shaw, *The Knights of England*, II (1906), p21; R. L. Storey, 'English Officers of State 1399–1485', *BIHR*, xxxi (1958), p92. It was a roundabout route by which he returned to where, over thirty years before, he had begun.

[144] He received a general pardon on 18 November 1485: *CPR 1485–94*, p44.

[145] Gairdner VI, p187.

[146] *CIPM Henry VII* vol I, pp204, 242, 263. Arthur was granted licence to enter his lands without proof of age in November 1507: *CPR 1494–1509*, p559.

more than names to us. Thomas we encounter twice and on both occasions, although they are twenty years apart, in association with William his brother and a man called John Dynley. In 1455–6 the Blythburgh bailiff noted the cost of meat and drink provided for the three men,[147] and in January 1476 John Dynley and Thomas Hopton esquire of Swillington were granted power of attorney by Sir John Pilkington, William Hopton and William Maulever to take possession of land in Whitkirk in the West Riding.[148] On his father's death Thomas had Easton Bavents, but he did not enjoy that small estate for long: he made his will only a few months after his elder brother's death in 1484 and died shortly afterwards.[149] He charged his stepmother Thomasin and Roger Townshend to see that his wife Margaret should hold Easton for her life, according to his father's will; Margaret was holding courts there in 1489.[150] Thomas desired that at the mass to be said for him at Easton £2 was to be disbursed for the good of his soul and the soul of his brother Sir William, and for the church there he wished his executors to buy a cope with his arms and the arms of his wife upon it. But he had not forgotten York-shire: at Swillington a priest was to pray for him for two years.

John, whom we have caught sight of at school, went on to Cambridge. He was there in 1469; ten years later on 6 June 1479 he was admitted a Bachelor of Canon Law.[151] By then he had been vicar of Reydon with Southwold for nine years. He had for a few months in 1474 held another local living, Wenhaston, immedi-

---

[147] SRO, HA 30/369/46 f101v.
[148] *Yorkshire Deeds* II, ed. William Brown, Yorks. Arch. Soc., Record Series, 50 (1914), p200. I take it that William was acting as Sir John Pilkington's feoffee in this transaction. How closely were they associated? As an early and influential Yorkist, Sir John could have done much to promote his Yorkshire neighbour's career, particularly in the 1470s when Sir John was a close connection of Richard, duke of Gloucester: *Test Ebor* III, pp238–41; Wedgwood, pp684–5.
[149] *Test Ebor* IV, pp5–6, dated 17 April 1484; it was not proved until July 1486.
[150] SRO, V5/19/2 no. 7. Margaret was the daughter of William Scargill of Whitkirk in the West Riding. He had been John Hopton's guardian in 1427 when the Saville marriage had been arranged, and was a feoffee of John's for Cockfield Hall and for Easton Bavents: BL, Lansdowne MS 255, f242; *Test Ebor* III, pp256–7; Davy's MSS collections, BL, Add MS 19136 f101; SRO, HA 30/369/124; Copinger II, p62.
[151] Emden, *Biog Reg Camb*, p313.

ately to the west of Blythburgh, but that he had quickly res-
igned.[152] It was twenty years before he acquired yet another local
benefice, one whose advowson was held by his own family: he was
instituted rector of Easton Bavents on 1 May 1499.[153] He died
four or five years later. To learn how this well-educated clergy-
man spent his time, and where, would be fascinating. Alas, we
shall never discover that now.

Nevertheless we have discovered, through his three eldest sons, a
little about John Hopton. For the eldest (after one false start) there
was a successful career in politics, though it would seem unlikely
that his father had any hand in arranging it. For his second son,
whom we take Thomas to have been, he made some provision,
small though it was, after his death. If John bought Easton Bavents
in the 1430s with his younger son in mind, that would be an interesting gloss on the inclination of fathers to leave some of the family
property to younger sons to support them, their wives and children,
or at any rate their male children. To do this not out of the patrimony but out of land acquired by purchase was certainly fitting, to
acquire land for that very purpose would have been even more
apt. For the third son the church was to provide; nevertheless in
order that it might decently do so, it was his father who saw that
he had a suitable education.

Two at least of John Hopton's three other sons also went to
school. Roger was at Covehithe in 1468–9, Robert finished at
Snettisham in 1477.[154] All we know of Roger thereafter is that in
1490–1 he received from the Westleton bailiff the £10 annuity
granted him by his nephew, Sir George, in his will.[155] Robert, who

---

152 He was instituted to Wenhaston (of which the prior of Blythburgh was
   patron) on 10 October 1474; on John's resignation Thomas Golofre was
   instituted, 17 January 1475: NRO, Norwich Diocesan Registry, Register 7,
   Institution Book 12, fs40v, 42v.
153 Emden, *Biog Reg Camb*, p313.
154 Roger had been provided with clothing in 1465–6 and 1466–7: SRO,
   HA 30/314/18 mss3, 4.
155 SRO, HA 30/312/424. Our Roger was *not* the yeoman of the crown,
   usher of the chamber, controller of the works and MP, for whom see
   Wedgwood, pp467–8. That king's servant was Sir Roger Hopton of
   Ackworth, of the Hoptons of Armley (from which family of course had
   almost certainly come our Roger Hopton's great-grandmother): *Test Ebor*
   IV, p5, footnote.

was much younger and who therefore was certainly Thomasin's son, had an annuity from the same source a dozen years before Roger did. It was in fact called a pension and was also for £10. He first received it in 1478–9, the year after he went to Lincoln's Inn. More to the point may be that 1478–9 was the first accounting year of the new lord, Sir William Hopton: had Robert been left his £10 pension by his father in his will? He was receiving it in 1481–2. That is the last we hear of Robert.[156] Of William we know only that, with Roger, he too was granted by Sir George an annuity of £10, which he received in 1490–1 from the Westleton bailiff, and that during the same twelve months he had been escheator of Norfolk and Suffolk.[157]

Of John Hopton's daughters we really know no more beyond (as we might expect) the names of their husbands. The Blythburgh bailiff bought a pair of shoes, price 4d, for the eldest daughter, Elizabeth, in 1448–9; cloth was purchased for the youngest, Anne, in the mid-1460s; we learn nothing from the accounts of their sister, Isobel.[158] It is their marriages which give them for us a resemblance of life, reflecting the situation whereby the spinster made little mark upon the world.

That his eldest daughter should make a substantial marriage was evidently a particular concern of John Hopton's. He was ready to pay 1200 marks to ensure that she did. Elizabeth was married to William Brews esquire, son and heir of Sir Thomas Brews of Whittingham Hall, in Fressingfield, Suffolk. They were married by 1456, when Thomas Brews' mother Eleanor made a bequest to William's wife.[159] It was a good match: Elizabeth was marrying into a well-established, comfortably off family. Sir Thomas Brews was a close connection, as well as a near neighbour of the Dukes of Suffolk: Fressingfield is next door to Wingfield where they had a house, and Sir Thomas turned out at Eye on behalf of the dowager Duchess in August 1454.[160] He struck a

---

156 SRO, HA 30/22/11/3; HA 30/369/39.
157 SRO, HA 30/22/11/3; *CFR 1485–1509*, p140.
158 SRO, HA 30/369/46 f46; HA 30/314/18, ms3, 4.
159 NRO, Norwich Cons. Court, Reg. Brosiard, f23, will of 6 October 1456.
160 BL, Egerton Charter 8779. The Dowager Alice Chaucer's initials are carved on one of the benches in Fressingfield church; no doubt she was one of the contributors to their cost.

stiff bargain with John Hopton; he was marrying off his son and heir and Elizabeth brought no property with her, but Thomas Brews seems to have been a hard man to deal with where the marriage of his children was concerned. The Paston family found that out when John Paston sought to marry Margery Brews in 1477. For that match, however, Elizabeth Brews, Margery's mother, was an enthusiast.[161] She cannot (once she became aware of its terms) have been happy with the marriage of her stepson, William, to Elizabeth Hopton. For John Hopton paid 1200 marks – and that large sum is a measure of his earnestness as well as of his wealth – for the settlement of two manors, one being Whittingham Hall itself, on Thomas Brews with remainder to William and Elizabeth. In other words, the possibility of Elizabeth Brews having a life interest in those estates was prevented: it was at her expense that the marriage was made. From the sequel it is clear how discontented with her lot she was. Thomas Brews died in 1482. By 1487, claiming that she did have an estate for life in them, she had ejected William from those estates.[162] As William died in 1489, he never enjoyed his lands in quiet for long. Elizabeth, his wife, may never have enjoyed them at all, for she died before her husband.[163] In the event her father might have felt he had spent so much of his money in vain, particularly as William and Elizabeth had no sons, only two daughters: Thomasin, who married Sir Thomas Hansard, and Anne, who married Roger Townshend, the son and heir of Sir Roger Townshend. That was a match, therefore, between John Hopton's granddaughter and Thomasin Hopton's grandson, very much a family affair; when it was made both were children.[164] Thomasin remembered her, but not him, in her will.

About the marriages of John's two other daughters we know only the names of their husbands. Isobel married John Jermy the

---

161 Elizabeth, daughter of Gilbert Debenham, was Thomas Brews' second wife: Wedgwood, pp108–9.
162 *CIPM Henry VII* vol I, pp265, 267–8.
163 The brass of William and Elizabeth, with its inscription, remains *in situ* at Fressingfield church.
164 Anne was said to be 15 in 1489, Roger was said to be 24 in 1500: *CIPM Henry VII* vol I, p265; II p302.

younger esquire, of Metfield, Suffolk. Almost certainly the son of John Jermy senior of Metfield, and of Buckenham Ferry, Norfolk, who died in October 1487,[165] the younger John died in 1504 and was buried at Metfield beside his wife.[166] Anne married John Buckenham of Snetterton, Norfolk, and Thelnetham, Suffolk; she was his first wife and died before him, but when he made his will in 1484 he wished to be buried beside her, and at Snetterton together they lie.[167]

What of the life these girls and their brothers had led with their father at Blythburgh? Can we piece together the details of the family's life at Westwood and Cockfield Hall to give us a picture which is at all revealing of John Hopton? I think not: the details are too scrappy, they remain merely jottings. Nevertheless they ought to be given the chance to speak for themselves.

For instance we know what he ate and what he drank, or rather we know what food and drink was supplied to him and his family; but what sort of an appetite did he have, was his a cellar always full of beer, was he a very epicure, free at his table, both in meat and wine, or was he temperate in diet, 'a very little eater and worse drinker'? Was he ever overtaken with liquor? Did he drink between meals? When did he eat his meals? How? Was he fastidious or was he slovenly?[168] Perhaps we do not need to know; nevertheless it is not said for nothing that manners make the man. As it is we shall never know whether he preferred mutton to pork, or how well-flavoured he liked the swans which were delivered from Easton or the rabbits which were brought from the Blythburgh warren. Did he have a particular fancy for cheese, considerable quantities of which the Blythburgh bailiff bought in, for Suffolk cheese in the fifteenth century was still of a high quality,

165 *CIPM Henry VII* vol 1, p140, *sub* Jermyn. His will (NRO, Norwich Cons. Court, Reg. Caston, f332) was made 24 October and proved 24 February 1488. He left 5 marks to each of his son John's sons and daughters. His feoffees in 1481 were James Hobart and Edmund Jenny, both of whom we shall meet in the next chapter: *Cal Anc Deeds* IV, A7688.
166 Blomefield v, p387 gives the inscription on their brass.
167 Blomefield I, pp420, 425 gives the inscription on their tomb. John's will is NRO, Norwich Cons. Court, Reg. Caston, f228v, dated 11 October, proved 31 October 1484.
168 I am using here Sir John Oglander, 'On his neighbours', *A Royalist's Notebook*, especially pp124, 143, 175.

though it was not long to be so.[169] We are however guessing, and that is not our game.

What is certain is that he and his family ate a good deal of fish, more sea fish one supposes than say the gentry of Northamptonshire. Living by the seaside had numerous advantages, of which this ample provision of fresh fish was one.[170] Herrings were brought in casks or by the thousand, salmon and eel by the ferkin, cod by the barrel, or (like ling) individually. Less common were turbot and sturgeon, and once there was from Easton Bavents a porpoise, which at 9s 2d, was a delicacy.[171] Oysters at 1s 3d a thousand were evidently not, though no doubt they went well with Rhenish wine. Perhaps there were local oyster beds, as there were mussel beds: in 1477–8 Hopton purchased mussels to create or restock a bed at Pallefen in Walberswick. Herrings, however, were the staple; they were normally supplied to the household by the ferryman at Blythburgh; no doubt he got them from the fishermen of Walberswick. Undoubtedly that was consistently the best part of being beside the sea. Whether John Hopton sailed on it we are not told. He could have done for he owned a balinger: water was pumped out of her in 1452–3.[172] Perhaps he preferred inland waters; John Moor, shipwright, built a boat for the river in 1456–7 and a fishing net was purchased the same year from one John Grey of Beccles, who himself came to have a look at things.[173] Possibly John Hopton pursued the gentle art of angling, though the provision of a net suggests that the taking of fish from the river was done by more straightforward means – by craft rather than by art, a task for menials not a sport for gentlemen.[174]

169 *Suffolk in the XVIIth Century*, pp40–1. For the cheese, the pork, the mutton, the saffron, the pepper, and much else, see Nicholas Greenhagh's notebook: SRO, HA 30/369/46 fs9, 9v, 21v, 46, 72v.
170 For what follows, see principally SRO, HA 30/369/46 fs9, 15, 30, 37v, 38; SRO, HA 30/314/18 ms4, 5, and 7; V5/19/1/16, 1468–9.
171 Indeed 12s was the price placed on a porpoise presented by the Walberswick churchwardens to master Hopton in 1478: *Walberswick Churchwardens' Accounts*, p43.
172 SRO, HA 30/369/46 f77.
173 SRO, HA 30/314/18 m4.
174 Here I am using E. F. Jacob, 'The Book of St Albans', collected in his *Essays in Later Medieval History* (1968), p209. On the other hand only one net was bought and it was specifically bought for the lord, so perhaps

The more ordinary revenues of a landlord whose estates were on the coast we have discussed elsewhere:[175] they did not amount to much for John Hopton. They were augmented by the occasional sale of timber from a wreck, or the salvaging of a ship's boat for Hopton's own use. Sometimes a pipe of wine came ashore; sometimes however it was shipwrecked sailors, and they had to be cared for and sent on their way: the twelve Dutchmen who got to land at Easton in 1463–4 cost the Blythburgh bailiff 6s 8d.[176] Probably what was more important was that household supplies might be bought directly from mariners and merchants. How much buying was done in this way we cannot say. No doubt salt was purchased from the Bretons who called with it each year; haberdashery and woad, however, we know were. The Blythburgh bailiff noted two transactions of this sort. Once over £40 was paid to John Young of Portsmouth for 15 'pokes wodde' out of a ship called the *Julian*, master Thomas Buckland. A little later four barrels of 'osmond', three barrels of haberdashery, two furs, 200 'rosyn' and four dozen pattens were bought from Gervaise Nutkin out of a ship called the *Mary Knight*. The custom on these items amounted to 3s 9d.[177]

Was the cloth which the bailiff recorded from time to time also obtained in this way, the nine pieces of narrow cloth which cost £6 and the sixteen yards of broadcloth at £2, for example?[178] Presumably it was cheaper than buying in London, and John Hopton regularly required considerable quantities of all types for his family and his servants. The varieties of cloth are bewildering: white kendal for the young John Hopton, russet for Anne Hopton, frieze for Roger Hopton, kersey, blanket, and medley, red, blue, green, and black cloth. In 1465–6 over one hundred yards of cloth were accounted for by the Blythburgh bailiff. As always it takes a lot to clothe a large family. Moreover, there were also servants, and not just those of the household; that year Robert Dolfinby, the ferryman, had six yards of blue cloth, and Richard Ulveston,

after all John Hopton was an angler, and therefore a man after the heart of Professor Jacob himself; see M. H. Keen, *England in the Later Middle Ages* (1973), p. x.

[175] See above, chapter 2.   [176] SRO, HA 30/134/18 m1.
[177] SRO, HA 30/369/46 fs1, 7v.   [178] *Ibid.*, f31v.

the son of the lord's supervisor, had five yards, for their robes.[179] Ten years later Robert Dolfinby was still receiving a gown; so also in 1477–8 were the custodian of the mill (William Mason's widow), John Godbald, John 'de Pinceria' and Edward 'Tutonicus'. Whereas their gowns were each made of four yards of cloth, John Everard, clerk, was given six yards, presumably unmade up.[180] Who chose all this material? Was it Thomasin in the 1460s, as the account suggests? And what happened before John married her? Who, for example, chose his hats in the 1440s? The straw (perhaps for fishing) that cost 3s 4d, the felt which cost only 1s 6d? No doubt he was capable of selecting his own, though a straw hat for 3s 4d (4d more than a sword purchased at the same time), makes one wonder whether that was a wise choice,[181] makes one wonder indeed whether he was not the sort of man who had to have a wife to see to things; in the early 1450s, after he had lost his first wife and before he married his second, the Blythburgh bailiff twice recorded sums spent on the washing of his master's linen, which surely was not a satisfactory arrangement.[182]

Clean linen then was important to him. What other comforts did he consider essential? Once more we are left vainly wondering. No household inventory survives to remind us of the silver and pewter of the hall, the carpets and cushions of the parlour, the chests and tables, the chafers and the laver basins, the pans and kettles of the kitchen,[183] the candlesticks and altarcloths of the chapel. Were there tapestries, was there panelling? Had the windows of the hall at Westwood, repaired in 1463–4, glass in them? Westwood was apparently where the family chiefly lived, though there was another house at Cockfield Hall in Yoxford, which Thomasin had in her widowhood. The present Cockfield Hall was built by Sir Arthur Hopton in the first half of the sixteenth century, and has been much altered since. The oldest part of

179 SRO, HA 30/314/18 m3.
180 SRO, HA 30/314/18 m5.
181 SRO, HA 30/369/46 fs21v, 38. So dear was it I wonder whether 'streyhatte' could mean something else.
182 *Ibid.*, fs84v, 102v.
183 For the binding of pans and kettles William Ramsey was paid 9s 10d in the 1440s; at about the same time Giles Coper received 8s for making 'stondes, factes and kelers' at Westwood: SRO, HA 30/369/46 fs11, 11v.

Westwood Lodge is also perhaps his work; it might be earlier. If it does date from John Hopton's time it can only be a fragment of the house of which we catch sight in the accounts.[184] It was a thatched house: the roofs were thatched in 1463–4 and again in 1490–1. Other chambers than the hall and chapel are not specified, save the long chamber 'prope portas manerii', and the kitchen, whose fireplace was renewed in 1465–6.[185] Whether all the house, or just part, was of brick, or whether it was timber-framed with wattle and daub infilling, we have no sure information: the five cartloads of wood from Wissett which Matthew Hunne, the carpenter, used in his work on the hall in 1466–7, and the daubing of walls, might suggest a timber and plaster house, but we cannot be certain. We do however know that there was lead guttering, repaired by Richard Nowell, the plumber, in the late 1440s.[186] Around this shadowy building were grouped others (we know not in what order): the bakehouse, the barn, which had a room within it, and the dovecot, and beyond them lay the fishpond, the garden, and the park.[187]

Did John Hopton lavish as much affection on his garden as, say, Sir John Oglander, who told himself that he had spent more money on flowers than a wise man would have done? It is through that pleasure of Sir John's – 'to solace myself in the garden'[188] – that we come to know him. There are no such ways of getting to know John Hopton. It is not only adversity which reveals character; how a man behaves in idleness, what he does with himself when he has nothing that *has* to be done, it is at these moments that he shows himself to us. Such moments, however, leave little trace. What moved John Hopton to delight or to despair, how he shrugged off the cares of business we can no

184 See Janet Becker, *Blythburgh*, pp56–8, for description, picture, and ground plan. The empty house was as melancholy in 1972 as it was when Miss Becker visited it – just as clandestinely it seems – in 1935 or thereabouts.
185 SRO, HA 30/314/18 m3. The long chamber is probably the 'long house' thatched in 1419–20 (HA 30/369/78); it was still there in 1614: *Blythburgh*, p59.
186 SRO, HA 30/314/18 ms2, 4; HA 30/369/46 fs11v, 12v; HA 30/369/281.
187 SRO, HA 30/369/46 fs30v, 38, 45v; HA 30/314/18 ms1, 2, 3, 5. I infer the existence of a garden from the payment of 9s to women of Walberswick for weeding at the hall: HA 30/369/46 f21.
188 *A Royalist's Notebook*, pp94–5.

longer know; no traces at all remain. He, at this great distance, resolutely stares at us with a formal face; it is a blank look which we get from him. We can come across him, for instance, one day in 1447–8, dining at Wissett when a buck was killed, or on a day at Blythburgh in 1464–5 when he entertained his fellow justices of the peace, or again on other days in 1477–8 when Elizabeth, lady Clinton and his lawyer friends came to hunt there, or when Elizabeth, the wife of Sir John Wingfield was a visitor.[189] We can detect him travelling to Swillington and to London, going to Ipswich and Framlingham, sending his servants to London, into Yorkshire, and about East Anglia on his business.[190] For his horses we know he paid between 35 and 50 shillings; Nicholas Greenhagh, the Blythburgh bailiff who supplied him with them, drew a sketch of himself in his rough account book: 'noverint universi per presentes me'.[191] Of John Hopton we have no such portrait, however rudimentary, nor can we, using such threads and tatters of information as we have just given, make one.

I suppose what we need to know most about a man is how well he gets on with others: if he does not, we may not get to know him at all. For historians, however, there is a paradox here. The less well a man gets on with his wife or children, or relatives or neighbours, the better we know him. The more strained the relationship between (say) king and nobility the more we hear of it, just as a scandal up the street is known quickly, discussed at length and remembered for many a long day. John Hopton, we think, got on well with his fellow men; there is no record to the contrary and that, on our argument, is testimony enough.

There are indeed a few positive indications of his attitude towards others: the annuity, for example, which he paid his step-father William Edlington,[192] his willingness to take on, if we may so phrase it, Thomasin and her children in 1457, the lack of friction between them all thereafter, and the length of time he

---

[189] SRO, HA 30/369/46 f38; HA 30/314/18 ms2, 5.
[190] SRO, HA 30/369/46 fs10v, 22v, 29v, 31, 45v, 53, 86; HA 30/314/18 ms1, 3, 4; HA 30/22/11/3.
[191] SRO, HA 30/369/46 fs38, 70, 77, and for the drawing f56v. Or is it someone else whom he has drawn?
[192] SRO, HA 30/314/18 m1.

kept his servants and his councillors. Richard Butler was a servant at Yoxford in 1463–4; he was still serving Thomasin there in 1492–3.[193] Richard Coppeshurst was active about John's business in 1463–4 too; Thomasin was particularly generous to him and his family when she made her will thirty-five years later. John Hoo was bailiff at Blythburgh for twenty years; it was not an easy post as it also involved being the lord's cofferer. John, and Ellis Lumhals, the bailiff of Yoxford between 1463–4 and 1479, frequently went about Hopton's affairs beyond Blythburgh and Yoxford, to supervise the husbandry at Easton Bavents for example, or to ride with their servants up to Yarmouth.[194] Other bailiffs, with more routine duties, served just as long as they did: John Keswick was at Wissett between 1463–4 and 1479, Philip Bosard and Henry Cobbe were at Ellingham and Pirnhow over the same period. Robert Dolfinby, the ferryman at Blythburgh and fishmonger to the family, held his post for at least fifteen years, and Matthew Hunne, the carpenter, was employed at Blythburgh and at Easton Bavents for at least eight. More important officers remained with Hopton for even longer: John Ulveston was supervisor from at least 1444 until his death in 1460, Walter Fulbourne was auditor for thirty-five years between 1445–6 and 1481–2. John's brother Robert was also his faithful servant and we may assume trusted adviser for more than twenty-five years.

We ought to know more about Robert than we do, if he was the Robert Hopton who sat for Wallingford in the parliaments of 1449–50 and 1467–8.[195] The seat indicates a connection with the Dukes of Suffolk and the crown. We know that Robert was a servant of the de la Poles in October 1450, when he, Edward Grimston and others were said to have been attacked by John Howard, Charles Nowell and others of the Duke of Norfolk's affinity.[196] The dates at which Robert sat, that is when the interests

193 SRO, HA 30/314/18 ms1, 3; HA 30/312/117.
194 SRO, V5/19/1/16, 1471–2, 1475–6; V5/19/1/17; HA 30/314/18 m3.
195 Wedgwood, p467.
196 PRO, KB9/118/2 part 1, no. 17. The dowager duchess's accusations to the justices of oyer and terminer date from the early months of 1453; in March 1453 Robert Hopton, for the only time of which we have record,

of crown and Duke were so in harmony as to be synonymous, show the way in which the royal connection was made. We can be reasonably sure, therefore, that the member for Wallingford was John's brother. Robert's association with the de la Poles does not, however, appear to have been greatly to his advantage; it might have been if the disasters of 1450 (the fall of the Duke) and 1453 (the nervous collapse of the king) had not happened. They did happen. Robert's political career did not take flight. His active life was spent in a limited and local framework, to which his second appearance in the Commons in 1467–8 was an exception.[197] Yet if he was a man of no importance in the broader context of East Anglian society he was important to his brother.

In the early 1450s the Blythburgh bailiff from time to time paid him monies on John Hopton's commandment; he may already have had an annuity, if so it was a small one compared to the one he had by the mid-1460s: 10 marks. He last received it in Michaelmas 1477, at any rate to our knowledge, and that is the very last we hear of him.[198] Almost certainly he lived at South-wold: he married the widow of Richard Skilman, bailiff of that town in the years around 1450, and they rented property there;[199] in 1464–5 3s 4d was paid at Southwold by our old friend the Blythburgh bailiff on behalf of Robert's wife; and in 1470–1, when the affairs of Easton Bavents were being unravelled, the arrears of the rent which were owed at Southwold were paid through him.[200] That he was on John's council is made explicit in 1466–7. During that year he was particularly busy on his brother's behalf, working with John Tasburgh, the supervisor, and others

was an elector in the county court at Ipswich: the two are linked by the temporary recovery of the government.

[197] He was never a JP, and he was only on two unimportant commissions, once with his brother in November 1470, once with his nephew in May 1472: CPR 1467–77, pp249, 353.

[198] SRO, HA 30/369/46 fs62, 62v, 70, 101v; HA 30/314/18 m4; V5/19/1/16, 1472–3; HA 30/314/18 m5.

[199] For his wife, see Mettingham College Register; BL, Stowe MS 934, f62v. For Richard Skilman as bailiff, see Southwold Accounts 26–30 Henry VI, Westminster Abbey Muniments 12165–7. Robert's property at Southwold was held of Mettingham College in right of his wife, as was the tenement, messuage and 50 acres of land he held of the college at Walpole: Stowe MS 934, fs62v, 72v.

[200] SRO, HA 30/314/18 m2; V5/19/1/16, 1470–1.

of John's council, on the final negotiations for a settlement with the Dunwich authorities over the old matter of the shifting mouth of the Dunwich river.[201]

This was a complicated business and it is not easy to follow now, because the continuing changes in the coastline have obscured the fifteenth century geography.[202] What happened was that while the port of Dunwich on its fragile cliff was eroded, the Dunwich river, which entered the sea below and beside the town to the north, was silting up. The original harbour was rendered useless by 1328. The river, however, forced its way through the shingle bank further to the north. By the 1390s the river mouth had moved so far north as to be about on the boundary between Dunwich and Sir Roger Swillington's manor of Blythburgh and Walberswick. Difficulties arose and disputes occurred. The agreement eventually reached between the town's bailiffs and Sir Roger in 1410 was that the new haven, as it was called, should serve as the boundary, as well as the harbour, and that the men of Blythburgh and Walberswick should be free of all tolls there on an annual payment of £1.[203] By 1435 that harbour in turn was said to have become blocked with shingle, and John Hopton gave his consent for the construction of a new cut for the river still further to the north and (so far as he was concerned at any rate) on his property.[204] Whether that cut was actually made is uncertain, but as Hopton continued to pay the £1 a year to the Dunwich bailiffs, and was still paying it in the first half of the 1460s,[205] it would seem that it was not. If it was not, then obvi-

---

[201] SRO, HA 30/314/18 m4. Robert may have had a direct interest in this affair, for he rented three pieces of marsh at Walberswick from his brother, Henneholm, Mistildam, and Burrysmarsh which Richard Skilman had previously held. The rent was 10d a year; so far as one can make out Robert never paid it: SRO, HA 30/50/22/10/17(6); HA 30/314/18 ms1–4; HA 30/314/1.

[202] See the maps in Gardner, *Dunwich*, Norman Scarfe, *The Suffolk Landscape* (1972), pp207–8, and the references in succeeding footnotes.

[203] *CCR 1396–9*, pp332, 497; *CCR 1399–1402*, p160; *CCR 1405–9*, pp336–8; *CPR 1408–13*, pp206–7, cf. BL, Add Charter 40705 (and the earlier 40737 and 40663); Gardner, *Dunwich*, pp12–13 (BL, Add Charter 40664), pp137–8; BL, Add Charter 40673, cf. SRO, HA 30/369/327. For the £1, see the Blythburgh accounts of 1419–20: SRO, HA 30/369/78.

[204] SRO, HA 30/50/22/27/2(1), printed in *Blythburgh*, pp76–7.

[205] SRO, HA 30/314/18 ms1–4, that is down to and including 1466–7.

ously the new haven, despite the grim description of it in 1435, was still in use. Either that or the cut had been made, but the Dunwich authorities did not recognize it as being on Hopton's land, and he continued to pay them the yearly £1 out of goodwill or inertia. Yet it is absurd to suppose that to have been the case. No landowner was likely to have allowed his rights to slip away either through goodwill or inertia; his council would see to it that he did no such thing.

John's council was active enough in the 1460s when the whole affair came to the surface again. There had been quarrels and disputes, some violence, much recrimination.[206] Negotiations for a settlement were, however, under way. In 1463–4 John had royal charters relating to Dunwich copied; in 1464–5 he and William Jenny were at Dunwich; in 1465–6 John, his son William, William Jenny and William Pickenham, doctor of civil law and yet another relative of Thomasin's, were at Westwood and Dunwich, at some expense, and no doubt in earnest consultation. Finally, in 1466–7 obligations between the town authorities and Hopton were sealed.[207] Royal intervention (as in Sir Roger Swillington's time) no doubt had speeded a conclusion. Edward IV sent a signet letter to the Dunwich bailiffs; it was blunt: Henry Sotell, the Attorney General, and William Jenny, sergeant-at-law, had been directed to resolve the dispute; the bailiffs, however, were not being cooperative; they were charged to stop their obstructiveness 'or else we will remit you to the law there you to chanysshe you at your peril without resort be had unto us for that cause hereafter'. It was a royal *diktat*, which the poor bailiffs of Dunwich, because they carried no weight in affairs and had no friends, could not resist.[208] For three days and nights in 1466–7 Henry Sotell was at Westwood with Robert Hopton and John's council; we can be certain it was Dunwich's defeat that they were

206 BL, Add MS 40721 relates to this phase of the troubles; SRO, HA 30/369/394 is a copy of the same.
207 SRO, HA 30/314/18 ms1–4.
208 SRO, HA 30/369/335 is a sixteenth century copy of this signet letter. It is dated at Westminster, 24 May. The year is almost certainly 1466, as in the Blythburgh accounts of 1465–6 the servant of Robert Blomville was paid for coming from Ipswich to Blythburgh with royal letters directed to the bailiffs of Dunwich 'pro materia domini'; SRO, HA 30/314/18 m3.

JOHN HOPTON

putting the finishing touches to.[209] Now it seems the new cut was
made, and from this time forward the annual £1 was no longer
paid.[210]

John Hopton evidently could count on receiving abundant
advice. That is what his council was for; that (he may have said)
is what brothers, and for that matter sons were for: Robert and
William had duties towards the family and the family estates, they
were sustained by them, they therefore must help maintain them.
Counsel was also to be had from the supervisor, the steward, the
auditors and the bailiffs. No doubt John frequently sought it from
them and from his other servants, like Robert Payn, for example,
the influential household officer and Blythburgh sheep reeve of the
1470s. In addition he had legal advice. He retained William
Bondes, a local lawyer, in the early 1440s, and as Bondes was
giving unpaid advice twenty years later, it looks as though he was
still being feed.[211] Perhaps Bondes had as his colleague over that
period Robert Banyard, another country attorney, who was called
of the lords' council in 1465–6, and who had been one of Hopton's
feoffees as long before as 1440.[212] As with his servants and officers
so with his lawyers, it looks as though once John had made his
choice he stuck to it. If he needed additional legal advice he either
paid for it on an *ad hoc* basis,[213] or he asked friends, neighbours
or relatives who were men of law for it, no doubt repaying them
with a good dinner, a tub of eels, or (in the case of William Jenny)
overlooking an unpaid rent.[214] The three men who came for a
day's hunting in 1477–8 could certainly have offered him heaps
of legal advice for all of them were to be judges within a few

209 SRO, HA 30/314/18 m4.
210 I am inferring this: by the time of the next surviving account, of 1477–8,
it was not being paid.
211 SRO, HA 30/314/14; HA 30/369/46 f10v; HA 30/314/18 m2, where in
1464–5 with the auditor Walter Fulbourne he was associated with
Hopton's fine for not taking up knighthood.
212 SRO, V5/19/1/17; HA 30/369/124.
213 Dr John Allen had nearly 10s in 1464–5: SRO, HA 30/314/18 m2. John
Bishop, the lord's attorney, had 12s 6d in 1477–8: SRO, HA 30/22/11/3.
214 Henry Sotell probably got something more substantial on the conclusion
of the Dunwich dispute. William Pickenham who was brought in to help
in 1465–6 may already have had his reward, for he had been rector of
Rayleigh since 1462.

years: William Jenny, his neighbour, John Sulyard, Thomasin's nephew, Roger Townshend, Tomasin's son-in-law and John's steward.[215]

How reliant was John Hopton on his councillors? How far were his decisions their decisions? Who, for example, first projected the idea of the new cut for the Dunwich river in 1435? Was it the 'good men of the coost and cuntre', those indeed who sealed the document of 1435,[216] who proposed the scheme, or John Hopton's officers and councillors, like Richard Daniel, still in 1435 his receiver general, or John Ulveston, who sealed the document and who was shortly to be, if he was not already, Hopton's supervisor, or was it John himself? We cannot tell, any more than we can know on whose initiative it was that in the 1460s the unresolved contest was reopened. Just as in his lifetime John Hopton would have been hidden behind a screen of servants and councillors, at any rate for some purposes and to some people, so now we (as prying outsiders) cannot penetrate the barrier of the documents left by them to come at the man himself. It is a familiar blank wall.

Another, and one which we may regret most, concerns his soul. We cannot enter into any man's soul, and perhaps we should not want to, yet we would like to know something of John Hopton's religion. As it is we have only circumstantial evidence and even that, lacking as we do his will, is not very great in quantity: all we know are a few of the things he did, or had done.

For instance, in the last year of his life in Blythburgh and Walberswick parish churches prayers for the souls of his parents, his friends and his benefactors were being offered, at Blythburgh at least on a regular basis by a priest who received £6 a year.[217] We do not know when John had begun this practice. John West, the priest at Blythburgh, was joined there by another, Robert Pilgrim, in 1479, who also received £6 per annum.[218] By 1490–1

215 SRO, HA 30/314/18 m5.
216 SRO, HA 30/50/22/27/2(1). The twenty-two included representatives from Southwold, Covehithe, South Cove, Easton Bavents, Blythburgh and Walberswick.
217 SRO, HA 30/314/18 m5; HA 30/22/11/3.
218 SRO, HA 30/22/11/3, see also HA 30/369/39.

George Hawes had replaced John West, and he and Robert Pilgrim (still each receiving £6) were then said to be praying for the souls of John Hopton, Sir Roger Swillington, and their friends.[219] Secondly, Thomas Crowe, the rector of Easton Bavents, celebrated 'a certitudine' for the souls of John's parents, friends and benefactors, once a year, every year, between 1464 and John's death.[220] The vicar of Westleton did the same in 1477–8,[221] though he apparently was not doing so in 1469–70. Undoubtedly John was grateful to the god who had been so beneficent to him; that his priests should pray for the souls of his benefactors, the chief of whom, Sir Roger Swillington, is named for us in 1491, shows that. And the depth of his gratitude is shown by his readiness to find a relatively large sum of money each year for the purpose.

Also, as we would expect, he was a benefactor himself, of the parish churches of Blythburgh and Walberswick. Blythburgh church was entirely rebuilt between the end of the fourteenth century and about 1470.[222] For how much John was responsible we can only guess. The Blythburgh estate accounts, with one exception which we will shortly discuss, do not tell us whether he contributed money, materials or men, and they cannot tell us whether his interest, perhaps even his enthusiasm, was essential for the completion of the building, or whether his taste determined that the design of the roof should be as it is. If he was closely involved with any particular part of the building it was likely to have been with the chancel and the chancel aisles, in the north one of which he founded the chantry for his first wife in 1451. Between the chancel and that north aisle his own tomb of Purbeck marble was put and in it, beside the body of Margaret Saville his body was buried, as later beside his, Thomasin's was laid. For that tomb, which we might consider 'swagger',[223] John was responsible.[224] We know that he also was responsible for glazing the east

219 SRO, HA 30/312/424.
220 SRO, V5/19/1/16, 17; he received 4s 4d for this service.
221 SRO, HA 30/22/11/3; he received 3s 4d.
222 According to Mr E. A. Gee, whose typescript notes on the church fabric were most kindly made available to me.
223 As Nikolaus Pevsner might have it: it is certainly not 'flashy' to use another word of that master.
224 According to a note taken of his will in 1753 he desired to be buried 'on

window, perhaps the east window of the north chancel aisle, rather than the east window of the chancel itself,[225] as in 1477–8 Martin Glasyer received £5 in full payment for his work: 'pro vitriacione fenestre ad orientalem finem cancelle de Blithburgh',[226] though it may be that in the end Martin received his money from Thomasin rather than from John. Neither the glass nor any record of what it depicted survives.[227] That alas is also true of the glass in the window at the east end of the south aisle of Walberswick church, which was also Martin Glasyer's work and for which he received £4 in 1477–8.[228] What other contribution John may have made to that church, which during the fifteenth century replaced an earlier building on a different site, to its construction or furnishing we, as ever, do not know. None, however, is recorded by the churchwardens.[229]

Spending some of his money on prayers for the souls of relations, friends, and even benefactors and even more to make local churches fit for the worship of god, hardly makes him distinctive. It was for a fifteenth century gentleman conventional enough.[230] That word conventional, however, has an air of condemnation about it; but we surely go far wrong in thinking a man who expresses his devotion under conventional forms necessarily shallow or complacent. His spiritual life might burn with a brilliance few even of his neighbours notice. How a man acts, whether he acts conventionally or otherwise, is what counts; the how of John

the north side of the chancel...under a tomb of marble set in an arch of the chancel...on the north side by him lately edified and built': Parr, 1, pp235–6.

225 *Blythburgh*, p49, citing BL, Add MS 6754.

226 SRO, HA 30/314/18 m5.

227 Apart that is, from the coats of arms noted by Harvey, which probably came from this window as they are composed of the arms of Swillington (viz. Hopton), Saville and Barrington: see Parr 1, p242, citing Harvey's notebook, BL, Add MS 4969.

228 SRO, HA 30/314/18 m5.

229 The contract for the building of the church tower is dated 1426: BL, Add Charter 17634. The church was not, however, consecrated until 1493, according to R. W. M. Lewis, *Walberswick Churchwardens' Accounts*, ppiii–v.

230 For the remainder of this paragraph I am indebted to two sources: Iris Murdoch, *The Sovereignty of Good* (1970), especially pp17–18; and Margaret Henderson-Smith, 'John Alcock, an English bishop c.1430–1500', a dissertation for the Keele BA, 1974.

Hopton's behaviour has disappeared; all that is left to us are a few remnants of the results of his actions. And they beg more questions than they provide answers.[231]

Here is one of those fragments. In 1445–6 the Blythburgh bailiff paid Stephen Kerver 2s for painting an image.[232] Such a simple jotting is a spur to our imagination, though before it carries us away we would do well to bear in mind an entry on the next page: paid Stephen Kerver of the gable making 3s. That East Anglian joiners were better at making roofs than painting images is demonstrated by the roofs and painted images they have left us. Here perhaps is another: in 1463–4 Robert Banyard and Walter Fulbourne rode to Eye where they spent a couple of days on business which lay between their master and the Duke of Suffolk.[233] Was it unimportant, was it all a matter of form (in 1463 the duke officially came of age), or was much at stake, and does our ignorance of it therefore mean our vision of John Hopton is flawed as well as distant? In short, like the universe itself, our curiosity has increased at a rate more rapid than that at which it has been satisfied.

[231] What are we to make, for instance, of the firewood worth 1s 8d given out of pity to the poor by order of the lord. SRO, HA 30/314/18 m2?
[232] 'pro pantyng of a emerge': SRO, HA 30/369/46 f22v.
[233] SRO, HA 30/314/18 m1.

4

ACQUAINTANCES, NEIGHBOURS
AND FRIENDS

Ryght Wurshypful and trusty Cosyn, y commende me unto yow yn
as hartly wyse as y can and as a Jantylman not gretly acqueyntdyd
with yow, trustyng yn tyme to come to be better acqueyntyd with yow.

>   Sir William Sandes to Sir William Stonor, c. 1481
>   *The Stonor Letters and Papers*, no. 298

>   These men, and those who opposed them
>   And those whom they opposed
>   Accept the constitution of silence
>   And are folded in a single party

>   T. S. Eliot
>   'Little Gidding'

If it is true that you can tell a man by his friends, then another
way of coming at John Hopton is through a study of his. There is
one snag: we do not know who were his friends. Our task is therefore more modest. If we cannot tell this man by his friends,
perhaps we can reveal something more of him and the world in
which he lived by an enquiry into the company he kept.

When we first encounter him it is in the society of Yorkshiremen. He was about to get married. The marriage was arranged
by his guardians, William Scargill and John Rushworth, and the
father of the bride, Thomas Saville; it was in the Saville house at
Thornhill in the West Riding that the indenture was sealed on
26 February 1427. The ruins of the hall, perhaps where all this
was done, remain, as do the ruins of the chapel where the following Easter John and Margaret were married. Although the fortunate couple, as fortunate they indeed became less than three years
later, moved to live in Suffolk, John did not lose touch with the
West Riding gentlemen who had been his earliest patrons. As he
came into possession of Swillington and other local estates he had
every reason to remain in contact with them.

William Scargill lived close by at Whitkirk; to the parish church there he added the south chapel as his chantry foundation.[1] He was John's feoffee, not only for the estates acquired in 1430, but also for the two properties John purchased, Cockfield Hall and Easton Bavents. He had, however, withdrawn as a feoffee for Cockfield Hall by April 1444.[2] While it is clear that Hopton's links with Scargill and other Yorkshire gentry were never broken – his son after all served with them or their sons on the commission of the peace in the West Riding in the 1460s and 1470s – it appears that in the late 1440s he was moving away from them. Two links were slipped then: in 1449 his father-in-law died, by 1451 his wife Margaret Saville was dead also. In 1447 Sir Thomas Saville had built as a chantry the north chapel of Thornhill church; possibly this was the last influence he was to have on his son-in-law, for when John founded his chantry for Margaret in Blythburgh church, it took the form of a north chapel.[3]

The Hoptons were not the only expatriate Yorkshiremen in East Anglia. The Wentworths of Nettlestead in Suffolk were another Yorkshire family who preferred the south to the north. It was with the younger members of the family that John's eldest son William Hopton associated in the early 1450s. As he had married the daughter of Roger Wentworth it was perhaps natural that he should be found in the company of his successful brother-in-law Sir Philip, who held office in the royal household and who was one of the dowager Duchess of Suffolk's foremost feed men.[4] Still, other young men rode with Sir Philip in 1454,[5] and while young and old rode with him to support the Duchess against Thomas Cornwallis at Eye in August that year, William was not named among them.[6] Nor did William share Philip Wentworth's

---

1 Licence of June 1448: *CPR 1446–52*, p167; Pevsner, *West Riding, sub nomine;* K. L. Wood-legh, *Perpetual Chantries in England* (1965), pp83, 187.
2 BL, Harley Charter 45 F41; SRO, HA 30/369/124, 180; Copinger II, p63.
3 Pevsner, *West Riding*, p510.
4 Receiving 20 marks a year in 1453–4: BL, Egerton Charter 8779; see also Wedgwood, pp934–5.
5 At a Cowhaugh Court to prevent their opponents' attempts to hold it, were 'Sere P. Wentworth and hise brothir, yong Hopton, yong Brewse, yong Calthorp, wyth xxiiij horse': Davis, II, p. 104.
6 BL, Egerton Charter 8779.

commitment to the Lancastrian regime, which began in earnest with his carrying of the royal standard at the battle of St Albans less than a year later (a standard which, according to hostile testimony, he threw down and deserted),[7] and ended nine years later at Hexham, where he was captured and beheaded. It was not an example to follow.

Many of the men John Hopton knew in Suffolk were attached to the de la Pole interest; he could hardly avoid knowing them. John Ulveston his supervisor, for instance, was the de la Poles' steward in Suffolk. Reginald Rous, one of his feoffees, received an annuity from the dowager Duchess,[8] who in 1454 could depend on two neighbours whom he may have known better than others, Sir John Heveningham and Sir Thomas Brews, turning out in her interest.[9] Long before then it was the society of men like these which he shared, and not that of the West Riding squirearchy. If John Hopton listened in the 1440s to the political opinions of Ulveston or of Robert his own brother, another de la Pole servant, he appears not to have acted upon them quite as they did; and if the de la Pole disaster of 1450 taught them a lesson it was one he did not have to learn.

By the later 1450s those whom John had known in Yorkshire, if he ever talked to them on his visits north,[10] might have offered him yet more advice. In his youth, when at a crucial moment he had needed a patron, he had turned to his local lord, Richard Nevill, earl of Salisbury, steward of the honour of Pontefract and constable of its castle.[11] Richard Nevill now was among that handful of noblemen whom the government considered its critics and opponents. By 1459, at the latest, he had been made irreconcilable. He carried with him into opposition a number of West Riding gentlemen. John was certainly not one of them, even though contact with the Nevills had not entirely ceased. In July 1455 John witnessed a charter in favour of Sir John Nevill,

[7] Gairdner III, p33; see C. A. J. Armstrong, 'Politics and the battle of St Albans', *BIHR*, xxxiii (1960), p43.

[8] BL, Harley Charter 45 F41; Egerton Charter 8779.

[9] BL, Egerton Charter 8779.

[10] For visits to Yorkshire see, for example, SRO, HA 30/369/46 fs22v, 45v.

[11] Somerville, *Duchy of Lancaster*, I, pp513, 515.

Salisbury's son, and later Earl of Northumberland and Marquis Montagu. With him witnessed William Scargill and Sir Robert Waterton of Methley.[12] Scargill died in spring 1459[13] and so had not to face a political choice which immediately forthcoming events may have forced upon him. One who by then probably had no choice at all was from another local West Riding family, the Sotells of Southill in Dewsbury. Henry Sotell was a younger son of a branch of the family settled in Lincolnshire, but at the outset of his brilliant legal career he had attached himself to the Nevills. In the transaction which Hopton, Waterton and Scargill witnessed in July 1455, Sotell was Sir John Nevill's feoffee. He was already Richard Nevill, earl of Warwick's feoffee, and by 1458 was his deputy at Pontefract. Hopton encountered him again; so shall we.[14] John Hopton, unlike the talented Henry Sotell, whom both the Duke of York and Sir John Fastolf employed at this time,[15] had little to offer the Nevills. But if they had little use for him, by 1458 John had none for them.

If he had no time for Yorkshire aristocrats, he appears also to have had little for those of East Anglia. Such contact as there was between John and the great ones of the region was slight:[16] mainpernor once for Sir William Phelip, lord Bardolf of Dennington, he witnessed a charter in favour of the Earl and Countess of Suffolk in 1441, and was on a commission with John Howard in 1455.[17] We have touched on all this before: he knew these important, influential men and women, yet to him they were not important, nor did they patronize him.[18]

In Hopton's later years, after 1461, John, duke of Suffolk and

12 *CCR 1454–61*, p62, cf. p78.
13 *Test Ebor* III, p257, admin. of his will 12 May 1459.
14 See below, pp183–6. For the Sotells of Redbourne and West Rasen, Lincs, see *CPR 1441–6*, p417; *CPR 1452–61*, pp107, 479; *CPR 1461–7*, p218.
15 *Cal Anc Deeds* IV, A6339; Davis I, p86.
16 His important contact with Ralph, lord Cromwell seems only to have been temporary; it was based on their mutual need to deal with Sir John Gra: see above, chapter 1, pp16–26.
17 *CFR 1430–37*, p49; *CCR 1441–7*, p57; *CPR 1452–61*, p301.
18 For his brief membership of the king's household in the later 1440s we have accounted above (chapter 3). It seems to have been entirely inconsequential.

John, duke of Norfolk were (in the absence of John, earl of Oxford for all but the years 1470–1) the dominant lords of the region. If they threw their weight about within East Anglia, outside it they were not men of great account; Edward IV, having such little regard for their abilities, did not for example appoint them to the council.[19] Both certainly lacked tact, let alone finesse. Both too had formidable ladies to reckon with, the Duke of Suffolk his mother Alice Chaucer, until her death in 1475, the Duke of Norfolk his wife Elizabeth Talbot, who lived another thirty years after he died in 1476. It was these two men, and these two women, who gave shape to the lives of the Paston family during the last eighteen years or so of Hopton's life. Whereas the Pastons could not shake them off, however, the Hoptons seem almost to have been unaware of their existence. When in 1463–4 Robert Banyard and Walter Fulbourne, two of Hopton's long-serving councillors, spent two days and a night at Eye on business which lay between their master and the Duke of Suffolk,[20] the matters discussed were as likely as not purely formal, relating probably to the duke's coming of age and perhaps to Hopton's manor of Westleton, which was held of the honour of Eye.[21] As it is all that remains to demonstrate any association between Hopton and the duke we are surely justified in thinking it was one which meant little or nothing to them.

Perhaps it was Thomasin not John who enjoyed the company of local lords, or at any rate of their womenfolk. During 1477–8 Lady Clinton came to Blythburgh to hunt, and also, on possibly the same occasion, Lady Wingfield with two women of her household.[22] Lady Clinton may have been visiting her father's estates,

[19] C. D. Ross, *Edward IV* (1974), p309.

[20] SRO, HA 30/314/18 m1. In 1463–4 how much of the new church tower might there have been for them to see? (HMC, *Tenth Report* (1885) appendix IV, p531.) One of the contributors had been the dowager Duchess Alice; she had given the churchwardens 20 marks in 1453–4 'ad novum facturum campanile ibidem pro perpetuo memorialium habendo inter tenentes domini ibidem pro anima preclarissimi domini sui Willelmi nuper Ducis Suffolicie nuper viri sui ac pro bono statu dicte Ducisse et Johannis filii eorundem': BL, Egerton Roll 8779.

[21] PRO, C140/72/70. 5s castle ward was paid each year: see the Westleton accounts.

[22] SRO, HA 30/314/18 m5.

for she was probably Elizabeth, wife of John, lord Clinton (who, having succeeded his father in 1464, survived her and died in 1488), and daughter of Richard Fiennes (created Lord Dacre of the South in 1459), who owned a number of estates immediately to the north of Easton Bavents, at Covehithe, Wrentham, Benacre, and Henstead, and even nearer, a manor in Thorington.[23] They were a Sussex family; perhaps Thomasin had become acquainted with them when she had lived at Battle in Sussex with her first husband William Lunsford, or at Kingsham with William Sidney, her second. Neither place was far from the fashionable new house Richard Fiennes' father Sir Roger had built himself at Herstmonceaux. Such acquaintance, however, would have been before 1457, when Elizabeth herself would not have been very old.

Lady Wingfield was probably another Elizabeth, the wife of Sir John Wingfield of Letheringham, Suffolk.[24] This Elizabeth was the daughter of Sir John FitzLewis of West Horndon, Essex, and so she and Thomasin may have known each other in earlier days; moreover her husband owned estates even nearer Blythburgh than Letheringham, such as Stradbroke and Laxfield.[25] She bore her husband twelve sons and four daughters, but none-

---

[23] Copinger II, *sub nomine*. Margaret, widow of John, lord Clinton (d.1464), would be a more attractive candidate than her son's wife, for her third husband was Sir John Heveningham. But were they married in 1477–8? Her second husband was Sir Walter Hungerford, second son of Sir Edmund Hungerford, who in turn was the third son of Walter, lord Hungerford (d.1449). They were married c.1470. The date of his death I have not discovered. Even so, as the wife of Sir John Heveningham would she in 1477–8 be called Lady Clinton? She died in 1496.

[24] Anne, wife of Sir Robert Wingfield, Sir John's younger brother, is the other, less likely, candidate. She was the daughter and heir of Sir Robert Harling of East Harling, Norfolk; he was Sir John Fastolf's nephew, and after his death in 1435, Fastolf became Anne's guardian (K. B. McFarlane, 'William Worcester: a preliminary survey', in *Studies presented to Sir Hilary Jenkinson*, ed. J. Conway Davies (1957), p200; see Davis, II, p152). The price Fastolf made Sir William Chamberlain pay for her as his bride was no less than £1000 'of gold in noblis': the marriage contract of 2 August 1438 is Magd. Coll., Oxford, Fastolf paper 17. Faint traces of the magnificence of this lady can still be savoured at East Harling church.

[25] For Sir John Wingfield, see Wedgwood, pp955–6, and for his estates, see M. E. Wingfield, *The Muniments of the ancient Saxon family of Wingfield* (1894), pp50ff, and his *IPM*: PRO, C140/81/59. John and Elizabeth's arms adorn the battlements of the grand tower of Laxfield church: Munro Cautley, *Suffolk Churches*, p287.

theless survived him by some twenty years. He died in 1481,[26] she in 1500.[27] She did not marry again after Sir John's death, and beside his body at Letheringham she desired to be buried.[28] If it was Elizabeth FitzLewis who came to Blythburgh in 1477–8, then perhaps she came to Yoxford during the next twenty years to see Thomasin frequently, for these two widows would have had much to gossip about; over a score of children between them and countless grandchildren.[29]

If Thomasin may have enjoyed the company of the great, John avoided it. We cannot deny their existence any more than could John. They loomed, so to speak, but it was at a distance: John gave them scant opportunity to get nearer. We have to look elsewhere if we are to discover any to whom John did give such opportunity. Let us therefore start at the bottom and on the outside, and work upwards and inwards in our quest.

We do not know how friendly John was with any of his tenants. They comprised a great variety of folk: the fact that one was a tenant did not define one's social standing. It never had. After all, all men were properly tenants save the king, and just as the king did not know all his tenants, we can be sure that John was not aware of all those who owed him rent. No more are we. Some men for one reason and another escaped his notice, much as they are, albeit for different reasons, beyond our attention. Moreover these categories may not coincide. A man whom he valued may have made no impression upon us; one whom we have selected, John Scothaugh or William Reve, for instance, may have meant

---

26 Will dated 10 May (the day before he died), proved 10 October: SRO, HA 30/50/22/1/8(16).
27 Will dated 14 July 1497, proved 22 December 1500: NRO, Norwich Cons. Court, Reg. Cage, f135.
28 For their tomb at Letheringham, see John Blatchly, 'The lost and mutilated memorials of the Boville and Wingfield Families at Letheringham', *Proceedings of the Suffolk Institute of Archaeology*, vol 33, part 2 (1975 for 1974), pp184–5.
29 Though we should note in passing that Thomasin and Anne Harling, who also died in 1498, may have had a good deal in common too. Anne also had three husbands, but alas she was childless; nevertheless her will (*Test Ebor* iv, p149ff) is full of the children of others, ending happily with one of her executors, 'my neveu Robert Wyngefeld esquyer, which I have brought up of a childe sythen he was iij yeres of age'.

nothing to him. Even if, however, these particular tenants played no part in his life, others like them may have done, for it was with the richer, more important folk of these communities of which he was the chief landlord, those whom we describe here, that he would willy-nilly have had some contact: they could hardly help but bump into each other from time to time. They may have done more than that. As John was not a lover of grand company, perhaps he enjoyed the society of these commoners, the yeomen and the husbandmen, the tradesmen and the fishermen of north east Suffolk. They were men with whom he cared to be perhaps more than he cared being with those who were his social equals, the Brews, the Calthorps, the Townshends. After all, they had only become his equals in 1430. Before then their society would have been very superior. May he not, therefore, have always been more at home among those of the level of society into which he was born and grew up?

Richard Cook of Yoxford, according to the 1471 terrier,[30] owed rent of well over £2, far and away the highest owed by any tenant there. In his case we know John knew him, for in July of the year the terrier was made Richard witnessed a confirmation of the Yoxford manors by Robert Banyard, a surviving feoffee, to John.[31] So did Richard's son John, who at this time held two small pieces of land at Yoxford. He soon succeeded his father in his properties. Richard died in January 1474, leaving his messuage and all his lands in Yoxford to his son, so long as he found a priest to sing for his soul in Yoxford parish church for a year. He also left to St Peter's, where he wished to be buried, £1 towards the making of an antiphoner. It is testimony to Richard's local standing that he named Roger Townshend supervisor of his will, and had among his executors William Botild, an attorney of Robert Banyard's in the 1471 charter and bailiff at Easton Bavents in the 1470s.[32]

John Scothaugh, unlike Richard Cook, had no son to leave his

[30] SRO, HA 30/369/1 fs9–9v.
[31] BL, Harley Charter 45 F41.
[32] BL, Harley Charter 45 F41; SRO, HA 30/369/1 fs9, 10v; SRO, V5/19/1/16. Richard's will is SRO, Reg. 2, f267v, dated 4 January, proved 11 January 1474. The family also held land at Yoxford of Sibton Abbey: A. H. Denney, *The Sibton Abbey Estates*, pp103–4.

lands to. Scothaugh was also a Yoxford man; in 1471 he held a close called Mellefield as well as a few other parcels, and in all owed rent of just under £1 a year. In 1484 he, like John Cook, held a little property in Yoxford of Sibton Abbey.[33] By that time he was probably renting a good deal more land in the village from the Hoptons, including three other enclosures and a large meadow; his rent had increased to 35s.[34] This would have put him among the most substantial tenants in the community. He was more than a mere farmer; as he left in his will leather, bark and bark vats ('barkefattes'), we may assume that he ran a tanning business. His tenure of so many closes would suggest his interest in animals, and he had plenty of cattle to bequeath in his will. He also had six servants, three women and three men. When he died in spring 1512 he left all his lands to his nephew Christopher Sampson; his widow Agnes, however, was to have 'her dwelling in the south end of my chief mease with free entering and outgate at her pleasure all the time of her life', and Christopher was to provide her with meat, drink and fuel at all times. In addition John gave to Agnes all his household stuff, eight of his cattle ('keen'), all his sheep and lambs, and all his grain, save only sufficient seed corn for Christopher for the next sowing. To Christopher went the bark vats, the bark and half the leather, the horses, and remaining cattle, but he was required to give each of the six servants a cow or 6s 8d. Christopher also had to provide 9 marks, a year's salary of the priest whom John wished to sing mass at Yoxford for two years. John also left 6s 8d to the abbot of Sibton and 1s to each of the brethren to pray for his soul. He desired to be buried in St Peter's church at Yoxford, before the image of our Lady of Grace, and he left the church 20 marks to purchase a silver gilt cross with the figures of Mary and John on it. Clearly John was a man of note in Yoxford, a man too who wanted to be remembered there.[35]

Another man who featured in the Yoxford terrier of 1471 was William Reve of Darsham. He held a few acres of land, pasture,

[33] SRO, HA 30/369/1 f7v; Denney, p106.
[34] In the 1471 terrier (SRO, HA 30/369/1 f6v) his name is written in a second hand over the holdings of Thomas Burnham and Robert Snelling.
[35] His will: SRO, Reg. 5, f246v, dated 16 March, proved 29 April 1512.

and marsh in Brendfen; his rent came to no more than 1s 4½d and a goose.[36] Yet, like many another tenant who was insignificant in one village community, he was no doubt important in another, in his case presumably Darsham. Seldom, if ever, do we have enough surviving material covering a locality of up to half a dozen villages to tell us who within *that* neighbourhood was substantial, influential and respected. William Reve, so far as his will[37] reveals him, was not such a one; Darsham alone was where he counted for anything. His chief messuage was in Darsham, his only pious bequest was of 3s 4d to the painting of the image of All Saints in Darsham church, and he named as supervisor of the will William Wiston, vicar of Darsham. His farming was on a smallish scale but it was mixed. He required his widow Katherine to deliver to his son and heir Harry, when he became 20, three kine and two horses; more immediately he left to her all his grain, pease, and hay, his horses, sheep, and cattle, his pigs, bacon, and hams, his ducks and geese, and his hemp, flax, and wool. The scale of his farming, the standard of his livelihood is well measured by the amount he left to his daughter Margery's marriage, 26s 8d.

Richard Love of Westhall, on the other hand, was a man of much wider interests. Katherine Love, who in 1481–2 was twenty-nine years in arrears with her annual rent of 8s 8d at Westhall, was perhaps his mother.[38] Richard, 'sike in body and knowyng my dayes very short and the perell of deth aprochyng ner', made his will on 6 August 1509.[39] He lived at Westhall; that was where his chief messuage called Lovys was; and he worshipped at Westhall church; there he was to be buried 'by my stolys ende'. However, he had property elsewhere: as he described it 'londes, tenementes, rents and services in the townys of Westhale, Brampton, Soterton or in any odur place withyn the hundred of Blithyng in the county of Suffolk'. The scope of his worldly concerns, as well as the range of his piety, is demonstrated by his bequests to local churches; not only was £1 bequeathed for the new bell at

[36] SRO, HA 30/369/1 f17.
[37] Drawn up in November 1510, proved November 1511: SRO, Reg. 5, f254.
[38] SRO, HA 30/50/22/20/9(13), see also SRO, HA 30/369/31.
[39] Nevertheless not proved until 19 February 1513: NRO, Norwich Cons. Court, Reg. Johnson, f244v.

Westhall, but other sums went to Brampton, Sotherton, Ugges-hall, Stoven and Redisham. Moreover, four bushels of wheat were to go to each of the four orders of friars at Yarmouth and Gorleston. There are other indications of his affluence, as there are of his devotion and the breadth of his local interests. His daughter and heir, for example, was betrothed to William Baret, of one of the most influential families in Blythburgh; all Richard's lands were to go to them, but they were to provide his widow Agnes with all that she required in food and drink and with a pension of 33s 4d a year for as long as she remained unmarried; she was to live with them at Lovys in the 'parlour and chamber in the East End of the Hall'. Also to remain at Lovys was Richard's 'Messe book and ij halff portes in prynte', unless John Crane his nephew were to become a priest, in which case he should have them. For his soul he made unostentatious provision: 10s to the college at Mettingham for prayers for his friends' souls as well as his own, 13s 4d to the nuns at Bruisyard for their prayers, and immediately upon his death five masses of the five wounds of Christ to be sung at the chapel of 'Scala Coeli' at Westminster. As supervisor of his will he named a Blythburgh man, probably the father of his prospective son-in-law, John Baret the elder.

The Barets of Walberswick were among the leading families of that fishing town in the thirty years after John Hopton's death. A Geoffrey Baret had rented a little land there in 1477–8,[40] and had worked for Hopton at Blythburgh and Easton Bavents in the years immediately before that, at timber felling and plastering walls.[41] If this was the father of the John Baret of the 1480s and 1490s, then the son appears to have gone a long way up in the world.[42] John was bailiff of Blythburgh in 1484–5 and 1490–1 and of Westleton in 1490–1, which in the later year brought him fees totalling just over £6, an income well worth the labour of ac-quiring it. In that year too he farmed the fish ponds at Westwood

[40] SRO, HA 30/50/33/10/17(4); HA 30/314/18 m5.
[41] SRO, HA 30/314/18 ms1, 4; V5/19/1/16, 1470–1.
[42] There was, however, a Geoffrey Baret of Halesworth who supplied timber to the Walberswick churchwardens in 1473–4 (*Walberswick Church-wardens' Accounts*, pp35, 37), and in the early 1450s there had been a Thomas Baret at Walberswick who owned two fishing boats (*ibid.*, pp90–1, 93; SRO, HA 30/369/46 f54).

for a mere 1s 8d, a profitable undertaking we might guess: during the minority of the lord it was well worth being a bailiff.[43] He was still bailiff at Blythburgh in 1496 when he bought from the Walberswick churchwardens a house in Blythburgh for 5 marks. It appears to have taken him beyond 1500 to pay off this sum at half a mark every Christmas.[44] He in his turn appears to have done a good deal for them and for the church; in 1492 when he rode to London, he had 7 nobles from them, and 3s 4d by way of reward; in 1493 he entertained them on St Andrew's day, the patronal feast day of Walberswick church; in 1495 he was (whatever it involved) constable and had 2s 9d as his expenses; in 1497 he supplied the cloth for the new crucifix.[45] Was it this John who died in December 1500 or January 1501?[46] He desired in his will to be buried in St Andrew's, his body to be covered by a gravestone costing £1. To the church he left £2 towards a pair of organs. His widow was to have all his wheat and malt, his ling fish and salt fish, a wey of salt, all the wood and coal in the yard, and candles, hops and trenchers, 'tappys and garlek'. As another John Baret was holding a 'plase called the Crowne' in 1505–6,[47] perhaps the John Baret who died at the turn of 1500 was, among other things, an innkeeper. That John Baret had four sons who survived him, John, Henry, Robert and Richard; none of them was twenty in December 1500. When each arrived at that age he was to have 5 marks, the same sum as John's daughter Rose was to have on the day of her marriage. As John named as one of his executors John Baret of Blythburgh, there was beside himself and his young son a third of that name. We cannot sort them out satisfactorily. By 1505–6 a John Baret junior was bailiff of Blythburgh; he was already bailiff at Westleton.[48] By 1509, as we have seen, Richard Love of Westhall made John Baret the elder supervisor of his will.

43 SRO, HA 30/134/18 m9; HA 30/369/281.
44 *Walberswick Churchwardens' Accounts* pp257, 268. The wardens noted the first seven instalments, but after the fourth did not record the year.
45 *Ibid.*, pp66, 68, 71, 73, 80. For the constable, see J. Charles Cox, *Churchwardens' Accounts* (1913), chapter XXII.
46 Will dated 3 December 1500, proved 9 January 1501: NRO, Norwich Cons. Court, Reg. Cage, f151v.
47 SRO, HA 30/369/44 f28v.   48 *Ibid*, f25; HA 30/369/38 f38.

John Hopton is likely to have encountered none of these six-teenth century John Barets. Two other leading men at Walbers-wick in earlier years, however, he had to have known, for one supplied his household with fish over a period of fifteen years or more, the other had him to dinner. Robert Dolfinby we have met before, as fishmonger to the Hoptons and as lessee of the ferry.[49] Nonetheless, it is evident from the Walberswick churchwardens' accounts and his will that he never rowed a ferryboat. In 1466 he was part-owner of a fishing boat, by 1468 he had a boat of his own, and some seven years later was owner of the *Andrew*, one of the larger vessels which went out after herring.[50] He rented the townlands from the churchwardens for ten years or more, and he himself was churchwarden in 1479.[51] In the 1470s and 1480s he often travelled to London or to Ipswich, sometimes with large sums of money: he went twice to London in 1480 with £3 and again with £4.[52] He was, as we would in these circumstances anti-cipate, a benefactor of the church, contributing for instance 3s 4d to the blessing of the bells in 1470, giving another 3s 4d in the year he was churchwarden 'for hys schyldren'.[53] Had they died? 1479 was a summer of plague. When Robert Dolfinby himself came near death in spring 1489 he desired burial beside his wife and children in the east end of St Andrew's.[54] He required his fish-ing boat to be sold and half the money to go to the making of an image of St John the Evangelist and its tabernacle, to be made like the image of St John the Baptist, and that both statues be painted at his cost. He left to a widow and a daughter considerable property and a quantity of bedding, pewter, spoons, basins and ewers. One of his executors was the rector of Easton Bavents, William Boswell. Six years later died Alice Dolfinby – neither the widow nor the daughter of Robert's will; it was however the rector of Easton Bavents, William Boswell, to whom the Walberswick

---

[49] He was leasing the ferry in 1463–4 and continued to do so until 1478–9; he supplied fish to the family over the same period.
[50] *Walberswick Churchwardens' Accounts*, pp130, 134, 163.
[51] *Ibid.*, pp129, 161, 178, 182.
[52] *Ibid.*, pp38, 43, 47, 50.   [53] *Ibid.*, pp139, 182.
[54] His will of May 1489 was proved in the following month: SRO, Reg. 3, f82v.

churchwardens paid £1 for her 'quethe word': the announcement of her death.[55]

Robert Dolfinby is easy to identify in fifteenth century Walberswick; William Ameringale, the man who had John Hopton to dinner in 1451,[56] was, on the other hand, one of a whole host of Ameringales. He may have been William, eldest son of Walter Ameringale who died in December of the year Hopton came to dinner, and who left money to the guild of St Andrew and for the building of a hall for the guild of St John;[57] but he could have been the William Ameringale who, with other men of Walberswick, indented with Richard Russel of Dunwich and Adam Powle of Blythburgh, masons, for the construction of St Andrew's churchtower in 1426.[58] William Ameringale died in 1465: his name ceases to appear in the churchwardens' accounts after that year, and his widow Margery sent out the fishing boat in 1466 and made the dole of sprats to the church.[59] Was this the William who was already a leading man of the town in 1426, or was this Walter's son who, having dined John Hopton in 1451, was prominent in Walberswick affairs over the succeeding years? The latter seems more likely.

He held land from Hopton at Walberswick, in fact his rent of 7s put him among those who paid most, and he contributed thirty-three sheep to the cullet flock recorded by Nicholas Greenhagh in 1453–4.[60] Nevertheless we have the impression that he mainly drew his living from the sea rather than from the land. In 1451 he had two sprat boats: in 1456 one was called his great boat, but the other had gone. By then however, he had a farecost for herring fishing. At the end of the 1450s it was called the *Trinity* and had Henry Bun as its master; William sent both vessels to sea every year until his death, and his widow sent them out in 1466.[61]

---

[55] *Walberswick Churchwardens' Accounts*, p253.
[56] At a cost of 7s 1d, *ibid.*, p2.
[57] Will, SRO, Reg. 1, f157v.
[58] *Walberswick Churchwardens' Accounts*, pvii.
[59] *Ibid.*, pp120, 121, 123, 125.
[60] SRO, HA 30/50/22/10/17/5 and 6; HA 30/369/46 *passim*, f87v for the cullet flock.
[61] *Walberswick Churchwardens' Accounts*, pp84, 91, 93, 94, 97, 108, 109, 113, 115, 117, 119, 122, 123, 125.

Nicholas Greenhagh bought fish from him in the 1450s,[62] so that William may have been the Hoptons' fishmonger whom Robert Dolfinby replaced in the mid-1460s. Unlike Robert, he appears not to have been closely associated with the church: only once is he noticed by the wardens other than as a regular contributor of the fishing doles. In 1453 he and Roger Passhelow – with whom he jointly held a messuage called Barkers some ten years later – gave 6s 8d for prayers for the soul of Thomas Seaton, his wife and daughter.[63] Perhaps if we had his will we would find that, like so many other of his fellow townsmen, he had as much affection for his town church as they had.

We are left in no doubt they had. In roughly the time John Hopton lived at Westwood the men and women of Walberswick built, decorated, and furnished the church which now, apart from the south aisle and the tower, is in ruins. It long has been; the remainder was pulled down in 1696.[64] The prosperity of the town was therefore brief. By the later sixteenth century the great days were gone,[65] almost as quickly as they had come, not two hundred years before. For that time sea, shingle, and river combined to create a coastline which favoured Walberswick.

> Soul (Southwold) and Dunwich, and Walderswick,
> All go in at one lousie creek.

Such says Defoe[66] was the 'rude verse' of northern coasting seamen, who knew how difficult it was to make the harbour. By then Southwold's turn had come: just as Walberswick had replaced Dunwich, so had Southwold overtaken Walberswick, though neither would match Dunwich in its heyday. In Hopton's day, however, the men of Walberswick would not have called

[62] SRO, HA 30/369/46 f71, see also marginal note 'in stuff owing him' 10s, on HA 30/50/22/10/17(6).
[63] *Walberswick Churchwardens' Accounts*, p88; SRO, HA 30/314/18 m1; William and Roger were amerced, and pardoned their amercements, the next year: *ibid.*, m2.
[64] Gardner, *Dunwich*, p162.
[65] *Ibid.*, pp167ff. The great bell was sold in 1585: *ibid.*, p159.
[66] Daniel Defoe, *A Tour through England and Wales* (Everyman edition, reprinted 1948), 1, p55.

their creek lousy, whatever others, even then, may have said of it. It was the making of their wealth and well-being.

So was the herring. Whatever the quantity of Suffolk butter and cheese carried out of Walberswick, it was fish which made the port such a thriving place in the fifteenth century. And North Sea herring was the fish men sailed out for. The churchwardens' accounts which cover the period 1450–99 reveal that; they show too that towards the end of the century the number of deep-sea boats, the herring boats, increased. In 1451 there were twenty-two sprat boats, thirteen herring boats; whereas the coastal fishing boats remained at around twenty in any year, by around 1480 the deep-sea vessels were up to a score or so and continued at that figure until the end of the century. Perhaps a less healthy sign was that by 1499 three men owned two herring boats apiece, and one man three; in the early 1450s almost all shipowners had just one ship and some of them were their own masters.[67] However that may be, this industrial enterprise, small scale as it was, meant work for a broader group of folk than just those of the port itself. The selling of the fish and the crewing of the North Sea boats were then, as they were in the early twentieth century,[68] ways in which (if they were lucky) men from villages behind the coast might augment their living from the land. Walberswick's fat years can only have meant better times too for Yoxford or Westleton, Wenhaston or Darsham.

Walberswick's wealth is reflected in its people leaving the old chapel down by the marsh,[69] and building the ambitious new church up on top of the ridge. Yet church towers and churches like theirs were being put up, or remodelled, made larger, lighter and grander over much of East Suffolk, indeed throughout most of East Anglia. They also were being fitted with finely wrought, expensive, precious objects – furniture and glass, ornaments, images, vestments, and books. Walberswick was in this not distinctive but typical. 'There is not a parish church in the Kingdom so mean as not to possess crucifixes, candlesticks, censers, patens, and

[67] *Walberswick Churchwardens' Accounts*: compare pp90, 93 with 265–6.
[68] G. E. Evans, *The Days That We Have Seen* (1975), pp206–9.
[69] Gardner, *Dunwich*, p152.

cups of silver' noted an Italian diplomat of England about 1500. Abbot Gasquet having recorded that comment added, 'what is most remarkable about the documents that have come down to us. . .is the consistent story they tell of the universal and intelligent interest taken by the people of every parish as a whole in beautifying and supporting their churches'. Elsewhere, he wonders how churchwardens raised money for all that was carried out by them, whether for routine work on fabric or furnishings or for any special purpose; it must, he says, 'always remain a mystery'.[70] What is the mystery? These people, at Walberswick as at a hundred places in East Anglia, put their money where their hearts were. By the fifteenth century the religion which was offered them in the parish church they participated in, they shared, even in some ways they created: it was popular religion. That, allied to intense local loyalties, meant the parish church was where their hearts were. All this, I imagine, was no mystery to Abbot Gasquet; it was where the money came from which mystified him. It came of course, and in so many parishes of England, not just from great men, Thomas Spring and John de Vere, earl of Oxford at Lavenham for example, but, as at Louth or Bodmin or as at Eye for its tower, from a great multitude of far humbler folk.[71] Whether it was from communal activity, like the three or four church ales a year at not far distant Cratfield in the 1490s,[72] or from individual

[70] F. A. Gasquet, *Parish Life in Medieval England* (1906), pp70, 123, 139. Not now a fashionable book because of its enthusiasm, it nevertheless deserves more than the casual touch of the forelock it gets from our generation.

[71] F. L. Ranson, *Lavenham* (1st edition, 1937), p22; *The First Churchwarden's Book of Louth, 1500–1524*, ed. R. C. Dudding (1941); 'Receipts and Expenses in the building of Bodmin's church, 1469–1472', ed. J. J. Wilkinson, *The Camden Miscellany* vii, Camden Society, New Series, XIV (1875); for Eye tower, see HMC, *Tenth Report* (1885), appendix IV, p531, a note in the town memoranda book of the sixteenth century: 'The steple of Eye was buylt in Ao 1470 as aperith by a book of Accompt I have of that yere T. Harvey clerk Robert Anyell & Jo. Fysk with Wm Hobert then being churchwardeyns & they receiving but £1 6s 2d of the former churchwardeyns gatheryd that yere partly with the plowgh, partly in churchales, partly in legacies given that waye, but chiefly of the frank & devowte hartes of the people the some of xlli. & litell odde money, Wherwith it aperith by ther sayd Accompt they dyd byld up the steple & wer at charges with the bells ther. . .'

[72] *Cratfield Parish Papers*, ed. William Holland (1895), pp18ff. I should not

offerings, like the shilling given by a woman in 1453 at Walberswick 'in devotion for her friends' souls',[73] the money came in.
Nor was there lack of it. Just as this was not simply a matter of
wealthy benefactors, nor was it either a question of the widow's
mite. The many smallholders, husbandmen, farmers, shopkeepers,
traders, craftsmen, artisans, and their wives who freely gave

forget obligation and social pressure, nor the desire to conform as part
and parcel of this generosity. All no doubt played their part even in the
following episode of the early sixteenth century, which bears repeating
here. It is described by Thomas Golding, vicar of Eye: '...Jhon Fiske,
Jesu have mercy upon his sowle, gave fower skore marks to the towne of
Eye toward a priestes service and it were purchased within fower yere,
and thei coulde not yette none by those yeres were expired, then forty
marks shoulde be songin in Eye Churche and thother part in Cambridge
for his sowle, we coulde not finde none in no place that was mete for vs.
I thanke Almighty God for it that my fortune that I desiered John
Fanner to breake his faste withe me in the vicaridge the daye before New
Yere in Christmas, and as we satte by the fyer we comonyd howe that the
towne should lose this service the whiche should be great rebuke on to all
the towne. Then the holy goste putte hym in minde. Saythe John Fanner,
Sir saythe he to me, what woll you saye and I will selle you. My good Jhon
Fanner, saide I vnto hym, Maye you selle it. Yea for God maye I sell it
for I bought it of my father and paide more for it than it was worthe.
What shall I give you for it, x skore marke, and I thought good to take
hym in his good mynde, I toke hym a peice of gold, saeing on to hym in
this manner, John Fanner this pece of gold I geve the on this condicion
that ye shall geve me respecte to give you an answer till the sunne gooe
downe on Sundaye next comyng, yf it be a bargayne, take that for yower
good will, and for the respyte that you geve me in the matter. I went into
the pulpet the next daye and shewed unto all the parishe that we were like
to lose the service the whiche should be great rebuke to all the town.
How saye, now saide I unto them if I have bought a ground for you so
that ye maye stonde in the church yard and see it, and I showed them how
I had made a bargaine with John Fanner and showed them the daies of
payment so that on Candlemas folowing he should have xxli. and at
Candlemas next mening xxli., and so xli, a yere forthe till it were paied
for, and if it be a bargaine because it [be] for the comon wele speake all
Una Voce and seye ye this was a godly hearinge; every man woman and
childe saide yea yea, dyverse men gave x marke a peice women fower
marke xxs. and xld. so that I gathered on Candlemas daye above xxli.
we toke never a penny of this fower skore marke we desiered lond for it
the whiche laye by John Fanner and I bought a peice of Watkin Pishmer
the whiche John Fanner had sold hym before in his neade and I gave it
for me and my frendes sowles, and on Candelmas daye at the first payment
putte the preste in possession Mr. Prime and an other Sir Stephen, after
hym Sir Webster, Mr. Dunston withe other moe.': HMC, *Tenth Report*
appendix IV, pp527–8.
[73] *Walberswick Churchwardens' Accounts*, p117.

money, and left money for their parish churches, could afford to. They had it, so to say, to give.

The guilds too were an expression of their well-being as well as their sense of community. Unlike the churches little survives to give us an impression of their place in parish society. Once again, however, the parishes of East Suffolk have more to offer than most; at Cratfield and Fressingfield, for instance, the guild hall close beside the church remains. It does also at Kelsale, by the fifteenth century a decayed market town,[74] but no doubt still a flourishing agricultural community, and at Laxfield; to both these guilds John and Thomasin made contributions.[75] The guildhouse at Walberswick has gone. It housed the guild of St John (and was sometimes called St John's house), and a shop or shops.[76] Was it also the home of the other guilds – of St Andrew, of Our Lady, and of St Barbara? Once there is mention of St Andrew's shop; but was that a separate establishment or in St John's hall?[77] These guild halls were not primarily for material commerce, they were chiefly places of recreation, taking over this function from the nave or the porch of the church itself, and so leaving the church much more the place for spiritual commerce. It was probably in the guild hall, therefore, that the Wenhaston 'game' was shewn in 1493, and the Bramfield 'game' in 1497. Were these 'games' plays?[78] In 1495 13s 4d was collected 'of game money the last game'; presumably this was Walberswick's own play. Was it in the guild house that Sir George Hopton was dined in 1489, at twice the cost of the dinner given the bishop that year?[79] The bishop was James Goldwell of Norwich, and the dinner must have pleased him: he came regularly thereafter.[80]

---

[74] Norman Scarfe, *The Suffolk Landscape* (1972), pp169–73.

[75] SRO, HA 30/369/46 f102; HA 30/312/117.

[76] *Walberswick Churchwardens' Accounts*, pp68, 114, 125, 132; see Walter Ameringale's will: above p172; in 1463 8½d was received for the shops of the guildhouse of chapmen: p114.

[77] For the guilds, *ibid.*, p117ff; for St Andrew's shop, p136. So far as I can detect no halls are mentioned for these other guilds.

[78] I owe this interpretation to Norman Scarfe. See the sixteenth century 'Game Place' at Walsham-le-Willows: Scarfe, *The Suffolk Landscape*, p201.

[79] *Walberswick Churchwardens' Accounts*, p60.

[80] *Ibid.*, pp63, 65, 66, 68, 71, 73, 76, 79, 80.

The churchwardens at Walberswick had much more to do besides entertaining. Not only, like most churchwardens, did they administer land and houses, they also, unlike others, were responsible for the quay. In the year Sir George and the bishop were entertained, for example, Edmund Wright was paid £3 13s 4d for 'keyemakyng', and his board came to another 5s. On top of this there were other workmen and their board to be paid for, and there was the cost of the timber and stone and its transport.[81] As we have seen, doles of the fishing catches were taken; these were levied for the profit of the town, not just the church;[82] thus the churchwardens of Walberswick had much more than church and guild business to see to. They were town managers.

Nonetheless the maintenance of the church building, its fittings and the enrichment of both were their main and abiding concern. As they were of most of the community they served. In the year the quay was so extensively repaired the churchwardens spent 15s on the organs, they had the church washed by Elizabeth Pye for 6s 8d and 3d went on the repair of the church lantern.[83] From time to time they had some heavy charges to meet: £5 to the bell-maker in 1466, nearly £7 to Harry Pay the mason for 'makyng of the batyllment of the cherche and for the wyndownys' in 1496, and in the following year over £11 for the painting of the crucifix and the ceiling.[84] Books too had to be bought, one for 8 marks in 1473, and then kept in good condition;[85] so had vestments;[86] so had everything else within the church. It was for all this that the people of Walberswick gave generously, not only individually but communally. For instance in 1495 two 'gatherings' in the church raised 37s 2d, in 1496 the wives of the town gave 10s for a glass window, in 1497 the 'maydynnys' collected for the painting of 'kyng herry tabyll' 6s 4d.[87] None of this is exceptional in fifteenth century England: it can be paralleled in parishes the length and breadth of the country. The brand new church at Walberswick,

[81] Ibid., p60.
[82] See the explicit statement (of 1489) ibid., p227.
[83] Ibid., p60.   [84] Ibid., pp22, 77, 80.   [85] Ibid., pp35, 56, 73.
[86] There is an inventory of 1482 or 1492: ibid., p199, see Gardner, p158.
[87] Walberswick Churchwardens' Accounts, pp253, 256, 261.

however, was especially the community's: it was the people's creation.

Blythburgh church was not quite that: John Hopton took a greater part in its building. Yet if Blythburgh can be said to be John Hopton's church in the sense that Walberswick was not, this still left room for it to be the church of others. Two of these others, William Colet and Alice Stapleton, Hopton tenants at Blythburgh, we shall end with.

William Colet paid a rent of 5s 8d in 1477–8.[88] He died late in 1503 or early in 1504.[89] He owned a shop and dealt in salt and probably much else; the churchwardens at Walberswick bought a yard of buckram from him in 1493.[90] He had property at Southwold and Walberswick as well as at Blythburgh, and as befits a traveller,[91] he left money for the repair of the footbridge between Blythburgh and Bulcamp and for the repair of the chapel of the Rood by the bridge at Blythburgh. He desired to be buried beside his wife Agnes in Blythburgh church, beneath a gravestone 'somewhat larger than the stone that lies upon Agnes'. Does that note of propriety capture the man? His bequests to the church where he had worshipped and where his body was to lie certainly show a sense of what is fitting, of what was right for a man of his standing. He left £1 for the painting of the image of the Trinity at the north end of the high altar, £1 for the purchase of a 'grayle', £1 for repairs, and his executors were to buy a red cope (like that bought for Simon Goading) and present it to the church. Prayers for his soul were to be sung for a year, the two orders of friars at Dunwich were to say a trental of St Gregory, and four honest clerks were to sing a dirge and a mass in the priory, and there too the bells were to be rung. Moreover, if his son John was disposed to become a priest he was to have £6 to celebrate for his father's soul (and the souls of his father's friends) at Cambridge for a year. If not, then a priest was to be added to the one at Blythburgh.

88 SRO, HA 30/50/22/10/17(4).
89 His will, dated 5 October 1503, proved 13 January 1504: SRO, Reg. 4, f122.
90 *Walberswick Churchwardens' Accounts*, p68.
91 Described as 'mercator de Blythboro' on his tombstone, according to Weever, *Monuments*, p761, see Gardner, *Dunwich*, p125.

Why Cambridge? That, William clearly envisaged, was where John would be at school. John was to be given 10 marks out of the sale of his father's salt when he reached 21; but if he wished to become a priest then the 10 marks was to go towards his schooling. One wonders whether, in the year his distinguished namesake was appointed Dean of St Paul's, young John Colet took a decision to go to school and follow him into the priesthood. If he was aware of such things, he could hardly have had a better model to pattern himself on. William Colet at any rate shared something with the Dean: an awareness of the need for education. It is no surprise to discover that awareness on the part of a man who described himself as a merchant. It is startling to come across it on the part of the brothel keeper.

Alice Stapleton was amerced (and pardoned) 6s 8d for keeping 'le bordelhous' in 1490–1.[92] She died late in 1494 or early in the following year. In her will[93] neither husband nor children are mentioned. She wished to be buried at Blythburgh; to the church she left 6s 8d towards the making of a canopy over the high altar and another 6s 8d for a 'masse' of silver, the money to be raised by her executors from the rent of her tenement. To the wife of one of her executors, Robert Hakon, went her second-best girdle and her second-best gown, to Alice Brende her best gown and best girdle. Ralph Brende was to have a featherbed and 'towards hys exhibycon to ye scole' 6s 8d. To what school, one wonders, was that? But let us not raise more questions. It is surely enough to know that Alice Stapleton, who was not thoroughly respectable, considered schooling for a boy absolutely so: isn't that beautifully in the tradition of such things?

Alice Stapleton and William Colet probably represent the opposite poles of Blythburgh society. Yet merchants and madams, fancy women and fishermen have always gone together pretty well. John Hopton's manor of Blythburgh and Walberswick had room enough for them all. John himself possibly never knew William Colet's enterprise – William may only have been at the outset of his career in 1478 – and, unless she had set up in business

[92] SRO, HA 30/369/281.
[93] SRO, Reg. 3, f171v, dated 13 December 1494, proved 17 February 1495.

before 1478, was totally ignorant of Alice Stapleton, but what he cannot have been unaware of was how both communities, and especially Walberswick, thrived; the longer he lived the more they flourished. It was to foster this economic and social wellbeing that he took on Dunwich in the 1460s. For that contest he needed friends too, legal allies to defend and extend his and those communities' interests.

There were plenty of lawyers to choose from in East Anglia. The compilers of a petition to the parliament of 1455 thought they were too plentiful: in Suffolk, Norfolk and Norwich, they said, there were eighty or more attorneys 'the most parte of theym not havying any oyer lyving'; they made more trouble than they alleviated, and the petition requested that their numbers be cut to six in each county and two in Norwich, to be chosen by the two Chief Justices. The petition was granted by the government, but nothing ever came of it: ten years later the over-abundance of lawyers was still a feature of East Anglian society.[94] It was of course none of the small fry the petitioners of 1455 had primarily in mind, whom Edward IV chose to sort out the Dunwich affair. William Jenny was after all a sergeant-at-law in the early 1460s, he was to go on to become a Justice of the King's Bench. His whole career was the law. He was therefore of much wider than merely local importance.[95]

William's estates of Theberto and Knodishall lay immediately to the south of Westleton. Moreover, he held a tenement, Beveriches, of John in Yoxford, bought rabbits from the

<hr>

[94] *Rot Parl* v, pp326–7. What was the genesis of this petition? Did it originate in Fastolf's circle? We are reminded of William Worcester's hostility to young men learning law and exploiting their fellows, whereas they ought to be learning the art of war and exploiting those foreign fellows: *Book of Noblesse*, ed. J. G. Nichols (Roxburghe Club, 1860), pp77–8.

[95] I have been much helped by the late Susan Flower's paper on the de Vere council (at the Essex Record Office, Chelmsford, among her papers). Her threefold categorization of lawyers is most useful: (i) of only local importance, (ii) those whose legal training was incidental to their career or life, (iii) those whose whole career was the law. The petitioners of 1455 were thinking of the first category, into which William Bondes and Robert Banyard fall. Miss Flower's early death was a great loss to scholarship.

Blythburgh warren,[96] and sat with Hopton on the commission of the peace. John may have sought his clever neighbour's advice on more routine matters of law than the Dunwich affair involved, but it is not likely that he sought his company for pleasure. William Jenny's reputation, like William Yelverton's, has suffered from his opposition to the Pastons over Fastolf's will, and their distaste for him enters into our thinking almost without us being aware we have become disapproving too, yet others than the Pastons did not care for him. In June 1464 Robert Banyard, no less than one of Hopton's councillors,[97] volunteered to John Paston the names of some 'that love not Jeney' whom he thought might be favourable in the plea of trespass Jenny had brought against him. It was not to be: Paston was convicted on 10 September 1464.[98] William Jenny after all was a hard man to beat and for that reason, if for that reason alone, he had friends enough. Sir William Calthorp, certainly a good friend of John Hopton's, was one of them. As sheriff in 1464, he explained to Richard Calle the dilemma he found himself in: he was well disposed towards John Paston but 'William Jenney hath bene hes goode frend and haue ben of hes councell this ij yere in all hes matres towchyng the lawe'; nevertheless, Calle reported, 'he seide leuer he hadde lose the lessere frend than the greete frende', and so undertook to write to the undersheriff of Suffolk to act on Paston's behalf.[99] As Paston eventually was convicted one wonders whether Calthorp's priorities were not really the reverse of those he gave to Calle. We can only sympathize with him: choosing among friends must always have posed problems for sheriffs, and fair words and faint actions was no doubt the policy of many of them. Nor are we ready to blame Calthorp if he in fact preferred Jenny to Paston in the summer of 1464. Already William Jenny was, as Colonel Wedgwood a shade dramatically put it, 'a man of great power, made by the law'.[100]

It was a group of powerful men made by the law which met at Blythburgh one day in 1477–8 to hunt. William Jenny, Roger

[96] SRO, HA 30/369/1 f4v; HA 30/314/18 m2.
[97] 'Old Banyard of Sibton Abbey': below p204.
[98] Davis I, pp526–7.   [99] Davis II, p229.
[100] Wedgwood, p501.

Townshend, John Sulyard;[101] Hopton was near the end of his life; it was Thomasin who acknowledged the 5s spent on their entertainment. Did they come only to hunt? Townshend and Sulyard were feoffees and executors of Hopton's, Jenny was neither, but perhaps it was enfeoffments, a will, even a testament that they discussed with John and Thomasin Hopton after their hunting, and for that business they considered Jenny a good man to have with them. We cannot know. No more can we know whether Jenny's role as arbitrator in the Dunwich affair was at Hopton's suggestion; were they in league to outwit the town bailiffs? That Jenny was *not* John's feoffee, was *not* among his executors, suggests that they did not have much time for one another. Maybe, therefore, in the Dunwich affair William Jenny was not in Hopton's pocket. William died in December 1483 and was presumably buried in Knodishall church, as John his father had been and Edmund his son was to be.[102]

Jenny's fellow referee in the Dunwich dispute was very much the senior partner in status if not in years, for Henry Sotell was Attorney-General. The three days and nights he spent at Westwood in 1466–7 with Robert Hopton and others of John's council may have seen the finishing touches put to the whole matter. Sotell, we must assume, was very much Edward IV's own man for this task. Yet, like Hopton, he was a West Riding man, or at any rate from a family of West Riding origins, and they had come across each other there ten years before. It was indeed in 1466 that William Hopton joined Sotell on the commission of the peace in the West Riding.

He had been a young man of great promise. As early as July 1450 he was on John Paston's council, and gave it as his opinion

101 SRO, HA 30/314/18 m5.
102 John Jenny's brass dated 1460 survives; it is aptly called comical by Norman Scarfe: *Suffolk, a Shell Guide* (1960). Edmund desired to be buried 'in the churche of Knodeshale under or by the walle devidinge the Chauncell and vestiary. That in that walle may be made an arche and a little tombe covered with a marble stone or some other stone under an arche that through that arche may be a sight to thaltare oute of the said arche for theym that wulbe in the said vestiarye to leyne upon the said tombe lokinge to thaultar. My wiffe lye undre the said tombe or by it': his will, NRO, Norwich Cons. Court, Reg. Brigge, f108. There is no trace of the tomb now.

that in the Oxnead affair Paston had the law on his side; no doubt his opinion would have been the same concerning Lord Moleyn's claims to the manor of Gresham which were disturbing Paston at the same time.[103] One ponders the lessons Henry may have learnt from that nasty business regarding the licence those with influence at court might have in the country. He cannot have had a more revealing experience of how local prestige pivoted on central power. Without friends at court and faced by an opponent who had, the Pastons were hamstrung. Only political changes at the centre saved them and the law from being defeated. Perhaps it was a very obvious conclusion; it required no subtlety on the young lawyer's part to reach it. Nevertheless the consequences of an entirely uncontrolled exercise of power by men such as Lord Moleyns came home to him, as it were, on the inside. Indeed, as he was also on Fastolf's council,[104] the evils committed by those who were the provincial agents of the establishment must have been dinned into his ears by his master, a born outsider if ever there was one. It would be too simple to believe it was this that led him to associate himself with those who actively set themselves against such a state of affairs; still, that is what we find him doing. He was a feoffee of Richard, duke of York and of Richard, earl of Warwick, and even if he entered Warwick's service before that nobleman became an opponent of the government, Sotell did not sever the connection after he had.[105] By the time his and Hopton's ways crossed again in the mid-1460s, and Henry came to stay at Westwood, he was reaping the harvest of his faithfulness to the Nevills.

The Leicestershire heiress Anne Bovill, whom he married, was probably not one of his rewards, for when he contracted for the marriage of his son and heir John to Elizabeth Plumpton on 11 February 1464, Elizabeth was no more than 3 or 4 years old, and it is unlikely that John was younger.[106] Henry gave 500

---

[103] Davis II, p38.   [104] Davis I, p86; II, p134.

[105] Magd. Coll. Cartae Misc., 303: Warwick's purchase of Collyweston from Ralph, lord Cromwell; *CPR 1476–85*, pp279, 341; *CPR 1452–61*, p49; *CPR 1461–7*, p270; *Cal Anc Deeds* IV, A6339; Somerville, *Duchy of Lancaster*, pp425, 454.

[106] *The Plumpton Correspondence*, ed. Thomas Stapleton, Camden Society,

marks for his son's marriage; in the light of what followed it turned out to be a high price to pay.[107] The indenture of marriage, as was usual, stipulated that Elizabeth was to live with her parents-in-law. Their home was at Stockerston in north eastern Leicestershire, or was shortly to be so, for John Bovill, the father of Henry's wife Anne, was still alive in 1464. He died in 1467.[108] Anne was one of three daughters and Stockerston fell to her as part of her share of her father's lands; in the following year she and Henry obtained confirmation of the licence John Bovill had been granted in 1466 to endow a chantry and almshouse at Stockerston.[109] During the 1450s however, Henry probably had little time to spare for Stockerston. If the Nevill success of 1461 made him into an establishment man and brought him the fruits of influence and office,[110] it must also have brought him far more work, not all of it, as the decade wore on and Edward's patience with the Nevills wore thin, congenial. As the king's attorney at the trial for treason of Thomas Hungerford and Henry Courteney in January 1469[111] he may already have felt uneasy, for this was very much an affair of Edward's and the group he had gathered around him, those indeed whom in July the Nevills would name as their and the community's enemies. Henry, it is clear, had not become a member, however distant, of that group; his connection with Richard, earl of Warwick seems to have been too close for him to have been able to attempt, or wish to attempt the

iv (1839), pplxxi–lxxii. In fact Henry was almost certainly married to Anne Bovill as early as 1451: *CCR 1447–54*, p265.

[107] What followed, indeed what had already taken place, was bizarre and complicated; but this is not the place to retell a story which is a revelation of fifteenth century attitudes towards land and the family, and the convulsions those attitudes could lead to: *Plumpton Correspondence, passim*.

[108] Brass in Stockerston church: Pevsner, *Leicestershire and Rutland sub nomine*.

[109] John Nichols, *The History and Antiquities of the County of Leicester* (reprint 1971), vol 2, part 2, p815, see *Cal Anc Deeds* v, A13122; *CPR 1461–7*, p486; *CPR 1467–77*, p113.

[110] The controllership of the great custom at London, granted him on 9 April 1465, was a large but rather late plum: *CPR 1461–7*, p423. Perhaps also he now had the means to acquire from Gerard Sotell the manor of Redbourne, Lincs: *CPR 1461–7*, p218. The 500 marks he offered for the Plumpton marriage has also to be borne in mind.

[111] Ross, *Edward IV*, p123.

crossing.[112] It is clear, because after Edward's ultimate triumph in
1471 Henry Sotell ceased to be Attorney-General: his tenure of
the post he had held for ten years ended on 11 July 1471.[113] He
was then, so to speak, put out to grass. He became what he had
not before had time to be, a country gentleman. In 1473 he ceased
to be on the commission of the peace for the West Riding; in 1475
he was on those for Leicestershire and Rutland, and he continued
to be on them until his death in 1485.[114] By then perhaps he
would have had rather more in common with John Hopton; but,
so far as we know, they did not encounter each other again after
1466–7.

An Attorney-General of the future John did encounter after
that date; it may even have been in 1466–7 itself that he first
became aware of James Hobart, for in 1466 Hobart first sat on
the Suffolk commission of the peace. He and John were thus
colleagues on the bench for four years. From 1473 Hobart had
William Hopton as a partner; but it was Sir George Hopton who
feed Hobart in 1487;[115] by then he had been Attorney-General
for just less than a year. His fee of 26s 8d was increased by
another half-mark in 1490–1 when Robert Clere and the other
trustees were in charge of Blythburgh. In September 1491 Hobart,
William Eyre, a lawyer with an even fatter fee from the estate,
and Sir John Heveningham, among others, were busy at Blythburgh: there must have been a great deal to do following Sir
George's unexpected death.[116] We ought to dwell no longer on
Hobart than we did on Sotell, but a short time we cannot resist,
for, however tenuous his connection with John, Thomasin and
the trustees of the 1490s clearly relied upon him, and besides a

112 Two of the feoffees he named in the Plumpton marriage contract of 1464
were very close to Warwick: Sir John Gresley and Sir Walter Wrottesley,
see *Plumpton Correspondence*, plxxi. Was Henry one of Warwick's councillors too?
113 *CPR 1461–7*, p6.
114 *CFR 1471–85*, p290. In Nichols' time Henry and Anne were depicted
kneeling with their names beneath their images in the glass of the north
window of the nave at Stockerston: plate facing p821 in vol 2 part 2 of
his *Leicestershire*. Henry's son John died in 1493 and Elizabeth in 1507:
North Country Wills, Surtees Society, 116 (1908), pp64–5. They were
buried at Stockerston where their brasses survive.
115 *CIPM Henry VII* vol 1, p242.   116 SRO, HA 30/369/281.

man of parts is hard to pass over in silence. Moreover we can also detect a man of charm. Sir John Paston wrote to his wife sometime after 1487:

Mastress Margery, I recomand me to yow, and I prey yow in all hast possybyll to send me by the next swer messenger that ye can gete a large playster of your *flose ungwentorum* for the Kynges Attorney Jamys Hobart; for all hys dysease is but an ache in hys knee. He is the man brought yow and me togedyrs, and I had lever then xl li. ye koud wyth your playster depart hym and hys peyne.[117]

If John Paston had so great an affection for him – and John took the trouble to write the letter himself – James is certainly worth our brief attention.

A Suffolk man by birth, he was at Lincoln's Inn in 1458,[118] and by the mid-1460s was, as we have seen, on the Suffolk bench. He had been retained by Sir John Howard by 1463,[119] and probably it was largely owing to Howard's patronage that in the 1467–8 parliament he sat as member for Ipswich.[120] This connection survived, and James continued to serve Sir John until Howard's death at Bosworth.[121] In April 1469 Anthony Woodvill, lord Scales wrote of him too patronizingly as 'my gode frend';[122] James was evidently close to John Mowbray, duke of Norfolk, whom Woodvill hoped he would try to restrain in his conduct towards the Pastons. There was little chance of that. Early in September when the duke had invested Caister he sent Hobart to London to Archbishop George Nevill, presumably to occupy him with soothing assurances;[123] the archbishop and his brother Richard, earl of Warwick had enough to worry about with the king a captive at Middleham; Norfolk had picked his time. Caister was surrendered by John Paston later that month.

[117] Davis I, p628.   [118] *Lincoln's Inn Admissions Register* I (1896), p14.
[119] *Manners and Expenses*, p180, see p215 for his gown of August 1463.
[120] Wedgwood, pp458–9.
[121] The Howard account books reveal this: *Manners and Expenses*, pp185–6, 257, 486 (1464); pp165, 287, 295, 297–8, 462, 464, 469, 471, 505, 583 (1465); 379–80, 474 (1466); 402, 420–1 (1467); *The Household Books of John, Duke of Norfolk*, pp60, 131, 192, (1481); p461, with Howard at Reigate late September 1483; p481, February 1484 when he undertook to find at his own cost 3 men and their military equipment to be ready to serve, under Howard, the king.
[122] Gairdner v, p19.   [123] Davis I, p403.

Norfolk, apart from being prized out of possession for a while during the Readeption, hung onto Caister until his death in 1476. This was despite all the pressure Sir John Paston and his brother brought to bear upon him and upon his councillors, of whom Hobart continued to be one of the most influential.[124] Sir John Paston, whatever his brother later may have thought of James, considered that he and the other councillors had dragged their feet in putting his case before their master; even after the duke was dead and the king's council affirmed the Pastons' title to Caister, Sir John had only hard words of them:

Not wythstondyng Sowthewell, James Hubberde, and Syr W. Braundon where at there owne desyryrs offryd to afferme and advowe my tytell for goode, and that my lorde off Norffolk that ded is hadde noo tytell thatt they knywe, they tolde my tale as ille as they cowde, and yit it seruyth them nott. They be knowen as they are, in cowncell be it seyde, and so most all thys letter be.[125]

It is likely to have been during the unavailing time John spent labouring to Norfolk's councillors before 1476 that he came to know James Hobart well. James may have got to know Sir Thomas Brews and thus his daughter Margery through this Mowbray connection, but by the mid-1470s James would anyway have known most men in East Anglia who were worth knowing. At any rate, and we have John's word for it, James it was who brought him and Margery together: they were married in 1477. In the unmistakable tones of a fresh spouse, whose wife is in her first pregnancy, John Paston wrote to his mother in February 1478. Not only, I think, can we sense here John's enthusiasm for his friend, but also why you might love him, even if he had not introduced you to the woman you loved. It is not just that he was a man who knew the right words; there is much more to him that that. John had been at London and talked to William Pickenham and Hobart about matters on which his mother wished for advice; Pickenham, whom we shall meet at Blythburgh, was too busy to come into Norfolk.

...he preyed Jamys that he shold in no wyse fayle to be wyth yow thys Lent. Not withstandying it was no gret ned to prey hym myche, for he told Doctore Pykenham that ther was no gentlywoman in Inglond of so lytyll aquentance as he had wyth yow that he wold be glader to do servyse on-to, and myche the glader for he purposeth fro hensforthe durying hys lyff to be a Norffolk man and to lye wyth-in ij myle of Loddon, whyche is but viij or x myle at the most fro Mautby. And in conclusyon he hathe appoyntyd to awayte on yow at Norwyche the weke next aftyr Mydlent Sonday, all the hole weke if nede be, all other maters leyd apart.'

Only when we recollect he was a Suffolk man can we appreciate the quality of his 'purposeth fro hensforthe durying hys lyff to be a Norffolk man'.[126]

It may have been about the vacant living of Oxnead that Margaret wished to be advised; one reason why James could help her was that he was 'grete with the Bisshop'.[127] This was bishop James Goldwell of Norwich whom we have discovered visiting Walberswick towards the end of his life. His chancellor was William Pickenham. In February 1479 Dr Pickenham had to write to Margaret a firm letter explaining why she could not have her young son Walter as parson of Oxnead.[128] Both he and Hobart would have had to draw on all their tact, and all their patience if they were to deal successfully with such a wilful, albeit guileless old woman.

Although the last Mowbray duke of Norfolk died in 1476, James Hobart is also to be found in the service of the first Howard duke, whom – as Sir John, then Lord Howard – he had, by 1483, served for twenty years. In 1483–4 he was Howard's steward in Suffolk; Richard Southwell, his fellow Mowbray councillor of the 1470s, was steward in Norfolk.[129] John Howard was killed at Bosworth and with him died temporarily the more grandiose ambitions of the family. The substitution of one king for another did not interrupt James' career, it may indeed have speeded it. On 1 November 1486 he was appointed Attorney-General; he was also a member of Henry VII's council and one of its most select committees, the council learned in the law.[130] He became a

[126] Davis I, pp612–13.   [127] Davis I, p183.   [128] Davis II, p365.
[129] BL, Add Charter 16559, East Anglian Receiver's Account 1483–4. They had fees of £5 each.
[130] *Select Cases in the Council of Henry VII*, ed. C. G. Bayne and W. H. Dunham Jr, Selden Society, 75 (1956), ppxxv, xxxi.

sergeant-at-law in 1501, and was knighted in 1503. His prodigious success is reflected in his spending and his giving. He lived – as he said he was going to in 1478 – at Hales near Loddon; there, only just across the Waveney from Suffolk, he built Hales Court, a substantial mansion the remains of which Pevsner 'found stimulating but tantalizing'.[131] He also built Loddon church, not just parts of it but all of it, and he or his wife gave the money for St Olave's (or Tooley's) bridge across the river, not unfittingly linking Norfolk and Suffolk.[132] Moreover he contributed towards the new council chamber in the guildhall at Norwich, of which city he was Recorder in 1496, and towards bishop Goldwell's vaulting of the choir in the cathedral there.[133] He died in 1517, as Blomefield says 'lord of many manors,' in fact no less than twenty-eight, all of which he had purchased.[134]

Hobart's testament and last will were drawn up on 27 July 1516;[135] they were, as we would expect of him, careful documents.[136] He strikes the attractive note right away: his body was to be buried in Norwich cathedral,

---

[131] *NW and S Norfolk*, p184.

[132] Blomefield IV, p241; see the 'very interesting painting' in Loddon church of James and his wife; the inscription says he built the church, she the bridge: Pevsner, *NW and S Norfolk*, p249. Nor should we forget Bacton church, Suffolk, and its inscriptions. That on the south aisle (outside below the eave) is now virtually impossible to read, but Cautley records it: 'orate pro animabus domini Jacobi Hobart et Margaretae uxoris ejus et parentum eorum'. Probably this refers (as does the inscription on the north aisle to Robert Goche and his wife) to the stone and flint panelled clerestory: it is of the very finest craftsmanship. James had lands in Bacton called 'haryngforthes', see his will: PRO, Probate 11/19, f257v.

[133] Blomefield IV, p241. He was an executor of Goldwell's, having £20, twice as much as any of the other executors: PRO, Probate 11/11, f283v.

[134] This is my count of the manors in his will. There is much other property mentioned too. As a younger son (of Thomas Hobart of Monks Eleigh, Suffolk, according to the pedigree in Blomefield IV, p241 and see also IV, pp25–6) his land had to be bought, for example, the manor of Plumstead Parva, Norfolk which he purchased on 20 June 1481 for £200. His will records many of those who sold to him; they comprise a great variety of folk. The will is a marvellous testimony to the landed estate a career in the law could bring, cf. B. H. Putnam, *The Place in Legal History of Sir William Shareshull* (1950), chapter 1, and *The Stonor Letters and Papers* I, ppxi–xvi.

[135] Proved 6 May 1517: PRO, Probate 11/19, 256ff.

[136] With so much property he was able to make ample provision for his wife and younger son. Although counting manors has long since been scorned

in the Northe side of the bodie of the saied churche as shall accorde
with my degree with oute worldly pompe or pride betwixte ij pillers
where a closinge of friese Stone of olde tyme was begonne. The which
closinge I wyll have made perfighte and finishede after the seyde
worke their apperynge in maner and fourme of a chapell in the
which I will have an awlter made for a preest to singe masse.'[137]

His worldly pomp nonetheless could not be disguised; it is to be
measured in the magnificence of his bequests. To each house of

as a pastime, here their enumeration is a useful shorthand to Hobart's good
sense. His wife Margery was to have for her life thirteen manors (and the
reversion of a fourteenth); she was also to have his considerable Norwich
property and his salthouse at Yarmouth. From this estate she was to give
Miles, the younger son, £20 annually; Miles and his wife Elen already
had one manor by way of jointure. Nine of Margery's manors were to go
to Miles and his heirs male on her death. The eldest son Walter on his
marriage to Elizabeth Heydon had been granted lands to the value of
£10, but

> 'forasmuche as that the same landis lye jontyly to the landys of the
> maner of lytyll plumsted [held by Margery] and be so medled to geder
> withe drryng up of merys and boundys that it is harde to know on
> frome oder, and for that ther shuldbe no varyaunce be twix my wyf and
> my sone water nor bytwix my sonnes nor ther heyres, my will ys that
> the same astate shalbe broken and so it is wherin ther ys none offence
> in consciens for it was doon and made by me and yett I will largely
> recompence it in this forme. I will that suche landis as I bought of John
> pulham lying besyde Bacton ner dyverse londys wiche I gave to the
> said water beyng of the yerly value of iiijli xs and my Maner of
> Lovelys and dageneys in Northwold of the yerly value of xxti marke
> wiche ar far above xli shall goo to the sayd water and to the heyres of
> the body of the said water if that he will take and accept it and this I
> doo to have rest and peace by twyx theim.'

Elizabeth had died and Walter had married again; on his marriage to
Anne, daughter of Lord Fitzwalter, they had received two manors.
By his father's gift he had had a further two manors. To these James now
added seven including Hales Hall itself. On Margery's death Walter and
his heirs were to have three of the manors granted to her for life. The
remaining two manors Margery had for life were to descend, on her death,
to Walter's son Henry and his heirs male. There is a splendid sense of
fairness about this settlement.

Margery and the executors were to have all the goods at Hales, including the growing corn; this they were to harvest and 'ley...in the Barnes
and other houses to the same maner belonging untill suche tyme as they
may have resonable utteraunce of the same'. One of the barns James
would have had in mind is the great brick barn that still serves the farm at
Hales Court. I am grateful to Mr Terence Read for showing me round one
blazing day in July 1976.
[137] All that survives is the unostentatious tomb chest without its brasses:
Pevsner, *NE Norfolk and Norwich*, p225. The chapel may once have
existed: Blomefield, IV, p26.

friars in Norwich he left £2, the same to each of five houses of nuns, including those at Bruisyard and Campsey, and 26s 8d to each of three other nunneries, including Carrow. Every house of lepers beside Norwich was to have 6s 8d and the 'ankers like rememberance'. To Mettingham College went £3 6s 8d and three books called 'Flores psalterij, and a Mantell and a masse booke which is delivered already'. His servants were not only to have their keep and wages for half a year, but £20 between them besides. To his children and their children he was just and generous; to his son Walter £100 in money, to his son Miles the same amount in money, and silver plate to the value of £40; to Walter's daughter Katherine £100 towards her marriage, to Margery, the daughter of Sir John Wiseman, a similar sum for the same purpose. Henry Hobart and James Wiseman, his grandsons, were to be helped to their learning at the discretion of his executors 'for I here say they be as yett well disposed thereto and I thynke they shall want helpe'. And, as a final example, he bequeathed to the cathedral at Norwich, because of the

...destresshinge of their ornamentes after the brennynge of suche as they hadde a sewte of vestementes the coopes for a preest deacon and subdeacon to the value of cxx li which is deliverede to that purpose and use to thonoure of god.

James was a man with far wider horizons than the merely provincial, yet how much of a provincial he was. He spoke truly when he said he intended to be a Norfolk man. None of the property he bought, and he bought freely, lay outside Norfolk and Suffolk, his pious bequests were all to churches or religious houses in those two counties, and his son and heir Walter's wives had both been the daughters of Norfolk men. One feels that, like John Paston, James was very conscious of the 'worship of Norfolk'.[138]

[138] In a famous passage John wrote to Margaret 'I pray yow ye woll send me hedir ij elne of worsted for doblettes to happe me this cold wynter, and that ye inquere where William Paston bought his tepet of fyne worsted which is almost like silk; and if that be moch fyner thanne that ye shuld bye me after vij or viijs., thanne bye me a quarter and the nayle therof for colers, thow it be derrer thanne the tother for I wold make my doblet all worsted for worship of Norffolk...': Davis I, p140. When one recollects John's usual parsimoniousness this patriotic extravagance becomes very striking.

Many of his connections were therefore with East Anglian men, particularly with his professional colleagues. One of the last services he was able to render his friend John Paston was in 1503, the year before John died, eight years after Margery's death. The service was of arbitration between John and Roger Townshend concerning the manor of East Beckham. The estate was awarded to John, he to pay Roger £100.[139] If the parties accepted it a long episode had been closed. John's brother Sir John had mortgaged East Beckham to Roger Townshend's father Sir Roger for 100 marks in the dark days of November 1469.[140] As Paston continued to borrow heavily from Townshend in the early 1470s and had to mortgage a further estate to him, that of Sporle,[141] East Beckham remained unredeemed. It must have done so until 1503. James made the award with John Yaxley. Yaxley was a Suffolk lawyer. He, Hobart, Edmund Jenny, the lawyer son of William, and Sir Henry Heydon (another lawyer son of a lawyer,[142] whose daughter Elizabeth had been married to Hobart's son and heir Walter), had been the arbitrators appointed by the king's council in 1489 to sort out the differences between Dunwich and Southwold. Poor, decayed Dunwich had few friends left; the award was that the people of Southwold were henceforth not to pay to Dunwich any customs or charges on vessels coming into the harbour, the entrance to which was shared by Dunwich and Southwold, and also by Walberswick. This time the defeat of Dunwich was made

---

[139] Davis II, p612. [140] Davis I, p410.
[141] See, for example, Davis I, p477.
[142] Sir Henry Heydon, like Sir James Hobart,, was a great builder, but unlike him bought and built outside Norfolk. He purchased West Wickham, Kent, in 1469 and built the house there in the years immediately thereafter. He rebuilt the church at West Wickham, and (apart from its west tower) that at Salthouse, Norfolk; he also completed his father's project of a great mansion at Baconsthorpe in their home county, Norfolk. The window in West Wickham church of Sir Henry as a kneeling skeleton, with above his head the Latin inscription 'Remember not O Lord our sins nor the sins of our fathers' seems so apt a text for a family of lawyers that we can only marvel at Sir Henry's perception, if indeed the window is his. See the paper by Mother Mary Gregory, 'Wickham Court and the Heydons', *Archaeologia Cantiana*, 78 (1963), pp1–21; and *Baconsthorpe Castle* (HMSO 1966). For Salthouse, see Professor W. G. Hoskins, *The Listener*, 5 February 1976, p136: 'The church at Salthouse is superb. Even when empty, it is so atmospheric that it talks to me, and, in its own way, reveals the former prosperity of the community'. *Eheu!*

final: by advice and act of parliament the king created Southwold a corporate borough.[143] The victory William Jenny and Henry Sotell had given to John Hopton and Walberswick in 1467 had been awarded too, and in a more thoroughgoing fashion, to Southwold in 1490. Dunwich was sunk by the sea, but these East Anglian lawyers helped push it under.

Two of those who did in 1489–90 were in 1490–1 receiving fees at Blythburgh. One of them, James Hobart, we have lingered over; the other was John Yaxley. He will detain us for less time. His fee was just £1, half what Hobart received.[144] He had in fact been appointed steward of the Norfolk and Suffolk lands of the Hoptons during Arthur's minority, on 18 February 1490.[145] These years were good ones for him: he sat for Ipswich in the parliament of 1491, and was made sergeant-at-law in that year or the next.[146] The faint impression we have that he was taking advantage of a minority to do well for himself, as we have noticed John Baret doing, is made stronger by a passage in the will of the third lawyer who was feed at Blythburgh in 1490–1, William Eyre. William himself took a large fee of £2 13s 4d. Moreover the Thomas Eyre, merchant of London, who was granted in February 1491, with Richard Southwell and others, the keeping of the Hopton lands during the minority, looks very much like William's brother.[147] Unlike Hobart and Yaxley, William Eyre was not of an East Anglian family. He came it seems from Buckinghamshire, and it was marriage which turned him into a Norfolk gentleman.

[143] *Rot Parl* vi, pp430–1; *CPR 1485–94*, p300.

[144] SRO, HA 30/369/281.

[145] *CPR 1485–94*, p317.

[146] Wedgwood, p978. He was really of Mellis, where he was buried, rather than of Yaxley: *CIPM Henry VII* vol ii, pp306ff; for his tomb, see *The Chorography of Suffolk*, pp103–4. He was unlucky with his eldest son: 'Item it is my last will... that Thomas myn unkynde son in consideration of his unnaturall demeanours towardes me and his moder have none of my londes ner goodes but oonly Pountrey hall and Baryngton's and that no more thereof but suche as wer my moders joyntour but Antony to be myn heir...' John set their value at no more than £12 per annum, not much for a gentleman's eldest son. Will: PRO, PCC 39 Holgrove, dated 12 May, proved 8 November 1505.

[147] *CPR 1485–94*, p334. For Thomas Eyre as William's brother, see the latter's will: PRO, PCC 16 Bennett. One of the other keepers was Sir Ralph Shelton, builder of the magnificent church at Shelton, Norfolk.

He married Elizabeth, daughter of Sir Thomas Barnardiston, and lived at Great Cressingham, where, in fine style, he lies buried.[148] In his will he wished a priest to be found to sing for the souls of his parents, Sir George Hopton's soul, the soul of Richard Bacon and the souls of all others 'which I have done wrong unto and made no restitution nor know not where to restore it'.[149] If he had made out of young Arthur Hopton's minority more than he thought he ought, he and Sir Robert Clere, as Sir George Hopton's executors, had also to go to some lengths to defend Arthur's inheritance against Sir George's widow Anne and her new husband, Sir Robert Curzon of Ipswich.[150] Certainly Thomasin trusted him, for in 1488 he was a feoffee of hers, and in 1492–3 he was supervising the bailiff's expenses at Yoxford.[151] So did the Walberswick churchwardens: at Easter 1497 they paid him £1 in fees.[152]

Someone else whom Thomasin trusted was Edmund Bowen; he was one of her executors in 1498. He had been feed (at 13s 4d per annum) as early as 1480–1, when he was one of Sir William Hopton's councillors, and he was still receiving his fee in 1490–1.[153] He was always described as 'of the Exchequer' in the accounts, in 1490–1 as 'auditor in Scaccario'. As an Exchequer officer he was already important in the mid-1470s, when he was particularly and closely associated with William, lord Hastings. John Paston wrote of him as 'a specyal frend of myn', albeit in the circumstances of awaiting payment from him at Norwich of

---

148 Blomefield III, p429. As for his Buckinghamshire origin, we should note that his father and mother were buried at Horseheath, Cambs: to the church there William left 5 marks: his will, PRO, PCC 16 Bennett.

149 *Ibid.*, dated 15 October 1507, proved July 1509. He died on 24 October 1507 according to his brass. Unlike John Yaxley with his three sons (one of them bad), he left an only daughter, Elizabeth; to her he bequeathed his 800 ewes at Cressingham, though his widow was to have the advantage and profit from them during her lifetime

150 Curzon appears to have entered Westleton forcibly on 21 March 1498, claiming Sir George had granted it to Anne for life. He and the executors also disputed other Suffolk property, a rent of £20 in Swillington, and household goods: PRO, Star Chamber 2/26/83; 2/9/241; 2/10/48, see also 2/17/36; 2/10/49, see also 2/25/144.

151 BL, Harley Charter 51 G14; SRO, HA 30/312/117.

152 *Walberswick Churchwardens' Accounts*, p71.

153 SRO, HA 30/314/18 ms7, 8, 9; HA 30/369/281.

his and his retinue's first quarter's wages in the spring of 1475.[154]
Early in the following year he mentioned him again in writing to
his brother: he wanted to borrow money from Bowen it seems,
£120 or £140, and was ready to mortgage a manor to get it.[155]
Two weeks later he wrote to Sir John with some urgency, though
possibly not on the same matter:

Syr, for Godys sake, in as hasty wyse as is possybyll send me woord
how ye feele my lord Chamberleyn and Bowen dysposed to me
wardys, for I shall neuer be in hertys ease tyll I vndyrstand ther
twoys dysposysyon.[156]

We ought to know more about this man; he has every appearance
of being one of those indispensable officials whom everyone dis-
covers he cannot do without.

He was not, however, of John Hopton's generation; nor was
William Eyre. It was Thomasin who lived long enough to put her
trust in both of them. John is unlikely to have retained an
Exchequer official, whereas Sir William would have needed to.
William Eyre would have been more John's sort of man, more his
level of lawyer than James Hobart. He did once employ a Doctor
of Laws, John Allen, in 1464–5. He may have used Dr Allen
(a man who was no well-willer to Sir John Fastolf,[157] and whom
the Pastons with reason heartily detested),[158] more than once, but
he is not likely to have had need of him often, certainly not before
1460, as until his death in that year John Ulveston, Hopton's
supervisor, was undoubtedly also his chief legal advisor. Hopton
also feed a local attorney, William Bondes, over a period of twenty

---

[154] Davis I, p593.   [155] Davis I, p598.   [156] Davis I, p599.
[157] Gairdner II, p233.
[158] He being, as they thought, one of the two principal advisors of the Duke
of Suffolk in his attack on Hellesdon and occupation of Drayton in
October 1465: Davis I, p324, and see p300. He appears also to have
caused trouble for John Paston at Norwich in September 1471: according
to news reaching Sir John at Winchester, Allen called John a traitor.
During these post-Readeption days the brothers had to watch their step:
'I pray yow be ware off yowr guyding, and in chyff off yowre langage,
so that fro hense forthe by yowr langage noo man parceyue that ye fauor
any person contrary to the Kynges plesure', counselled Sir John: Davis I,
pp440–1. Dr Allen was not one for political half-measures; friar Brackley
considered him one of the prime movers of the bill attainting the Yorkists
which was approved in the Coventry parliament of 1459: Davis II, pp210,
221.

years or more: the last we hear of William is in 1464–5, the year John employed Dr Allen.[159] William was surely just the sort of lawyer of whom the 1455 petition considered there were too many in East Anglia, one of those legal busybodies William Worcester had in mind in the *Book of Noblesse*.[160] William Bondes would certainly have been busy: he was also retained by Mettingham College and by Sibton Abbey.[161]

Such attorneys had innumerable uses, and if it is easier to see the Pastons or the Plumptons in need of their knowledge and experience of the strategy and tactics of the guerilla warfare, partisan fighting and terrorist activity which comprised fifteenth century litigation, there was nonetheless a good deal that a John Hopton, free of large legal problems as he was, needed to know from the likes of Bondes or Ulveston, How to get out of being made a knight was not the only thing.[162] The powers of a Justice of the Peace were not known to every gentleman who was on the commission; Sir William Stonor, for instance, seized grain which was being hoarded; evidently not entirely sure of his conduct he wrote to his legal advisor; he was told that he could not do such a thing, and must release the corn, 'but I wold not ye confessid yourself to thaym that ye have mys don in that case'.[163] It is for this that you paid these men: to avoid making a fool of yourself, or if you had, either to get away with it or out of it. There were other tasks too which even the most retiring of gentlemen could not escape: the shrievalty, for example, which John Hopton endured twice, or (less prestigious but no less onerous) the escheatorship. John was never escheator; Robert Clere in 1444 was: William Bondes was his deputy and, one feels certain, just as committed as his master to the arrangement of a return favourable to the Pastons by the jury of inquisition held after the death of judge William Paston.[164] Bondes clearly was closer to the Clere family

---

[159] SRO, HA 30/314/14; HA 30/369/46 f10v; HA 30/314/18 m2.
[160] Pp77–8.
[161] Mettingham: BL, Add MS 33986, fs9, 136: 1448–9 and 1456–7, his fee increasing in the interval from 6s 8d to 10s; Sibton: SRO, HA 50/9/15/7/1 f37v, a fee of 6s 8d. From Hopton he had 13s 4d.
[162] SRO, HA 30/314/18 m2.
[163] *The Stonor Letters and Papers*, II, p59.
[164] Davis II, p24.

than he was to that of John Hopton.[165] He did not, however, live
long enough to draw up the marriage alliance between them:
Sir William Hopton's daughter Anne married Sir Robert Clere,
yet another lawyer, almost certainly after Bondes disappears from
view in the mid-1460s.[166]

The making of marriage and other settlements occupied a great
part of these solicitors' time. What made a settlement was of
course not knowledge of the law – affection or distaste, trust or
distrust, necessity or greed were mainly the makings – but men
who knew the law had to give these untidy things legal shape.
It is no cause for surprise, although William Worcester and the
petitioners of 1455 thought it cause for alarm, that in such a great
age of settlements and trusts there was an abundance of men
whose living was got by making, administering, and trying to
break them. It is therefore not a matter for wonder (or concern)
that John Hopton employed so many lawyers. For while he was
not forever battling in the court, he had always settlements to
make, sometimes perhaps complicated, as when he married
Thomasin, at other times perhaps more simple, as when he
married off his sons and daughters. Not only did lands have to be
settled, they also had to be managed, and the men on them had to
be managed too, particularly during a time when rents were not
easy to collect, in full at any rate. Here, where negotiation –
even solicitation – was required, the skills of these professional
persuaders, the men of law, were essential.[167] Thus it was as his
supervisor that John Hopton employed his lawyer neighbour
John Ulveston of Henham for fifteen years or more.[168]

165 See the will of Edmund Norman of Filby, Norfolk, in Gairdner, II, p67:
Edmund, William Bondes and the brothers Robert and Edmund Clere
were, on this testimony, closely connected. Bondes was also a feoffee of
Edmund and Robert Clere: *ibid.* IV, p105; *Cal Anc Deeds* IV, A7758,
7774, 7857, 7874.
166 Was the journey of Hopton's bailiffs John Hoo and Ellis Lumhals to
Yarmouth and Ormesby in 1465–6 concerned with matters connected
with either the Clere family, who lived at Ormesby, or William Bondes?
Bondes was probably recently dead and he almost certainly came from
these parts. See: SRO, HA 30/314/18 m3.
167 A good example of a gentleman's legal advisor pleading on behalf of one
of his farmers, apparently against the steward, is Richard Page to Sir
William Stonor: *The Stonor Letters and Papers* II, pp85–6.
168 Wedgwood, p895, has him of 'Debenham'; he is, however, more generally

Ulveston, attached to the Suffolk claque in the 1440s and thus a royal servant, we have come across before. On the commission of the peace with Hopton, and of the quorum, he can have had ample opportunity to instruct his more innocent fellow justice.[169] What he did for Hopton as his supervisor in the 1440s, like the fee he received for the office, was small change however compared with his activity on behalf of his more influential employers, and what he got for that. The £1 fee he took from John Hopton from 1444 or earlier is to be measured, for example, against the fee of £10 which he had as steward of the dowager Duchess of Suffolk ten years later.[170] Of course, the hazards were slighter, the risks slimmer; when you worked for the great and gathered, so to say, the crumbs which fell from their table, you risked the table being cleared away all of a sudden. The leavings and pickings ceased for John Ulveston in 1450. When Suffolk's richly burdened, overladen table crashed, among the wreckage was John. He was omitted from the commission of the peace in October of that year and in the following two months was accused, frequently maliciously no doubt, of a variety of misdemeanours, as is the normal fate of those who have fallen from power.[171] His connection with the

called 'of Henham', for example in the 1450 King's Bench proceedings and in his pardon of 1455: in Wedgwood read H for B. He purchased the manor of Cravens in Henham from his brother-in-law, William Micklefield of Blyford, sometime after 1441; he had already acquired Mickfield itself from him by that date. Mickfield lies beside Debenham: Ulveston Hall is still there on the map.

[169] They were also together on other commissions: *CPR 1441–6*, p463; *CPR 1452–61*, pp302, 517, 560.

[170] BL, Egerton Charter 8779. He was probably a de la Pole officer or councillor before that: in the course of the accounting year, 1450–1, the de la Pole East Anglian receiver-general, Andrew Griggs, once was delivered money 'per manus John Ulveston': Staffs RO, Jerningham Papers, D641/3, packet 5, Costessey Accounts 29–30 Henry VI.

[171] R. L. Storey, *The End of the House of Lancaster* (1966), p218. Memories were long and had no doubt been worked up into travesties of truth: at Beccles on 7 December 1450, for example, he, Robert Micklefield of Blyford, his brother-in-law, and a Westleton husbandman were accused of maltreating and wounding three men at that place on 12 October 1440; Ulveston alone (but originally with John Tasburgh, the John Tasburgh who was probably Ulveston's successor as Hopton's supervisor, whose name however was crossed through), on 6 May 1443 at Gorleston was stated to have obtained money from various men by menaces, and from John Davy of Yarmouth, merchant, he wrung (by threats of death and

duke's widow survived, but the exciting days were over; he was gladder now to have his £1 a year from that undisturbed Justice of the Peace John Hopton. He remained his supervisor until his death in 1460.

Although the impression we may have given of him is of a small fish who for a little time swam successfully in a very large pond, Ulveston was, so far as Suffolk society went, a rather superior person. He was after all John Ulveston esquire, Member of Parliament, albeit for a borough, receiver of Eton College (a crumb from the table if ever there was one), a lawyer and a gentleman.[172] While, therefore, he was quite prepared as escheator (like Robert Clere and every other escheator) to tamper with a jury of inquisition,[173] did he really have enough knowledge of the

mutilation) an obligation of £2. More likely, if only because it was both more recent and its detail was more circumstantial, was what we might call the Buxlow incident of 20 July 1450. The detail is worth giving for what it tells us of the stained glass of a long ruined church of a long deserted village: Buxlow since 1721 has been part of Knodishall parish. John was accused of being one, probably the principal one of the maintainers of Robert Drane, franklin, and John Drane, husbandman, of Buxlow, who broke into their parish church and smashed
'quandam fenestram vitream Cancelli Ecclesie predicte orientalem... vocatem le Glaswyndowe ad valenciam v li. in qua quidem fenestra quedam ymago cum tunica armorum Willelmi Bokele armigeri nuper veri patroni Ecclesie predicte ac quedam ymago cum tunica armorum Johannis Bokele armigeri quondam eciam veri patroni Ecclesie illius filii et heredis predicti Willelmi Bokele armigeri antecessorum Willelmi Jenney quorum heres ipse est nunc veri patroni eiusdem Ecclesie ac quoddam scutum armorum predictorum tempore Regis Edwardi tercii in perpetuam memoriam ipsorum Willelmi Bokele et Johannis Bokele posita et confecta fuerunt... '
As there was little love lost between Jenny and Ulveston perhaps there was some justice in Jenny's accusation; on the dorse, after all, are the words 'vera billa', so the jury thought so. But would the Dranes need to be put up to it, or did they have it in for Jenny on their own account? Might not their new landlord have given them grievances? Was it now that the 'depopulation' began at Buxlow? All this is in PRO, KB 9/267 fs13, 14, 18.

172 Wedgwood, p895.
173 This at any rate is what Fastolf wished to indict him for in 1450, 'foryete not Ulveston, Andreus, and the othyrs that forged a fals office to cast my maner of Bradwell yn to the Kyngs hand': to Howes and Bocking, 4 December 1450: Gairdner II, p194 (cf. the abstract printed on the preceding page). I take it that this relates to Ulveston's term as escheator, 1442–4, and Fastolf only now dared to raise the matter (or took the opportunity to make this charge).

lands at Easton Bavents to draw up new arrangements with the farmers in 1459–60?[174] Was he not, in other words, a little too grand to be Hopton's supervisor? Was he in turn advised, say when he was negotiating the Easton Bavents leases, by others of Hopton's council, who knew better about farming that sandy, crumbling coastline? Yet we are probably making too much of Ulveston as a lawyer and a gentleman, and we would probably place him better if we described him as a man of business, expert in, or at least thoroughly familiar with the administrative and financial as well as the legal aspects of estate management. If he was appointed receiver of Eton College, then it was as a skilled businessman that he was appointed. For running estates efficiently was a business. If landowners themselves were not businesslike – and although so many gentlemen were seeing that they had to be and getting the training for it at those schools of business studies, the Inns of Court, there were others who had neither inclination, aptitude nor ability for it – then businessmen had to be brought in to do it for them. Hence, we suspect, John Hopton's reliance on John Ulveston and others. Nonetheless there is more to estate management than the analysis of accounts and the drafting of valors. There remain always the men, who have to be managed, and the land itself, which has to be intimately known. John Ulveston may have had a winning way with yeomen and husbandmen, and been able to conjure crops from the most recalcitrant clay, yet we cannot imagine it. He seems somehow too distant from the soil, we do not detect very much on his boots, we find it not easy indeed to detect, on the receiver of Eton College, boots at all. With John Tasburgh however, it is otherwise.

Tasburgh became supervisor on Ulveston's death. We are given uninformative glimpses of him at work at Blythburgh and at Easton Bavents in the 1460s.[175] We have no record of his fee; employed many years before in 1448–9 by Mettingham College

---

[174] SRO, V5/19/1/15: the new agreements were on a bill attached to the account roll. The bill has disappeared.
[175] SRO, HA 30/314/18, ms1–4; V5/19/1/16, 1461–2; V5/19/1/17. He in fact held the Christmas court at Blythburgh in 1460: SRO, HA 30/369/397.

he received 10s.[176] It is his will of 1473 which enables us to know
him at all.[177] He was of St Peter's parish, South Elmham, and in
the chapel of the Virgin on the north side of the church of St Peter
he was buried.[178] His formal pious bequests were not extravagant:
towards the glazing of a window 'in the west ende of the stepille',
and for the making of an alabaster reredos at St Peter's; small
sums, with a manual and a processional, to the church at Flixton;
to the church of Ilketshall St Margaret 'ten qwayers of a grayle
redy wretyn' and 6s 8d 'to make with the seyd grayle'; to St
Michael's, South Elmham 3s 4d; and to each of the other parish
churches of Elmham 1s 8d. To the poor of each of these places
1s 8d was to be distributed. He took longer over the distribution of
his lands. His one manor of Boys he left to Margery his wife, with
remainder to his son Thomas. Margery also was to have for life a
meadow and two closes; these on her death were to go to Thomas
too. If she did not remarry she was to have a newly built house
with its lands, meadows and closes, some of which John had
purchased, and these were to be hers to do with as she pleased.
If she did not remain a widow his executors were to sell them to
provide for masses and other charitable works pleasing to God and
profitable for his soul. For the immediate provision of a priest to
sing in the chapel where his body was to be buried Margery was
granted various tenements, some of them in the West town at
Yamouth; but this property was also entrusted to her 'to fyndyn
Raf' Toppesfeld younger to skoole'. We are faced here, as we
have been so frequently before, by that concern with education
which is such a mark of the society we are exploring. Moreover,
it is so incidental a reference: John Tasburgh was trying to ensure
that the young Ralph Toppesfield would have what presumably
he had provided for his own sons, a good schooling.[179]

[176] Mettingham accounts: BL, Add MS 33986 f9.
[177] NRO, Norwich Cons. Court, Reg. Gelour, f27v. The month is left blank;
proved in October.
[178] For his tomb, see *The Chorography of Suffolk*, p88.
[179] Unless only the youngest of the five, destined to be a priest, like Ralph
perhaps, went to school. This was Edward, admitted to a degree at
Cambridge in 1473–4, Bachelor of Canon Law 1479. He became rector of
Barningham, Suffolk, in 1481, vicar of Assington, Suffolk, in 1494:
Emden, *Biog Reg Camb*.

Margery then, with all John's moveable possessions as well, was adequately provided for. Thomas was left directly John's chief messuage, lands, tenements, meadows, pasture, 'fedyngs', and woods, which were held of the Duke of Norfolk, and pieces of land recently bought from John Manning. As between Thomas and Margery there seems to have been a rough equality, though for his father's one manor Thomas would have to be patient. All the properties left to Thomas and those which were to fall to him on Margery's death, were left to him and his male heirs. Remainder then was to the next son Edmund and his heirs male, then to John, the next son, and his, then to the fourth son Robert and his, and finally to the last son Edward, the celibate cleric. These younger sons got not a great deal more than remainders.[180] One of them, Robert, got nothing more. Edmund however was left £20, John was to have property in St Peter's Parmintergate parish, Norwich, and Edward received his father's religious books: 'my best portewos a grayel a processionarii with a primer'. Anne, the only daughter named, was to have £40, so long as she was obedient to her mother and married after her advice. So much for the family.

There were a few others to remember too. Elis Lumhals, Hopton's bailiff at Yoxford in the 1460s and 1470s, an executor with John Hoo, the Blythburgh bailiff, of Tasburgh's will, and quite clearly a friend, was commended to John's feoffees: they were to make a lawful estate to Elis, Agnes his wife, and their heirs according to a charter 'to hym ther of plenely mad'. There was also William Ruste. He was to have for life 3 acres of land with a house; after his death the house was to be for 'pore folkys to dwelle in withowte ende', and the 3 acres were to return to the Tasburgh family, the proceeds from them to be used for the maintenance of the house. If in sentiment such provision for the poor is familiar enough, its form is unusual. A single almshouse kept in repair by the donor's descendants was a small and novel enterprise, particularly as John laid no obligations of prayers for his soul upon the poor folk of South Elmham who might live in

---

[180] Also, of any properties which Margery or the executors might sell, John's children were to have first and reasonable offer.

this house he sought to provide for them; also he put all his trust in future generations of Tasburghs to see that this somewhat secular, informal arrangement worked. One wonders whether it did and for how long. Not being at all connected with prayers for the dead, the Tasburgh poorhouse should have survived, if it then still existed, the holocaust of charitable institutions made in the 1540s. Surely it deserved to.

Although we can come at John Tasburgh a little way in his will, we cannot arrive at him at all where we would most want to, at his work. Dare we fancy John as sharp about his business as Chaucer's reeve? Was it John, for example, who detected the need for change at Easton Bavents, he who initiated the new policy? We can be pretty sure that the comfortable life his will displays was obtained by the exercise of such skills as he shared with that Norfolk reeve of Chaucer's:

> And he could judge by watching drought and rain
> The yield he might expect from seed and grain.[181]

After all, if the supervisor could not judge such things, who else on Hopton's council would?

The answer might be most of them including Hopton himself. One who almost certainly would have been able to was 'old Banyard of Sibton Abbey',[182] for Robert Banyard was involved in the decisions made at Easton Bavents in 1470–1, 'evidence' on which those decisions were taken being in his custody when he died some time during 1471–2.[183] By then he had spent over thirty years advising Hopton. Possibly one of his first pieces of advice had been to buy Easton Bavents, as he was a feoffee at its purchase in the mid-1430s.[184] He acted in the same capacity at the acquisition of Cockfield Hall in 1440,[185] and was at an early stage also a feoffee for much of Hopton's other Suffolk property,

181 *The Canterbury Tales*, translated N. Coghill (Penguin, 1951), pp41–2.
182 As John Paston called him in 1464, Davis I, p527.
183 The bailiff was rewarded with 3s 4d 'pro evidencia nuper in custodia Roberti Banyard scrutanda et domino fideliter liberanda': SRO, V5/19/1/16, 1472–3. Record of Robert's activity ceases in 1471.
184 Copinger II, pp62–3. A Robert Banyard was at Lincoln's Inn in 1423 (for his first Christmas). Was this him? *Lincoln's Inn Admissions Register* I, p4.
185 SRO, HA 30/369/180; HA 30/369/124.

outliving all of his fellows.[186] Some twenty years later, in 1461–2, he is detected visiting Easton with his master, and a couple of years after that he rode to Eye with Walter Fulbourne, the auditor, to discuss business with the young Duke of Suffolk.[187] In the years between we can only guess at what services he performed as Hopton's councillor, or for that matter as the councillor of others besides Hopton.[188] By the early 1460s he was regarded as having sufficient experience of Suffolk society to be appointed a collector of a parliamentary subsidy, of which John Hopton was an assessor,[189] and to be consulted by Margaret Paston as to who in that county might as jurors in a court of law speak up for her husband in the case of trespass brought against him by William Jenny. When Margaret broached this to him, 'he knew non that wold pase vpon the mater at his desyir' but could name 'dyuers...whyche he kowd thynk wold pase vpon it at yowr [John Paston's] desyir if ye spak wyth hem youyrselue'. This is the authentic voice of an agent of, not an actor in county society.[190] He was nonetheless a gentleman, or was called such in February 1457,[191] and although he was described as of Sibton both by the Pastons and the patent roll clerk of 1463, it was not there but at Spexhall, next to John Hopton's Wissett estate, where he owned a manor, that of Banyards.[192] At Spexhall his father Richard died and was buried in 1441.[193] He left money to the brothers of the guild at Wissett, where Robert rented property from John Hopton, as Robert's son did after him.[194] Is not Robert another of

---

[186] BL, Harley Charter 45 F41.
[187] SRO, V5/19/1/16, 1461–2; HA 30/314/18 m1.
[188] He too was feed by Mettingham College in 1456–7: BL, Add MS 33986, f136.
[189] *CPR 1461–7*, p104.   [190] Davis I, p527.
[191] *CCR 1454–61*, p282.   [192] Copinger II, p158.
[193] His will: SRO, Reg. 1, f144 dated 21 May, proved 15 June.
[194] SRO, HA 30/50/22/8/3; in 1473 Henry: SRO, HA 30/369/294; in 1479 Thomas, perhaps Robert's grandson: SRO, HA 30/369/31. Robert's wife had been Margaret, daughter of Thomas Knevet of Norfolk: in his will of 1458 Thomas made bequests to her, the wife of Robert Baynard esq. (PRO, Probate 11/4). That our Robert's wife was a Margaret would possibly explain Copinger's error in confusing her with Robert's daughter Margaret, who married John Bacon of Baconsthorpe, Norfolk (Blomefield, III, p708). John Bacon refers to Margaret Banyard, 'matri mee', in his will of 1462; he is referring to his mother-in-law, and his bequest to her of a

those indispensable men of business whom we have encountered before, and whom indeed we meet at every turn in the England of the later Middle Ages? Of those who are marvellously successful, of those who become indispensable to lords and princes we hear much, but of the Banyards and Bondes of this world, who serve esquires and gentlemen, and whose own gentility is possibly precarious, we are lucky to hear anything. Of Robert Banyard we have one rare glimpse, and it is of him doing what he spent so much of his time doing, what he was paid for, and what he was good at: giving his opinion. Of the countless other men like him so little survives.

Of John Grickis, however, Hopton's auditor in 1477–8, collector of Sibton Abbey rents at Norwich in Richard III's reign, retained by Mettingham College for more than thirty-five years,[195] something tangible does remain. It is the terrier or drag of the Westleton manors, a paper book in 96 folios bound in parchment,[196] which took him five weeks to compile in 1478.[197] Before the sixteenth century we seldom learn who are the authors of estate documents. In John Grick's case we know nothing of the man, but we do have his book to remember him by, and even at a range of five hundred years, it is testimony to the skill as a surveyor of this man of business whom one employer retained for a generation. For how long he served John Hopton we do not know; in 1477–8 Hopton was paying another auditor besides Grickis, a man who had been for a generation *his* auditor and sub-steward.

silver salt immediately follows his bequest to his father-in-law Robert of an overcoat of marten fur (NRO, Norwich Cons. Court, Reg. Brosiard, f304ff, dated 10 July, proved 25 November); Robert and John Banyard, with the elder John Paston, were John Bacon's trustees for certain estates, the revenues of which were to be set aside to send John Bacon's son Thomas to school. In 1474 John Banyard of Norwich left to Margaret, who was presumably his niece, a silver vessel ('cratera') with a cover 'sculpata cum heyrons'; on her death it was to descend to her son Thomas Bacon and his heirs 'in perpetuum' (NRO, Norwich Cons. Court, Reg. Gelour, fs56v–58, dated 6 March, proved 7 June 1474).
195 SRO, HA 30/22/11/3 at a fee of £1; Denney, p33 (SRO, HA 50/9/15/7/1 f49v); Mettingham accounts: BL, Add MS 33986, f9; MS 33987 f203v: 1479–80, fee 33s 4d; MS 33988 f43: 1483–4, fee 40s.
196 SRO, HA 30/50/22/27/7(1).
197 SRO, HA 30/22/11/3.

Walter Fulbourne had been feed as far back as 1444–5. We can trace him in the 1460s busy at Easton Bavents or at Blythburgh, receiving a livery of cloth, and (perhaps dressed in it) riding to Eye with Robert Banyard, or with William Bondes disposing of the threat of knighthood that hung over their master. In 1469–70 we have our first indication of his full annual fee: £2 13s 4d, charged on the Westleton account.[198] Then in 1477–8 we find not only Grickis feed at £1, and Walter's fee, perhaps as a result, reduced to 26s 8d, but also that Walter's thirty years' court keeping for Mettingham College has come to an end.[199] Perhaps illness or more possibly work for others more grand had prevented Walter doing all he had done before for John or the College,[200] for his Mettingham colleague John Grickis, no younger than he, went on there for years yet, and was called in to assist him in Hopton's service. Walter received his diminished fee in the immediately succeeding years. He did not die until 1489. One wonders whether the arrangement of 1478 pleased the two men, or alternatively was the occasion for friction. It ought not to have been on Fulbourne's part for he was a religious, though not necessarily a charitable, man. His will demonstrates that, and thus we are enabled to know more about him than about John Grickis. Yet one thing the two men share, for Fulbourne also has left us a visible remembrance of himself, though it has been more trifled and tampered with than the Westleton terrier. It is the brick south aisle which he built onto his parish church of Wickham Market, and in which his body was buried.[201] His will has a great deal to say about this mortuary chapel and the services which were to be chanted there for his soul.

It was dated 3 October 1489 and was proved on 29 Novem-

198 SRO, HA 30/369/393; V5/19/1/17, 1465–6; HA 30/314/18 ms1, 2, 3; HA 30/314/10.
199 BL, Add MS 33986, fs9, 129; MS 33987, f168; at f183v John Everard has taken Walter's place.
200 He was, for instance, both a feoffee and an executor of Sir John Wingfield in 1481 (PRO, C140/81/59; SRO, HA 30/50/22/1/8(16)) and had been present at Sir John's election as knight of the shire for Suffolk in December 1477: see below, p210.
201 Pevsner, *Suffolk*, p453. There are nineteenth-century windows; there is no trace of his tomb and little sense of what church and chapel were like before the last century.

ber.[202] It is solely a religious document. So far as provision for his
widow went, and the disposal of his lands was concerned, his
feoffees might see to that; we can be assured that not only would
the settlements he had made have been adequate, they would have
been as secure as this man of law in his lifetime could have made
them. We may be pretty certain too, that he and his wife were
childless. It was this sorrow which allowed him to be so occupied
with his own soul and to be free with his town property to provide
for it and the mausoleum where his and his wife's bodies would lie.
He gave to Thomas Gerling of Wickham Market and his heirs the
new tenement which he had built in the town, under condition
that annually and forever £1 would be paid to his executors and
those to whom they assigned this charge. Ten shillings of that was
to go each year to the nuns at Campsey to celebrate the anniversaries of his and his wife's deaths. Three shillings and fourpence
was to be given to the churchwardens at Wickham for the same
celebration in Fulbourne's chapel, Walter specifying how they
were to distribute it: 8d to the vicar, 2d to the parish clerk, 1s 8d
to the choir, and so on; and the remaining 6s 8d the churchwardens were to spend on five wax candles, each of 5lbs, which
were to be lit on certain high festivals, all carefully and character-
istically listed. Any of the 6s 8d left over was to go to the repair
of the chapel. Walter also set down the services which were to be
sung at his interment and for the thirty days thereafter. For the
time which stretched beyond that handful of days he had also
taken as careful precaution as a man of law might: he had entered
into indentures with the two priests who were his chaplains for the
masses they were to sing to assist his and his wife's soul in their
ordeal. John Cade, 'capellanus meus', was to have a salary of £6
a year and the chamber with the sitting room ('solar') over it and
the garden beside it, which lay at the south end of the new hall
Fulbourne had built to the east of the churchyard; in return Cade
was to pray for the salvation of Walter and Katherine's souls and
to keep his rooms in good repair. William Clerk, also 'capellanus

---

[202] SRO, Reg. 3, f89v. It is in a poor hand with an unusual number of
erasures, corrections, interlineations and a large omission rectified by an
entry at the foot of the folio. I hope I have the gist of it accurately.

meus', was to have 8 marks a year to perform the same service; where he lodged, however, was his own affair. The two priests were to use in their celebrations the missal, chalice, vestments, antiphoner and ornaments, with which Walter and Katherine had furnished their chapel. For the better security of them 'intitulata in meo missale': a touch we might have anticipated from this man. So much then for the Fulbourne chapel of Jesus and St Mary, a foundation where as little was left to chance as a man with a lifetime's experience of the law could devise.[203]

Others besides Cade and Clerk and the sisters at Campsey were to pray for Walter and Katherine's souls. Those others were the canons of Leiston Abbey. Walter bequeathed to the abbot and the convent the profits of his lands in the fields of Glevering in order that the anniversaries of his and his wife's deaths should be celebrated at the abbey. They would also surely remember him for his generosity to them in another way, every time (he might reasonably have expected) that they turned their faces towards the high altar, for he bequeathed them £10 in money, furniture and plate, to have made within four years of his death two tabernacles, one of the Virgin, the other of St Thomas of Canterbury, which were to stand upon it. The nuns at Campsey would also perhaps recall him, at other times than on the anniversary of his death, and at other places than at the high altar, as he left to their refectory pewter and six silver spoons, and to their infirmary two beds, though for the latter they would have to wait until his wife had died. Every sister too was left 2s, each having therefore double the cause for grateful remembrance that the canons at Leiston, left only 1s apiece, had. Finally, and we hope with affection (possibly as they spent it), the members of the Framlingham guild may have remembered him, for to them he left 6s 8d.

It is easy enough to think how typical all this is of a well-to-do and childless solicitor in the England of 1489: it is what we might expect. Yet on closer examination it is only half of what we

---

203 The familiarly possessive 'my chaplain', the terms of the indentures, and the whole tone of reference to the chapel in the will, indicate that it had not only been built before 1489 but also that it was being used as a family chapel, served perhaps by Cade from the Fulbourne house across the churchyard.

have come to expect: where are the good works? The piety is self-centred, the preoccupation is with prayers. This is not to say Walter was a selfish man, for about that we cannot speak, but that he was single-minded in his devotion to the salvation of his soul is a conclusion we can reach. Through the conventional expressions of that devotion, or rather *in* those conventions themselves, is not a passionately religious man to be discerned? It is perhaps what Walter Fulbourne did not do in his will that gives us our clue to his character.

Was it, one wonders, a character that drew any sympathetic note from John Hopton? Over thirty years of rubbing along together suggests some sort of harmony, even if they never got beyond talking shop. Yet in an association which lasted so long they must have got further than knowing only how to cope with each other over the annual audit of the estates.

How far did John get with those other agents of his who also often served him for many years at a stretch, his bailiffs? With Nicholas Greenhagh, for example, who bought him hats and sold him horses, or with John Hoo, at whose house he ate and drank in the mid-1450s?[204] How did these men get on with each other? What did John Hoo and Elis Lumhals do for pleasure at Christmas 1463 in London, after they had delivered their master's money safely?[205] One December day fourteen years later they were together again and we can be sure on this occasion had a good time, as they were in familiar company. At Ipswich on Monday 15 December 1477, 'circa horam undecimam ante nonam' Sir John Wingfield and John Broughton esquire were elected knights of the shire for the county. Among the electors were Elis and John, Walter Fulbourne, James Hobart, Robert Payn and John Everard (both of whom we shall shortly encounter), and John Bishop, an attorney Hopton was employing at this time.[206] Hopton himself was not there, but some of his friends, Sir John Heveningham and Henry Wentworth for instance, as well as his

204 SRO, HA 30/369/46 fs21v, 70, 102v.
205 SRO, HA 30/314/18 m1.
206 He received 13s 6d out of the Westleton issues during the accounting year 1477–8: SRO, HA 30/22/11/3.

officers, were.[207] If the successful candidates spent as much as Sir John Howard and Thomas Brews esquire had on their election as the county's knights of the shire ten years before, then Elis and John would have sat down to a splendid feast. On 20 April 1467 8 oxen, 24 calves, 24 sheep, 30 pigs, 108 capons, 120 rabbits, and 140 pigeons, among other things, were consumed, and 20 barrels of strong beer, 16 of small beer, and nearly £4 worth of wine were drunk. To prepare the banquet in the kitchens, under the supervision of 4 chief cooks, had toiled the hired help: 12 labourers and 6 lads. The cost to Howard and Brews was £40:[208] getting into parliament was (as always) an expensive business. We have, however, left Elis Lumhals and John Hoo too far behind us.

These two were also on good terms with the man who oversaw their labours on their master's behalf, for they were, as we have noticed, the executors of John Tasburgh's will in 1473, and Tasburgh left land to Lumhals. Did Elis also get along with John Lunneys, who rented a little property at Yoxford,[209] and who was the bailiff of the Duke of Norfolk's neighbouring estate of Kelsale?[210] As men with similar responsibilities perhaps they compared notes and shared grievances over their drink; but where? At Yoxford, at Kelsale? Perhaps sometimes they went to Dunwich, at the invitation of the Westleton bailiff, Robert Vincent,[211]

207 PRO, C219/17, part 3 no. 70. Could Sir John Wingfield's wife's visit to Westwood this year have been connected with the election? Hopton's employees (or whatever we want to call them) had turned out in force.
208 *Manners and Expenses*, pp398–400. I owe this reference to Mr Victor Gray at the Suffolk Record Office, who realized with a logic which was beyond me that Wedgwood's meaningless Ipswich Account Books (*Register*, p358, footnote) could be the Howard Account Books. There were 47 named electors (PRO, C219/17, part 1 no. 79); surely more than that number were required to eat and drink these quantities.
209 The 1471 terrier: SRO, HA 30/369/1/ fs5, 13v.
210 In 1483–4: BL, Add Charter 16559.
211 He was bailiff in 1477–8 when he was busy with John Grickis and Robert Payn about the making of the terrier: SRO, HA 30/22/11/3. In the very same year he headed the list of those tenants who had provided information for the drawing up of a new extent of Mettingham College's manor in Bramfield: BL, Stowe MS 934, f43. He would almost certainly have been working with Grickis here too, for Grickis was also the Mettingham college auditor. Exactly thirty years before Grickis had received £2 13s 4d

for Robert, one of the foremost tenants at Yoxford,[212] and a tenant too at Sibton and Bramfield,[213] was bailiff at Dunwich in the 1460s.[214] He was therefore a man of broader experience. Yet they were all men of broad experience. They were men, one feels, who could be relied on, the pillars of these communities of north east Suffolk. Hopton, for one, relied on them: in a transaction concerning the Yoxford manor of Brendfen in 1476 his attorneys were Richard Coppeshurst (whom we have met before),[215] Robert Payn, Robert Vincent, Elis Lumhals and John Hoo.[216] Still, however much Hopton and others depended upon them, however real his friendship with them or theirs for each other, however vivid their personalities, they are no more than names to us. We cannot breathe life into them, we have no means of raising them from oblivion. Our single and small consolation is that the mere listing of their names is a bede-roll which does some justice to them.

Only with one of them may we go the slightest way beyond that. Robert Payn seems to have been one of the most versatile of them all, at any rate in Hopton's service, and we have a brief, sad will. Robert was bailiff of Westleton in 1469–70; he was also on Hopton's household staff, for his fee of just over £3 covered his work in that capacity too.[217] In the 1470s we find him frequently at Easton Bavents, clearing up the situation there in 1470–1, renewing the Covehithe rental in 1472–3, enquiring about rents in 1475–6 and with John Hoo and Elis Lumhals discussing matters that lay between Hopton and Richard Cook and others. In 1477–8 he it was who sorted out the cash liveries and testified to the arrears of the demesne farmer John Deynes before the auditors when they came round after Hopton's death in autumn 1478.[218] He was called then the lord's clerk, and in another place, clerk of the lord's kitchen. That year too he was testifying to the

for making an extent of the same Mettingham manor: BL, Add MS 33986, f9.
[212] He was paying a rent of 28s 7d for land, closes and pasture in 1471: SRO, HA 30/369/1 f3.
[213] Of Sibton Abbey at Sibton, Denney, p105; of Mettingham College at Bramfield, see note 211 above.
[214] Gardner, *Dunwich*, p80.   [215] See above, p121.
[216] BL, Harley Charter 51 G13.   [217] SRO, HA 30/314/10.
[218] SRO, V5/19/1/16.

demesne farmers' arrears at Blythburgh, and receiving 6s 8d as payment for his office as sheep reeve.[219] Moreover, he had been at Westleton only a few months before with John Grickis and Robert Vincent going round the fields and farms gathering information for the new terrier; he it was who presented the bill of their expenses to the auditors. At Michaelmas indeed he took over as bailiff there from Robert Vincent.[220] He had already been, during that hectic year 1477–8, bailiff of Westhall; now, in the years immediately after John Hopton's death, he continued as bailiff of Westleton and Westhall, and of Thorington, while in addition supervising the farmer of Pirnhow and the bailiff of Ellingham: it was he who kept their accounts and carried the money they owed William Hopton to John Hoo at Blythburgh.[221] He seems to have been as indispensable to William during his first years in control of the estates as Richard Daniel had been to William's father during his.

In 1481 Robert leased the Westhall manor house and the adjoining 32 acres of enclosed arable and pasture. If he lived there then, when he died five years later he made his will at Wrentham,[222] in Wrentham church he desired to be buried, and to the poor of Wrentham he called upon his executors to distribute corn after his death. The only property he mentions, moreover, is his tenement at Wrentham; he left that, his nineteen cows, and all his other stock and grain to Joan his wife. Upon her death the holding was to go to her son Robert Hyde. Robert Payn does not seem to have had much, nor had he any children to leave that little to. Can this undemonstrative Robert Payn be the bustling Hopton official of a few years before? One thing only connects them but it seems decisive: Robert Payn of Wrentham required John Everard, priest, to pray for half a year in Wrentham church for his soul, those of his parents, benefactors, and friends, and of all the faithful dead. It was John Everard, priest, who received by

219 SRO, V5/19/1/16, 1477–8; HA 30/314/18 m5.
220 SRO, HA 30/22/11/3.
221 SRO, HA 30/369/31; HA 30/314/18 m1; HA 30/50/22/20/9(13); HA 30/369/39.
222 NRO, Norwich Cons. Court, Reg. Aubry, f97v, dated 12 July 1486, proved 12 January 1487.

command of John Hopton six yards of cloth in 1477–8, who was a feoffee of Thomasin's in 1488 (with the Blythburgh bailiff who had brought him his cloth in 1477–8, John Hoo),[223] and whom Thomasin in her will wished to have to sing for her soul for a year. This John Everard,[224] who appears to link Robert Payn of Wrentham to the Hoptons, brings us to those clerics with whom John and his family associated.

Both the type of cleric and the sort of association with each varied enormously. On the one hand there was, for example, Clement Rollesby, vicar of Yoxford, on the other Dr William Pickenham, archdeacon of Suffolk (and much else). Clement for one thing was a rent collector; William, among other things, collected benefices; and whereas the clever doctor will occupy us for a good while, the obscure parson we can quickly deal with, so demonstrating how perverse a process the turning of the past into history can be. Clement became vicar of Yoxford in 1419; as he died vicar of Yoxford in 1457 and in his will has nothing to say of other places, or of people of other places, it is obvious that this one parish was his only care over a lifetime. Was it lack of talent which kept him from getting on in the world? Or for him was there no world worth bothering about beyond the confines of his parish, save the next? Do we have (in other words) a dull and dreary vicar here, or such a priest that we are minded to call on Chaucer again, this time for his parson? Collecting rents was no part of that parson's business, and rent collection (like tithe collection) is not, one would have thought, a pursuit which can readily be combined with popularity. Still the circumstances and the context are, amid so much else, lost to us. Clement collected them for the manor of

[223] SRO, HA 30/314/18 m5; BL, Harley Charter 51 G14.
[224] Was he the John Everard Hopton presented to St Margaret, Westwick, in Norwich in 1462? That John Everard had vacated the living by 1467: Blomefield II, p669. Also what relation (if any) does he bear to the John Everard whose brass survives in Halesworth church, dated 1476, or the John Everard who replaced Walter Fulbourne as court-keeper for Mettingham College in 1477–8 (BL, Add MS 33987, f183v), and who collected Sibton Abbey rents at Fressingfield in the 1480s (Denney, p33)? One, or more of these was probably of Linstead by Halesworth (Copinger II, p118), another was of Cratfield (*Cal Anc Deeds* IV, A7688).

Meriells in Yoxford, and had ceased to do so by 1435, when his arrears stood at £1; he cleared the last 10s 10d of this sum in 1443–4.[225] Possibly he had not collected rents since before Hopton came to Suffolk. We know nothing more of Clement until his will of 15 October 1457.[226] It is succinct enough: he desired to be buried in St Peter's, Yoxford; he left to the church his antiphoner and processional, and to the fabric 3s 4d; to the poor and decrepit he left the same sum; and Clement Carter of Yoxford he wished to have an acre and a rod of land in that place before any other man. Who, we wonder, was Clement Carter, and who (perhaps we wonder too) was his mother? The remainder of his goods – and they cannot surely have been many – he made his executors, the vicar of Sibton and John Orderne of Yoxford, responsible for disposing of for the salvation of his soul and to the pleasure of God. It looks as though he was as poor as Chaucer made his parson; whatever other qualities Clement may have shared with that admirable man, he appears like him at least in that he was 'a shepherd and no mercenary'.[227]

What did John Hopton make of Clement? We know what he made of William Pickenham. He made him one of his feoffees, and Thomasin also made him one of hers.[228] This is not surprising. William had been called in during 1465–6 to help defeat Dunwich;[229] at that time he had not yet become the important man he was when John and Thomasin made him a trustee. How then had they come across him? He was in 1465–6 rector of Rayleigh, Essex, the home of Thomasin's family, but that was a consequence of the Barringtons knowing him, rather than the reason for their, and hence the Hoptons, getting to know him. For the Barringtons were related to him. In his will of 1469 Thomas Barrington left to William 'consangineo meo' a silver basin and ewer;[230] Thomasin

225 SRO, HA 30/50/22/8/3; HA 30/314/14.
226 NRO, Norwich Cons. Court, Reg. Brosiard, f62, proved 3 November 1457.
227 *Canterbury Tales*, translated Coghill, p39.
228 PRO, C140/72/70, see *CPR 1476–85*, pp142–3; *CIPM Henry VII* vol II, p99.
229 SRO, HA 30/314/18 m3.
230 PRO, PCC 6 Wattys. William in his will of 1497 left £10 and two long gowns to Thomasin Rysele, his sister (PRO, PCC 9 Horne); this was presumably Thomasin, wife of John Risley esq., influential councillor to

was Thomas' brother. William's Barrington relatives had not however been this very bright young man's first patrons. He had grander friends. He had been appointed to Rayleigh in August 1462. Henry, lord Bourgchier, later Earl of Essex, presented him to Little Hallingbury, Essex, his first living, before 1461.[231] He was then probably a fellow of All Soul's, where as a Cambridge graduate he had gone in the mid-1450s. Despite being fined for carrying arms and for assault in 1456, he kept to his studies in the canon and civil law. It must have been apparent to anyone who had the eyes to see these things that this was one of the cleverest young men of his generation, one moreover who would reap in due course the rewards cleverness in such studies produced in the fifteenth century. Someone indeed, perhaps a Barrington, would have seen that promise even in the boy and sent him to Cambridge. By 1465–6, when he came to Westwood, his career was beginning to take flight: in the previous year he had received his doctorate in civil law, and he was already holding two other rectories besides Rayleigh. So it went on. By 1470 he was rector of Hadleigh, Suffolk; in 1472 he became archdeacon of Suffolk; in 1479 he was appointed rector of Wrotham in Kent, in the 1480s he became a canon of Lincoln and a canon of Lichfield, in 1493 he was made dean of the college of St John the Baptist, Stoke-by-Clare, Suffolk. These were not all his benefices, but all of these he held until his death in 1497. His connection with the Bourgchiers continued; after all he served the regime they had helped bring into being, and one of them was archbishop of Canterbury. William was a trustee of Earl Henry's estates and a feoffee for his sons; he became Thomas Bourgchier's chancellor at Canterbury in 1481, a prelocutor of the convocation of Canterbury in the same year, and he was the archbishop's executor in 1486.[232] He was a great man, only at the last denied his bishopric by the change of dynasty in 1485.

Henry VII. She was (according to Wedgwood, p717) daughter and heir of Richard Turnaunt of Tottenham.

[231] L. S. Woodger, 'Henry, third Earl of Essex and his family (1408–1483)', unpublished Oxford DPhil thesis, 1974, p309. For other details of his career mentioned in the text, see A. B. Emden, *A Biographical Register of the University of Oxford to 1500* (1957–9) pp1530–1.

[232] L. S. Woodger, pp311–12.

Nonetheless he was not too grand to ignore John and Thomasin. There was no reason why he should: fifteenth century churchmen who had risen in the world did not tend to forget their kin, nor indeed their origins. Pickenham did neglect his place of birth and nurture, unless it was Hadleigh, where he founded, endowed and built. There were the twelve almshouses for 24 men and women with their chapel, and there was the palace. Only the gatehouse of the latter survives; in the smartest style and of fashionable brick it testifies to what we might expect from him: the very best taste.[233] He also had a house in Northgate Street, Ipswich; here too the gateway, also of brick, remains; it has a refinement which caused Sir Nikolaus Pevsner to call it 'remarkable'.[234] As moreover he left to the college at Stoke-by-Clare – not, we may note, to All Souls' – all his books of canon and civil law and theology, perhaps it was Suffolk which he loved.[235] Whether that was so or not, he did have time for his Suffolk relatives, even if she was from Essex and her husband came from the West Riding. He had time too, or was obliged to make time, for the Pastons of Norfolk; it is his contacts with them which enable us to obtain a glimmering insight into his character.

It is a very correct character. That, I think, is the impression we gain from his courteous letter to Margaret Paston of 2 February 1479.[236] Her son Walter was shortly to graduate at Oxford; six years before, when he was going up for the first time, she wrote, probably to James Gloys who was accompanying him:

And bydde hym that he benot to hasty of takyng of orderes that schuld bynd hym till that he be of xxiiij yere of agee or more, thoff he be consaled the contraré, for oftyn rape rewith. I will loue hym bettere to be a good seculare man than to be a lewit prest.[237]

[233] Dean Spooner, 'The Almshouse Chapel, Hadleigh, and the Will of Archdeacon Pykenham', *Proceedings of the Suffolk Institute of Archaeology*, VII (1891), pp378ff. Did he, perhaps as benefactor, have anything to do with the guildhall at Hadleigh, just across the churchyard from the palace?

[234] *Suffolk*, p281.

[235] The nuns of Campsey and Bruisyard were left money to sing a requiem for him: PRO, PCC 9 Horne.

[236] Davis II, p365. It is also 'probably autograph', according to Professor Davis.

[237] Davis I, p370.

Now however, circumstances had altered, and it was Margaret who wanted Walter to be a priest; more accurately she wanted to present him to a Paston benefice, probably that of Oxnead, which at this time seems to have been vacant.[238] She had therefore changed her tune, and had written to Pickenham. He was polite, firm, and to the point:

> ..I have resyuyed yowre letter and vndrestonde yowre desyre, wyche ys ageyns the lawe for three causys. Oon ys for yowre son Watre ys nott tonsewryd, in modre tunge callyd Benett; a-nodre cause, he ys not xxiiij yeere of aghe, wyche requiryd complete; the thyrde, he owte of ryghte to be preyst wythin dwelmonthe after he ys parson, wyth-owte so were he hadd a dyspensacion fro Rome be owre holy fadre the Pope, wyche I am certen can not be hadde.

He had not for these reasons made her wish known to Bishop Goldwell, and he advised her to think no more of it, for, he wrote concisely, 'yt ys not goodely nether goddely'; she should present 'a-nodre man abyll'. In a postscript he was equally frank: 'I sende yow yowre presente agen in the boxe.' What had Margaret tried to tempt him with? He was not to be tempted, not at any rate this time, on such a matter. He knew that what he had to say was the opposite of what Margaret wanted to hear: he tried to lighten the blow, even crossing out at the last a phrase which put conditions on his goodwill. He wrote 'Be not wrothe thow I send vn-to yow thusse playnly in the matre, for I wolde ye dede as wele...', and at first continued 'that ys wyth rygth', but then crossed this through and added over it 'as any woman in Norfolke', and so wrote on 'to yowre honor, prosperite, an to the plesur of Godde, wyth yowre and all yowres...' It is surely a letter which has style, both of language and of manner; it is the letter of a man who had style, a man who knew how to carry things through, even though they were unpleasant and embarrassing as they were on this occasion. Although Sir John Paston wrote of him in 1473 that he had not been 'kynde and just',[239] it is just

---

[238] Davis I, pp177–80; Gairdner v, p327; vi, p1 footnote. The advowson was in Agnes' gift, Oxnead being her jointure: Gairdner iv, p251.

[239] Sir John was in the thick of difficulties and was not disposed to be generous (Davis I, p469); in 1478 William responded at once to John

these qualities which he displays in his letter to Sir John's mother half-a-dozen years later. For what we can see and see clearly is him trying, not without success, to temper justice with kindness. He seems therefore to have been exactly the man to have as a feoffee. He died in April 1497. Thomasin, who had married for the third time while he was still at Oxford and probably still waiting for his first benefice, survived him by nine months.

There were other clerics than these very different ones, Clement Rollesby and William Pickenham, with whom John Hopton might have had greater communication than ever he had with them. Thomas Crowe at Easton Bavents may have been one, William Yarmouth, who taught his sons may have been another. His own son John was a priest, and there was his confessor, or rather over a lifetime the many priests who heard his confessions. These may have been drawn from his chaplains, though we get no evidence that he ever had a chaplain until the very end of his life when we come across John Everard, Robert Pilgrim and John West. The two last may in fact have been more chantry priests than chaplains, celebrating as they did at Blythburgh. George Hawes, Thomasin's chaplain, replaced West in this role in the mid-1480s.[240] When George drew up his will in December 1506[241] he desired that his body might be buried 'in the Estende of the churchyard ayenst the ende that I synge at'; that this was the end of Blythburgh church is shewn by his choice of executors: besides John Hawes his brother, these were John Baret the younger and John Baret the elder of Blythburgh. Moreover he left to Blythburgh and Walberswick churches 6s 8d apiece. George was seemingly rather better off than Clement Rollesby, or at least he had looked after himself better. He bequeathed to the chantry altar a corporal of green and white silk, to John Baret his round

Paston's prompting to put in a word on Edmund's behalf, when a marriageable mercer's daughter was in prospect: Davis 1, p613.
[240] West wrote a bill of the cash Thomasin had received from various tenants and farmers at Yoxford in 1483–4: SRO, HA 30/369/391. Hawes was paid a small sum and given herrings worth 12s by the Blythburgh bailiff in 1484–5: SRO, HA 30/314/18 m9. Pilgrim and Hawes were celebrating together at Blythburgh by 1490–1: SRO, HA 30/312/424.
[241] NRO, Norwich Cons. Court, Reg. Spyltimber, f14v, proved 11 August 1507.

table in his chamber, to Margaret Pakke a 'bakke' chair and a mattress, and to someone simply called Thomas his sarsenet tippet with a lace of silk and a 'tache' of silver. He wanted his feather-bed, two pairs of sheets, a blanket, his best gown, and his short gown to be sold. His best coverlet was to go to John his brother, and 6s 8d to George his godson 'yf yt may be born'. His old 'portruas' he left to Bruisyard Abbey with £1 which was to be divided among the nuns and friars there. The short gown, the gorgeous tippet, the featherbed and the single *old* portruas suggest a man who cared to look well, sleep well but not to read or study well. Don't they create – or is it we who are creating – the stock image of a late medieval priest? He did have a table and a chair, yet we feel they were for eating and drinking not for working. We must not be unjust to Sir George, but that tippet cannot be ignored: its gaiety shines through nearly five centuries, if not to damn him, still to make us wonderfully uneasy as to what his whole heart and mind were set upon. Perhaps indeed he was a man to be loved – it is when all is said and done not a frivolous tippet; if so it was Thomasin not John who loved him, for George was after his time. Would that piece of finery have disturbed John? Alas, we cannot know whether this sort of priest or that sort, or any priest at all would have made him uneasy; whether there was one indeed who ever made him feel easy. He did not, I think we can say, seek the company of clerics; if he had done so we surely would have known something of it.

Hopton had plenty of opportunity, for so many of his neigh-bours in his part of Suffolk were religious. Sibton and Leiston abbeys were next door, Bruisyard nunnery was just beyond Sibton, and Snape priory and Campsey nunnery were not far off. Rumburgh priory was near Wissett, and Wangford priory was near Blythburgh, while at Blythburgh itself there was a priory. Just how these particular religious houses 'fitted into' the part of the world of which they were so much a part is not easy to grasp. Most houses were at home in the world in ways which their founders and early benefactors could not have foreseen. This is true of these Suffolk houses: their religious function was so inte-grated with other aspects of their existence that they had become veritably part of their environment. Such integration does not mean these religious houses were not religious, rather it shows that religion itself had become so much part of the *mise-en-scène*, it no longer was distinct or different. Piety was so commonplace, you ran into it everywhere, not only, not necessarily in religious houses. The result was that you treated the members of such houses with no more and no less reverence than you did anyone else; what merit they had lay in themselves not in their calling; the consideration they might anticipate was for the quality of their lives not for the habits they wore. Of any such merit and consideration in our part of East Suffolk we have no inkling. Neither would have left much trace.

Rumburgh, Wangford and Blythburgh were all small houses; at Blythburgh in 1473, for instance, there were three canons and the prior.[242] Hopton regularly gave the prior rabbits in the 1460s and once sent him swans from Easton Bavents;[243] otherwise we know only of their relationship as landowners in the same place. Hopton appears to have had nothing to do with the equally small and even more insignificant house at Snape, but nor did he, so far as we can tell, with the far grander establishment of Campsey near Wickham Market. There were about twenty nuns at Campsey in the late fifteenth and early sixteenth centuries and five secular clergy serving the Ufford chantry, 'the only instance of which we are aware where a small college of secular priests was actually established within the precincts of a nunnery'.[244] They sang for the souls of William Ufford, earl of Suffolk, who had collapsed and died as he had entered the chamber where the Lords were sitting in February 1382, and his wife Isobel, who survived him unmarried for thirty-four years. Both were buried at Campsey. As William left no direct heirs, Richard II took the title for his chancellor Michael de la Pole, while the Suffolk properties of the Uffords, after Isobel had enjoyed them for a generation, came to Robert, lord Willoughby, grandson of a nephew and co-heir of William Ufford. With these lands went the advowson of the

[242] *VCH Suffolk* II, p93.
[243] SRO, HA 30/314/18 ms2, 3, 4; V5/19/1/16, 1467–8.
[244] *VCH Suffolk* II, pp113–14.

JOHN HOPTON

nunnery,[245] and when the Willoughby title and lands went out of
the family with Robert's only daughter on his death in 1452, the
Ufford properties and the advowson came, by an entailment on
male heirs, to a cadet branch: these Willoughbys lived at Parham
between Wickham Market and Framlingham and gave their
patronage to the priory, their womenfolk to be sisters and their
bodies to be buried there.[246] Bishops on visitation in the later
fifteenth century invariably discovered all was well.[247]

Bruisyard was another nunnery where all was well. Its endowment had originally been for a chantry college at Campsey,
but this foundation was transferred to Bruisyard in 1354 and
was shortly thereafter changed into a house of Poor Clares.[248]
Willoughby women were here too, Jane for example in 1498.[249]
So were other East Anglian ladies: Alice Clere was abbess in
1489, Margaret Calthorp in 1497.[250] Earlier in the century
grander women than they had been sisters at Bruisyard: Elizabeth
Fitzalan, widow of Michael de la Pole, earl of Suffolk, killed at
Agincourt, and her only surviving daughter Katherine were nuns,
and Katherine may have become abbess.[251] Another daughter,
Elizabeth, who died before she was ten, had begun her education

245 *CCR 1413–19*, p341; *CFR 1413–22*, p180.
246 All trace of the tombs has gone, along with most of the buildings, but
stone Willoughby shields fixed to the north wall of the chancel of Parham
church possibly come from them: Norman Scarfe, *Shell Guide*, *sub*
Parham.
247 *Visitations of the Diocese of Norwich, 1492–1532*, ed. A. Jessop, Camden
Society, New Series, xliii (1888), pp35–6, 133–4, etc.; *VCH Suffolk* II,
p114; D. Knowles, *The Religious Orders in England* III (1959), p75
footnote.
248 *VCH Suffolk* II, p131. This chantry of five priests was founded by Maud
countess of Ulster, daughter of Henry, Earl of Lancaster (d.1345), after
the death of her second husband, Ralph Ufford (d.1346), brother of the
Earl of Suffolk. She herself entered Campsey and also transferred to
Bruisyard to become a Poor Clare; there she died in 1377: *CP* XII, part
2, p179. She clearly set the tone of the house. These late fourteenth
century foundations: Bruisyard, the Ufford college at Campsey, Mettingham College, Wingfield College, are splendid examples of the not quite
circular tour of ecclesiastical taxation via soldiers' pay and soldiers' profits:
K. B. McFarlane, 'England and the Hundred Years War', *Past and
Present*, 22 (1962), pp6–7. They had a vigorous life, as one would expect.
249 Sir Christopher Willoughby's will: Lincs RO, 2 Ancaster 3 A25.
250 *VCH Suffolk* II, p132.
251 *CP* XII, part II, p443.

222

here in 1417 when she was five, under one of the friars.[252] The Hoptons too were known at Bruisyard; Sir William was there with John Hoo in 1480–1; Thomasin left the nuns £1 and Jane Wentworth 10 marks to make her a nun there.[253] Of the Hoptons' relationship with the sisters, indeed of this socially important house itself, we would like to know more. If bequests are any indication, then the house was held in affection by many in these parts of Suffolk. Evidently in county society Bruisyard had a place; just what place we no longer can discover. The abbeys of Leiston and Sibton too had a social role to play. Leiston was a large house, in 1488 of sixteen canons and the abbot;[254] Sibton was not large but it was wealthy.[255] Apparently however, the Hoptons had with the abbots only what we might call an economic relationship: in 1465–6 John bought rabbits from the abbot of Leiston; from 1457 the abbot of Sibton leased the Westleton demesne.[256] If there was more than this between them we do not know of it.

What of John's secular neighbours? Were any of them his friends? None so far as we can see were his enemies. Middleton, which divided Yoxford from Westleton, was owned by the Audleys. When James, lord Audley was killed at Blore Heath in September 1459, Humphrey (his son by his second wife), had Middleton.[257] While his elder half-brother John, lord Audley accommodated himself quickly and profitably to the new regime, Humphrey like his father gave his life for the old, though in what changed circum-

---

[252] McFarlane, *The Nobility of Later Medieval England*, p245. The friar was called 'le president'. What does that mean, and who were the old men at Bruisyard, to every one of whom Sir Christopher Willoughby left 10s in 1498? To each friar he left only 6s 8d. In 1383 Nicholas Gernoun, in his old age and infirmity, had been allowed to live there 'ex devocione' (*VCH Suffolk* II, p132) Bruisyard was much more than a mere nunnery.

[253] SRO, HA 30/314/18 m7; PRO, Probate 11/11.

[254] *VCH Suffolk* II, p119. Here was another house where we know all was well. In Bishop Redman's visitations of the later fifteenth century it 'receives unstinted praise' and 'the management of the estates is frequently praised': R. C. Mortimer, 'An Edition of the cartulary of Leiston Abbey', unpublished PhD thesis, University of London 1977, p56.

[255] For Sibton, see Denney, introduction.

[256] SRO, HA 30/314/18 m3; HA 30/369/325.

[257] For courts in his name, see SRO, HD 79/AB 1–10.

stances: he was beheaded after the battle of Tewkesbury in 1471. Politics also played havoc with the lives of another family who were John Hopton's neighbours, though they were at a little distance from Westwood. The Willoughbys of Parham did not suffer at all in the way the Audleys did, and for the Audleys there was more suffering, indeed a disaster, to come in 1497. What happened to the Willoughbys happened so to speak at a remove; deaths and disputes elsewhere kept them on tenterhooks: would they inherit the Willoughby of Eresby lands?

Robert, lord Willoughby died in 1452. He had been a great soldier; at least he was spared the sight which his old companion in arms Thomas, lord Scales and Sir John Fastolf had to endure: the collapse of English government in England itself.[258] On his permanent return to England in the mid-1440s Lord Willoughby was mainly active in Lincolnshire but he was on the Suffolk commission of the peace with John Hopton.[259] By his first wife[260] he left a single daughter, Joan, who was married to Richard, son and heir of Lionel, lord Welles; Richard was summoned to parliament as Lord Willoughby from 1454. His father Lionel was killed at Towton in 1461 and subsequently attainted. Not therefore until that attainder was reversed in 1467 did Richard become Lord Welles, as well as Lord Willoughby. By then Joan had died. She had given her husband a son, Robert, and a daughter named after herself. Father and son, caught up in local rivalries in Lincolnshire, were supported by the dissident Earl of Warwick who, tempting them into revolt, brought them to disaster in March

[258] The heavy expenses of this English soldier in France in the latter days are probably reflected in Davis II, pp3–4. According to Sir John Fastolf, he and Willoughby had received only 1000 marks apiece for the ransom of the Duke of Alençon whom they had captured at Verneuil; 4000 marks was still owed to each of them over thirty years later: Davis II, p135.

[259] CPR 1446–52, p595.

[260] By his young second wife, Maud Stanhope, he had no children. She was one of the three nieces and heirs of Ralph, lord Cromwell, another infertile English aristocrat. Maud's second husband Thomas Nevill was killed by the Lancastrians at Wakefield in 1460, her third, Sir Gervase Clifton, was beheaded by the Yorkists after Tewkesbury in 1471. She lived a widow for another twenty-six years, and died and was buried at Tattershall in 1497. She could have had a great deal to say about the Wars of the Roses, particularly as her wedding to Thomas Nevill at Tattershall in August 1453 was the occasion for their beginning.

1470: both were beheaded by Edward IV. Robert, though married, left no children. Joan therefore, remained the sole heiress of Welles and Willoughby. She was already married in 1470: her husband was thus the beneficiary of infertility and political ineptitude. He was Sir Richard Hastings, younger brother of William, lord Hastings and one of Edward IV's foremost advisors, particularly after the king's recovery of the throne in 1471. But by 1474 Joan was dead,[261] and Richard Hastings was put in the position Sir John Gra had been in 1429: as there had been no children of the marriage, he could not hold Joan's lands by courtesy, they would go to the right heir of each. Nevertheless necessity can find a way, even against the law, if political power lies to hand. So it did for Hastings. By act of parliament in 1475 he was confirmed in possession of the Welles and Willoughby lands.[262] This was just one of the instances, and not the most blatant, of Edward IV's use of a compliant parliament in the later part of his reign to override the laws of inheritance, so that his family and friends might hold onto or accumulate property. Every time he did so, of course, he disinherited someone. There we come to the Willoughbys of Parham.

Parham was an estate of the Uffords, earls of Suffolk in the fourteenth century. It, with the castle and town of Orford, the quay and the town of Woodbridge, Ufford itself and other Suffolk manors, fell to Robert, lord Willoughby in 1416 as one of the heirs of William Ufford, earl of Suffolk. On Robert's death in 1452, leaving Joan as his heir, these properties by a male entail went to Robert Willoughby esquire, his nephew.[263] Robert went to live at Parham and was thereafter a commissioner in Suffolk, frequently with John Hopton;[264] he joined John on the commission of the

---

[261] She was dead by January 1474 when Richard Hastings was confirmed by his feoffees in his possession of Willoughby and other estates: Lincs RO, 2 Ancaster 3 A23.

[262] *Rot Parl* VI, p148.

[263] *CCR 1413–19*, p341; *CFR 1413–22*, p180; *CPR 1452–61*, p396; Davis I, p119. Robert Willoughby esq. was in control of Orford in 1453–4; the Duchess of Suffolk's receiver could not get £20 out of him which was owing: BL, Egerton Roll 8779.

[264] *CPR 1452–61*, pp402, 409, 490, 491, 606. He had been on one commission before that, with his uncle in the year of his death, in Lincolnshire: *CPR 1446–52*, p579.

peace in December 1455; both went off it in January 1459. John, as we know, returned in July 1461; Robert never did.[265] Nor was he ever a commissioner of any sort after February 1460. He comes out of obscurity to witness, with John Hopton, both John Pastons, and others a series of charters in February 1464,[266] and he became, after that date and before his death in May 1465, a knight, but that is all.

In 1465 Robert's son and heir Robert was a minor; his lands and marriage were granted to Hugh Fenn and William Jenny;[267] Robert died, still a minor, in March 1467. Sir Robert's second son Christopher succeeded. He also was a minor; almost certainly Fenn and Jenny had his wardship[268] and marriage too, for his wife was to be William Jenny's daughter Margaret. His guardians sent him to Lincoln's Inn, where he was admitted in Hilary Term 1470.[269] He was given livery of his lands in July 1474,[270] a few months after he had become, by the death of a childless Joan Willoughby, the heir at law of the title and lands of Willoughby of Eresby. It was therefore Christopher Willoughby of Parham who was disinherited by the parliamentary act of attainder of 1475.

The right heir of Welles who was disinherited by that same act was John Welles esquire of Maxey, Northants. By the time of Richard III's coronation, at which Christopher was knighted, both may have been hoping for the reversal of the attainder of 1475. Richard Hastings, who had been summoned to the last parliament of Edward IV as Lord Welles – an extraordinary thing, as his wife had been dead for eight years past and there were no children – can only have been reflecting upon what, after the murder of his elder brother, the usurper had in mind for him. Perhaps predictably, Richard III left the Hastings family alone, and Richard Hastings was, for a while at least, secure. Christopher Willoughby and John Welles were disappointed. They took their disappointment differently. John Welles joined the rising of October 1483, and after its collapse went to his half-nephew

[265] CPR 1452–61, p678.   [266] CCR 1461–8, pp208, 227–8.
[267] CFR 1461–71, p159.   [268] CFR 1471–85, p44.
[269] Lincoln's Inn Admissions Register 1 (1896), p17.
[270] CCR 1468–76, p338.

Henry Tudor[271] in Brittany. Christopher on the other hand accepted his lot and settled down to a country gentleman's life in Suffolk. He was on the commission of the peace from June 1483, and on commissions of array in 1483 and 1484.[272] Sir William Hopton was (until his death early in 1484) one of his fellow commissioners; one wonders whether, if they ever talked at all, they conversed of such matters as these: the relief Sir Christopher owed Sir William for lands at Wissett, which at £27 had been scheduled as a desperate debt in 1479,[273] and secondly, this complicated history of how Sir Christopher had been, and was being denied his right. If Sir Christopher did feel he had a grievance, and nothing is more sure than that he did, his sitting still and doing nothing about it proved the wrong course; John Welles' political commitment in 1483, seemingly then the foolish choice, turned out to be the right one. He came back in August 1485, and with the success of Henry Tudor had his reward. Christopher once again got nothing.

In Henry VII's first parliament, amid all the other restorations and recoveries, was the reversal of the attainder of Richard, lord Welles and his son. This, though only momentarily, deepened the embarrassment of the occasion, for there were now two Lord Welles at this parliament, Richard Hastings and John Welles. The duplication of title was simply remedied: John Welles was created a viscount. The more important matter of lands was taken care of by an accommodation which denied only the now entirely right heir of Willoughby all that was properly his. By act of parliament John, viscount Welles recovered from Richard Hastings the Welles inheritance, but Richard was allowed to retain for life the Willoughby lands: he had become, we have to remember, a member of a dead hero's family. Sir Christopher, to whom no one owed anything, could be ignored. He was.[274]

Yet he was not entirely ignored. On the last day of December 1485, even as parliament was assembling, Richard Hastings sealed and with his own hand signed a grant to Sir Christopher

---

[271] For the relationship, see S. B. Chrimes, *Henry VII* (1972), p35 footnote.
[272] *CPR 1476–85*, pp397, 490, 574.   [273] SRO, HA 30/369/31.
[274] *Rot Parl* VI, p287.

'consanguineo et heredi Roberti Willoughby militis domini de Willoughby et de Eresby', of an annual rent charge of 43 marks 10s during Richard's life; the grant had one condition: if Maud, lady Willoughby should die before Richard did, then he would no longer be obliged to pay 40 marks of that sum.[275] What determined this condition was that Maud, widow of Robert, lord Willoughby (d. 1452), was still enjoying her dower after thirty-three years, but that on her death these dower estates would fall to Sir Christopher, the right heir. On her death in 1497 they did. Thus in November 1498 he made a new and final settlement of all his estates, and of reversions 'post mortem Richard Hastyngs knyght'. What a company of feoffees he had by then! Robert Willoughby lord Broke, Sir Reginald Bray, Sir Thomas Lovell, Sir Henry Heydon, Sir William Boleyn, Sir John Paston, Master Simon Stalworth the archdeacon of Lincoln, among others, had joined James Hobart, Edmund Jenny, and Thomas Banyard.[276] Sir Christopher had already drawn up his will and he had not more than a week to live,[277] yet one thing at least must have cheered him and it showed in the number and quality of his feoffees: how much better the situation was for his family than it had been in 1485, let alone in 1465.

There was a simple reason for that, the sterility which, as the late Bruce McFarlane liked to remind us, so frequently brought to nothing the elaborate and expensive schemes men, ambitious for their families, put together. Christopher had mature sons to succeed him; Richard Hastings, childless in 1474, was childless still in 1498, despite a second marriage. That second marriage was probably made a little before 1485,[278] and although the act of Henry VII's first parliament (like that of 1475) allowed Richard to have the Willoughby lands for his life only, we can be sure that

---

[275] Lincs RO, 2 Ancaster 3 A24.
[276] Lincs RO, 2 Ancaster 3 A26, see also *CPR 1476–85*, p16.
[277] His will (Lincs RO, 2 Ancaster 3 A25) is dated 1 November, the settlement is of 9 November, the writ of *diem clausit extremum* was issued on 17 November: *CFR 1485–1509*, p270.
[278] He married Jane, widow of Richard Pigot, sergeant-at-law, who died in spring 1483: *Test Ebor* III, p.285. His will, dated 15 April, was proved 21 June, just eight days after its supervisor, William, lord Hastings, had been murdered by Richard III.

if a son had been born to him by his second wife, Richard would not have let that provision deter him from making every effort to divert at least some of those estates towards himself and away from Sir Christopher. But no son had been born, and by 1498 Richard knew one never would.[279] By then too it had long been clear to Richard that political favour was not to be had: the act of 1485 was, so to speak, all that this new regime felt it owed to him, an embarrassing survivor from other days. He was never summoned to parliament again, even though he bravely styled himself Lord Willoughby. Sir Christopher, on the other hand, left off the commission of the peace for Suffolk in 1485, was restored to it as early as July 1486 and remained upon it until his death;[280] he was also often on other commissions. By November 1498 he was calling himself Lord Willoughby, and on his death in the same month so did the royal chancery.[281] Thus, although Christopher himself never enjoyed all that was properly his on his deathbed he knew that his son at some point would enjoy his.

Richard Hastings lived on for another five years. After his death in September 1503 and the return of the Willoughby lands to William, lord Willoughby, Christopher's son and heir, the opportunity was taken for a settlement in parliament of the Welles estates. John, viscount Welles had died in 1498, a few months before Sir Christopher; he had left all his estates to his wife Cecily, a daughter of Edward IV; there were no surviving children. Henry VII made typically harsh terms with the prospective heirs: he was to have all the lands for ten years after Cecily's death. There were four co-heirs, of whom William, lord Willoughby was one.[282] Cecily Welles died in 1507, but William did not have to wait the agreed ten years for some at least of his share of the

---

[279] It may of course have already been clear in 1485 that Richard's second marriage was to be childless.

[280] *CPR 1485–94*, p501; *CPR 1494–1509*, p659.

[281] See his will and the writs of *diem clausit extremum: CFR 1485–1509*, p270.

[282] *Rot Parl* vi, pp542–4. It was only in February 1504, at about the same time as the parliamentary settlement of the Welles inheritance, that William, lord Willoughby had licence to enter his father's lands: *CPR 1494–1509*, p370. This delay may indicate one of the means used by Henry VII to get such favourable terms in the Welles settlement.

property: he was granted lands in Essex in 1508.[283] Thus the Willoughbys of Parham, after thirty years during which princes and politicians had abused the law in its highest court to keep them from it, got their right.

Probably it was William rather than his father who built the Moat Hall at Parham, that 'wonderful survival' of 'a moated early sixteenth-century timber-framed house with substantial brick parts'.[284] Possibly there William, lord Willoughby entertained Sir Arthur Hopton; did they ever in conversation after dinner touch upon those accidents, sad for others, happy for them, which had made the fortunes of the houses they in their successful persons represented?

The Willoughbys of Parham were a family who, with patience and endurance, achieved nobility and at a time when a gulf was being firmly fixed between it and gentility; there was a real measure of social distance between Lord William and Sir Arthur. Other, and earlier aristocratic neighbours of the Hoptons were neighbours more in the sense of landlords who owned nearby estates, than in the meaning of families who had their homes not far off. The de la Poles probably did come to their house at Benhall from time to time, but they cannot be said to have had their home there: they mainly lived at Wingfield, at Ewelme, or

283 *CP* XII, part II, p670 footnote j.
284 Pevsner, *Suffolk*, p361. How far responsible were the Willoughbys of Parham for the fifteenth century work in Parham church, which (see Cautley, p303) 'must have been a very fine one'? Sir Christopher left £6 13s 4d for the repair of the church in 1498. There is also Ufford church with its fifteenth century south porch, clerestory, roofs, benches, painted screen, font, and font cover, that 'prodigious and delightful piece reaching right up to the roof' (see Pevsner), which even from that iconoclastic philistine William Dowsing on his errand of destruction in August 1644 brought forth an unlikely 'glorious' and he left it alone for us to enjoy too: *The Journal of William Dowsing*, ed. R. Loder (Woodbridge, 1786), p15. The fifteenth century font it dwarfs bears the arms of Ufford and Willoughby, and one of the misericords of the stalls in the chancel also has the arms of Willoughby carved upon it. Might these stalls not have come from Campsey at the dissolution? As for the rest, who can doubt that the Willoughbys were in some way, and in some part, responsible, as the church was surely associated by them with their ancestors and benefactors, the Uffords. This would be true too of the church at Combs near Stowmarket (Copinger VI, p153); one would like therefore to associate its fine stained glass of scenes from the life of St Margaret with the Willoughbys of Parham: the date at least is suitable.

in London. The Mowbrays also presumably came to lodge at Kelsale and hunt their park there occasionally. As we have seen, there is little evidence of a lively association between these two great families and the Hoptons. John Hopton may, however, have known the Tropenells of Kelsale, who held land of him at Yox-ford,[285] rather better. They may even have discussed education, for at his death in 1469 John Tropenell required the supervisor of his will, Walter Fulbourne, and his executors to send his son John to school at Cambridge for a year, and, if he should take holy orders at the end of that year, to find for him there for a further three. As John Tropenell left £8 to the guild of St John the Baptist in Kelsale parish church, and his widow mentions in her will of 1477 three or four tenements and a close, they were parents who could obviously afford schooling, even at Cambridge, for one of their sons. It is perhaps their wanting it, rather than their being able to afford it which interests us. Walter Fulbourne was also the supervisor of Isobel's will: she called him her brother. When Thomas Tropenell, John and Isobel's son, came to make his will in 1485, however, he named Edmund Jenny 'my master' its supervisor.[286]

Edmund, also an executor of his brother-in-law Sir Christopher Willoughby,[287] was the son and heir of William Jenny and was a lawyer like his father. The Jennys owned Theberton and Knodis-hall, and lived at Knodishall; they were therefore, with Leiston Abbey, John Hopton's immediate neighbours to the south. To the north his immediate resident neighbours were relatives of Thomasin's, the Micklefields, who lived after 1441 at Blyford.[288] Before 1441 they had lived first at Mickfield near Debenham, then on their manor of Cravens in Henham, which lay beside

285 SRO, HA 30/369/1 f13; HA 30/369/357.
286 John's will, dated 1 August 1469, proved 29 September 1469: SRO, Reg. 2, f188; Isobel's will, dated 20 June 1477, proved 3 July 1477: SRO, Reg. 2, f341; Thomas' will, dated 8 February 1485, proved 7 May 1485: SRO, Reg. 3, f81v.
287 Lincs RO, 2 Ancaster 3 A25. Sir Christopher married Edmund's sister Margaret.
288 They had 40 acres of land, marsh, pasture, and meadow in Blythburgh, which they held for half a knight's fee and 4s per annum: SRO, HA 30/50/22/27/6(2).

Blyford. Henham was where William Micklefield drew up his last will in 1439; it is a long, elaborate document and it helps to explain the move of the Micklefields to Blyford.[289]

William had no children. He left to Isobel his wife the manor of Cravens in Henham for her life; the reversion was to be sold to John Ulveston, a man whom we know well, for £400, the payment of which was to be made under specific terms over fourteen years. The manor of Mickfield William had already granted by charter to John Ulveston 'in recompence and satisfaccion for 200 marcs which Thomas Ulveston his fadre befor payid for ye seyd maner of Cravenes'. Later in the will we learn that William's sister Elizabeth was John Ulveston's wife; this, however, is not enough to explain why William had granted away the estate which was his inheritance. What pulls everything together is the information[290] that Isobel, William's wife, was the widow of Thomas Ulveston. Thus John Ulveston was William's wife's son. At what point had John married William's sister Elizabeth? Probably, one suspects, before his father's death, and before his mother had married his brother-in-law. Would it not have been at the time of John and Elizabeth's marriage, therefore, that Thomas had given the money towards the purchase of the manor of Cravens? Perhaps moreover, the other side of the bargain had been the settlement of Mickfield on John Ulveston. William hoped in 1439 that his heir, his brother Robert, would be reconciled to the loss of Mickfield by being given Blyford and other properties which he had purchased. Nonetheless Robert had to find an annuity of £10 for Isobel, and he had to continue to pay Robert Banyard his annuity and fee for life. William was worried that Isobel might not receive her annuity from his brother, but he was far more preoccupied with John Ulveston's attitude towards the cessation of a £10 annuity paid to him out of the manor of Cravens 'for his surete of the seid Maner of Mekilfield pesible to be had'. If John was not satisfied then an award should be made by disinterested parties, and if their arbitration failed, the Earl of Suffolk and

---

[289] NRO, Norwich Cons. Court, Reg. Doke, f145, dated 21 September 1439, proved 30 June 1441.
[290] Supplied by Wedgwood, p895.

William, lord Bardolf were to do what they could to pacify him. The impression which we derive from William Micklefield's apprehension is that his stepson shared one quality with Shylock.

William's arrangements for his lands thus favoured his stepson at the expense of the true heir, his brother, and in this he was perhaps influenced by his wife. It would not be the first nor the last time that had happened. Some forty years later for example, the king himself appeared to do more for his queen's sons than he did for his own brother. Edward IV and Elizabeth Woodvill had sons of their own however; William and Isobel Micklefield did not. It was this sad fact which also allowed William to be so generous to local churches and houses of religion, as well as to his servants: 40 marks for a new aisle to be made at Wangford parish church, £20 'to the helpe and amendying' of the church at Blyford, £2 to the priory at Blythburgh, £1 to Sibton Abbey, to John 'my shepherd' 2s, to Hopton 'my man' 2s. His goods he left to his wife; he, or whoever composed his will, describes them well:

I wil that my seid wif shal have alle my stuf longyng to my household as in halle and chambir except myn armur and certyn chestys which I have yeve and assignyd. also she shal have alle myn hostysments and other necessaries longyng to Boterie Kechin Bakhous Bruerie with alle my plowes cartis oxis hors and harneys therto longyng except iiij oxis. also she shal have al my deyerie and other bestes of stor and porcerye and half myn sheep alle the cornys in my berne and gernez that shall leve over my seed to my londys to be sowe. and also half my cornes tho be sowe and this yer shulde be sowe with alle myn hey now housid to her proper use and profyt.

To John Ulveston's son Richard, and to his brother's son William he was indifferently open-handed: he left them each 10 marks. It is with these two that we get back to John Hopton.

Richard Ulveston was with the Hoptons at Westwood in 1465–6; he received five yards of cloth for his robe.[291] If this was the same Richard Ulveston he would no longer have been a child, nor even a young man; moreover, while his father had died in 1460, his mother was still living, indeed Elizabeth did not die until 1495.[292] One wonders therefore why Richard Ulveston

[291] SRO, HA 30/314/18 m3.   [292] Wedgwood, p895.

should be treated by John Hopton as one of the family at that particular time in his life. With the William Micklefield esquire who was paid 10 marks by the Blythburgh bailiff in the previous year, 1464–5, we are on safer ground.[293] He had been a minor in 1441, and had married a niece of Thomasin's, Elizabeth, daughter of Thomas Barrington of Rayleigh, Essex.[294] Moreover, when Robert his father died in 1471 or 1472, having been ill for some while, he did not mention his son in his will, only his wife Margaret.[295] William became a feoffee of Sir Christopher Willoughby,[296] who left him 10 marks in 1498, the same amount as he had had from his uncle almost sixty years before; probably William and Christopher had become kin by marriage, for Sir Christopher also left £5 to 'my aunte Margery Mekilfield'.[297] Thus William Micklefield, altogether an obscure figure from an obscure family, at any rate once John Ulveston had got through with them, was a kinsman Hopton and Willoughby had in common. At Westleton on 28 July 1471 William witnessed Robert Banyard's release, as a surviving feoffee, of that manor to John Hopton.[298] With him as a witness there that day, if in this respect the document means what it says, was the last neighbour of the Hoptons whom we shall mention, Sir John Heveningham of Heveningham.

There were three Sir John Heveninghams whom John Hopton

---

[293] SRO, HA 30/314/18 m2. In September 1465 'Mykelfylde' was one of William Jenny's company who were beaten to it by Paston's supporters, and so deterred from holding a court at Caldecott Hall as they had arranged: Davis I, p319.

[294] See Thomas Barrington's will (PRO, PCC 6 Wattys): to Anne Micklefield, daughter of William Micklefield and Elizabeth late his wife, my daughter, £20 towards her marriage; to Robert son and heir of William and Elizabeth, £10.

[295] His will (dated 4 April 1466, proved 27 February 1472: NRO, Norwich Cons. Court, Reg. Jekkys, f259), opens unusually: '...senciens corpus meum nedum senectute vehementi sed eciam gravi infirmitate dedentum sanus tamen mente et recolendus memoria...' Margaret died in 1480. Robert Micklefield was not her first husband; she had been married previously to Richard Calthorp of Cokethorp, Norfolk, and she desired to be buried beside him at Cokethorp. She does not mention any Micklefields at all in her will: NRO, Norwich Cons. Court, Reg. A Caston, f67, dated 20 February 1478, proved 12 December 1480.

[296] *CPR 1476–85*, p16.   [297] Lincs RO, 2 Ancaster 3 A25.

[298] BL, Harley Charter 45 F41.

new. The first died in 1444,[299] the second, his son in 1453, and he third, his grandson, in 1499. The first was also, and possibly better known to Sir Roger Swillington, for whom he was a coffee;[300] he must have watched with sadness the deaths of Sir Roger's sons,[301] and then followed with attention the unravelling of the settlement of 1413. In the odd way of such things he was scheator of Norfolk and Suffolk when John Hopton was found to be the heir under that enfeoffment, and therefore it was he who on February 1430 gave seisin to John of the East Anglian estates.[302] With the next John Heveningham, who succeeded his father in 1444, Hopton was on the commission of the peace. How far his contact with this faint friend of Sir John Fastolf's went beyond that we do not know.[303]

He is a man who for us comes to life only on 3 July 1453, the day he died:

And on Tuysday Sere Jon Henyngham ghede to hys chyrche and herd iij massys, and cam hom agayn nevyr meryer, and seyd to hese wyf that he wuld go sey a lytyll deuocion in hese gardeyn and than he wuld dyne; and forthwyth he felt a feyntyng in hese legge and syd doun. Thys was at ix of the clok, and he was ded or none.[304]

How remarkable it is that a consequence of the unexpectedness of Sir John's death should be, five centuries later, our deriving from it insight into his life. Almost a window is opened into his soul. How much too we may learn of the devout laymen: after hearing three masses in church he returns, not to dinner, but to walk in his garden to 'sey a lytill deuocion'. As Agnes wrote her description

[299] His will; NRO, Norwich Cons. Court, Reg. Wylley, fs47–8, dated 19 August 1425, proved 14 July 1444. See Davy's collections, BL, Add MS 19135, f263.
[300] *CFR 1422–30*, pp314–18.
[301] In the year of Sir Robert's death Sir John Heveningham's son visited Blythburgh: SRO, HA 30/369/78, accounts of 1419–20.
[302] *CPR 1422–9*, pp244, 305; *CPR 1429–36*, p48; *CFR 1422–9*, p313.
[303] Thomas Brews to Sir John Fastolf, 9 May 1451: 'Also to knowe som of your feynt frendes, at that tyme that my Lord Norfolk sat at Norwich up on the oyer determyner, Sir John Hevyngham myht nat fynde it in his hert to go iiij furlong from his deullyng place to the shirehouse, but now he cowd ryde from Norwich to Walsyngham to syt as one of the Commyssioners.': Gairdner II, p239.
[304] Davis I, p39.

from Norwich, Sir John was presumably at his house in that city,[305] and the church where he could attend so many masses before nine o'clock was, therefore, not the village one at Heveningham, but a town one.[306] Did he read from a book as he went up and down in his garden? That is how I understand it. If it were not for the collapse which immediately overtook him the picture of Sir John walking there would be a felicitous one: a welcome image from an age not generally noted for its felicity.[307]

More typical for those who are stern interpreters of the men and manners of the age would be the way in which John Wyndham sought to take advantage of another consequence of Sir John's unlooked for death: his widow left to cope with debts of 300 marks. Wyndham wanted to marry Lady Heveningham, and what he had to offer her was payment of those debts, the manor of Felbrigge as her jointure, 'and oder large proforys'. John Heveningham the son thought his mother would not refuse. But how was Wyndham to raise 300 marks?

And by thys mene, as he seyth, he hathe bargeynid with j marchande of London and hath solde to hym the mariage of hys son, for the qwyche he scal have vij c marc; and of that the iij c marc schoulde be payd for the forseyd dettys...

Which seems as coldblooded as sending children away to be educated. If, therefore, Wyndham was to be prevented, and John Heveningham wished to prevent him, then it would have to be with hard facts not soft feelings. 'I pray yow', wrote Margaret

305 For his house there, see note 303 above.
306 Was it St Michael Coslany? This was the only Norwich church his son left money to in his will; he left it the large sum of £1: PRO, Probate 11/12 f72.
307 So far as walking and pleasure are concerned I am reminded of Sir William Sandes walking for pleasure in Hampshire; he wrote to Sir William Stonor c.1480, 'And as y undyrstonde sumtyme as y walke yn my recreacon y may see that yn yowr wodys [your farmer is doing damage]': *The Stonor Letters and Papers* II, p132. And where reading in the garden and happiness are concerned I cannot resist the recollection of Marcel Proust at Combray: *Remembrance of Things Past*, vol I (Chatto and Windus paperback ed., 1966), pp111–17. As for devout laymen: was Sir John following some pious programme such as that set out for a Throckmorton at about this time? (See W. A. Pantin, 'Instructions for a devout and literate layman' in *Essays presented to R. W. Hunt*, ed. J. J. G. Alexander and M. T. Gibson (1976), pp398–422.)

Paston to her husband 'sende me a copy of hys petygre, that I may schew to hyr how worcheppfull it is, for in goode feythe sche is informyd...that he is mor worcheppfull in berthe and in lyuelode ther-to than they [Wyndham's supporters] or ony odyr can preue, as I suppose.'[308] Margaret had every reason to detest Wyndham, and to deride the quality of his breeding, for he had once called her and her mother 'strong hores' to their faces and taunted her with the Pastons' own low birth, about which they were extremely touchy.[309] No wonder she was someone the young John Heveningham knew he could turn to as an ally. If John Paston did send her the pedigree, it did not do what Margaret wanted it to: convince Lady Heveningham that Wyndham was not worth it. For she married him.[310]

It looks as if Alice, the dowager Duchess of Suffolk's influence prevailed, as it was her active support for his marriage that Wyndham had won. Was it Alice who finally won over the young John Heveningham, as Wyndham hoped she might?[311] This third John Heveningham certainly appears to have been easily won over by the great. Alice was an imperious woman,[312] and John Heveningham had turned out before in her interest, at Eye in August 1454;[313] he did so again on her son's behalf in October 1465, when the duke's men attacked Drayton and Helsdon. Margaret wrote to John

And asfor Ser John Hevenyngham, Ser John Wyndefeld, and othere wurchepfull men ben mad but here doggeboltes, the which I suppose

308 Davis I, p256.
309 Davis I, p224. See Caroline M. Barron's convincing reconstruction of Wyndham's phrase, 'charles of Gemyngham', which John Paston attempted to remove from this letter: 'Who were the Pastons?', *Journal of the Society of Archivists*, vol 4, no. 6 (October 1972), p533. The Pastons had reason to be concerned: at Gimmingham bond tenure survived for as long as anywhere in England, see Somerville, *Duchy of Lancaster* I (1953), pp315–16.
310 Blomefield IV, p309. John Wyndham's father was, it seems, a leading citizen of Norwich: M. A. Wyndham, *A Family History 1410–1688, The Wyndhams of Norfolk and Somerset* (1939), p1.
311 Davis I, p256.
312 Apart from the Pastons' view of her, *The Stonor Letters and Papers*, no. 148 impresses.
313 BL, Egerton Roll 8779.

wull turne hem to diswurchep here-after. I spake wyth Ser John
Heuenyngham and enformed hym wyth the trough of the matere,
and of all owyre demenyng at Drayton, and he seid he wuld that all
thyng were wele and that he wuld enforme my lord as I seid to hym,
but Harleston had all the wordes and the rewle wyth the Duke here
and after his avyse and Doctour Aleynes he was avysed here at this
tyme.[314]

The weakness of that 'he wuld that all thyng were wele' comes
through as sharply now as it must have done then. Nor was he
only the de la Poles' dogsbody; he also did dirty work for the
Mowbrays. At the Duke of Norfolk's siege of Caister in the late
summer of 1469, as Margaret wrote to Sir John Paston,

...my lord hath mad hym on of the capteynes at Cayster of the
pepill that shuld kepe the wetche abought the place that no man
shuld socour them if my lord departed. I desired hym to favour them
if any man shuld come to them fro me or you, and he wuld not
graunte it; but he desired me to write to you to vnderstand if that
my lord myght be mevyd to fynde suerté to recompense you all
wronges and ye wuld suffre hym to entre pesibilly and the lawe after
his entré wuld deme it you. Be ye avysed what answere ye wull
geve.[315]

Margaret knew what she was about when she wrote, 'Be ye avysed
what answere ye wull geve': it took long enough for the law to get
the duke out once he got in. This then, the Pastons' faintest of
faint friends, was the Sir John Heveningham John Hopton knew.
    Apparently, they were related by marriage. Sir John's first wife
is said to have been Alice, daughter of Sir John Saville of Thornhill; thus she was Hopton's first wife's niece.[316] As however

---

[314] Davis I, p324.   [315] Davis I, p340.

[316] Davy's pedigree, BL, Add MS 19135, f263. Alice Saville, otherwise un-
authenticated, is a trifle wraithlike but the Saville arms did adorn the
North chapel in Heveningham church: *The Chorography of Suffolk*, p87.
Sir John's next two wives are better evidenced. Alice Bruyn, whose third
husband in less than ten years he was, he married between 1466 and 1473.
She was one of the two daughters and heirs of Sir Henry Bruyn of South
Ockendon, Essex, and Beckenham, Kent; Sir John had his son George
by her, and thus on her death in 1473 held by courtesy her part of the
inheritance: her father had died in 1461, her grandfather in 1466, her
grandmother (a Lincolnshire heiress) in 1471. There was valuable

Margaret Saville had died by 1451, and John Heveningham did not succeed until 1453, this relationship may not have meant much to either of them.[317] They were on the commission of the peace together in the 1460s, and on one occasion Hopton acted as a feoffee of Sir John's.[318] It was the only time (which we can discover) that Hopton was a feoffee: perhaps that is one measure of their acquaintance. Another is given by an entry of the Blythburgh bailiff in his rough account book: 'vendit my mayster Hevenyngham 100 redes of the quech my mayster gaf hym 1 quarter 9s.'[319] Yet they were not of the same generation, and Heveningham may therefore have got on better with Sir William or even Sir George Hopton. The evidence that he might have done is his being busy at Blythburgh with James Hobart and William Eyre after Sir George Hopton's death, and it was from his house at Heveningham that Sir George's household stuff was carted back to Blythburgh that year.[320] Sir John called a son of his George too.

property involved. It comes as no surprise therefore that there was trouble over the division, especially as the husband of the other daughter, Elizabeth, was young William Brandon. These Bruyn estates did not however remain with the Heveningham family after 1499, as Alice had had a son by her second husband, Robert Harleston esquire. For all this see: *CIPM Henry VII* vol 1, pp236–8, 283–4, 329–30; *CFR 1461–71*, pp4, 78, 177; *CFR 1471–85*, pp1, 59; *CPR 1467–77*, p538; *CPR 1477–85*, pp524, 550. Philip Morant, *The History and Antiquities of the County of Essex* (2 vols, 1768), 1, p100, and Edward Hasted, *The History and Topographical Survey of the County of Kent* (4 vols, Canterbury 1778–99), 1, p80 have the right number of husbands for Alice Bruyn, but not in the right order, nor with the right names. Sir John's third wife was Margaret, widow of John, lord Clinton; she died in 1496: *CFR 1485–1509*, p241. We are presuming that Thomas, who succeeded Sir John in 1499, was the son of Alice Saville, though the jury of inquisition were themselves not sure about Thomas, nor about his age; their confusion arose, I believe, because of his half-brother George's decisive role in their deliberations, as son of Alice Bruyn. It was George who was 30 in 1499, Thomas who was 50: see for example *CIPM Henry VII* vol 1, p237. Poor Thomas! He died within a year of his father: *CFR 1485–1509*, p287.

[317] Heveningham was however married by 1451, as Thomas his son and heir was said to be 50 and more at his father's death in 1499: see the last note. He was without a wife when he wrote Davis II, no. 723.

[318] BL, Harley Charter 51 F3, in a quitclaim by Heveningham to Sir William Brandon and Elizabeth his wife of the manor of Cravens in Henham in 1473. For the importance of the date, see note 316.

[319] SRO, HA 30/369/46 f98v: the date was 1455–6.

[320] SRO, HA 30/369/281. This was in 1490–1. As these household goods (valued at 4000 marks) were to be fought over by Sir George's widow

This suggests that Heveningham, like Sir William Hopton, but unlike John Hopton, got on with the great. We have indeed seen him doing so earlier in his life. He kept it up until the end. As supervisor of his will, drawn up on 11 March 1499, nine days before his death, he named Thomas, earl of Surrey.[321]

If, as we have seen, he had sometimes been in opposition to Margaret Paston, one concern he did share with her; in their wills they both were mindful of the lepers at the five gates of Norwich. Margaret left them 3d,[322] Sir John 1s, each. Sir John left the same sum to the lepers in the hospital at Dunwich. He was also generous to those who were more fortunate; he left 6s 8d apiece to the four guilds at Halesworth, the guild at Laxfield, the Kelsale guild, and the same sum to the 'amending' of the Framlingham guild. He remembered the nuns at Bruisyard, leaving them 20s, and to Anne Berney, one of them, he left 5 marks. To his servants he gave in due proportion to their status, every gentleman 10s, every yeoman 6s 8d, every groom 3s 4d, each woman 3s 4d, and we can estimate the social standing of John his servant from the two pairs of 'yoman shetes' which he wanted him to have. Sir John was equally correct in his wide remembrance of local churches: half-marks were bequeathed broadly. To his own church of Heveningham, however, he left only his best antiphoner – the sole book mentioned in his will: perhaps, unlike his father, he did not read in the garden. Nonetheless, in his lifetime he had been a benefactor of Heveningham church, having built a chapel 'on the North parte'; there he wished to be buried, and there he desired a priest to sing for his soul continually, setting aside 200 marks to purchase land for his endowment. Tomb[323] and, if it ever was founded, chantry have gone; the chapel survives containing the pew of the family which came after the Heveninghams: they in turn have gone, leaving their prayer books behind them. Apart from his and his wife's souls, Sir John had another particularly

Anne and Sir George's executors, of whom Eyre was one, their removal to Heveningham had probably been some sort of precautionary move: PRO, Star Chamber 2/10/49.

[321] PRO, Probate 11/12 f72.   [322] Davis I, p385.

[323] For which see *The Chorography of Suffolk*, pp87, 122. The brick windows of the clerestory are also of *c*1500, see Pevsner, *Suffolk*, p246.

on his mind: that of Dame Margaret Pole. He left silver plate to George his son that he might be minded to pray for Lady Margaret's soul, and, in a postscript, he left a further 13s 4d to the nuns of Denny, Cambs, to pray for her soul and only half that sum to pray for his.

Margaret Pole had, no doubt, been a real friend to Sir John Heveningham. Moreover it is his will which enables us to detect their friendship. For John Hopton we have no will; as to who his friends were we have to remain ignorant. Yet, with the last group of his associates we have to consider, we shall perhaps stumble across a real friend or two.

Hopton had two sets of feoffees in his last years; the sets over-lapped.[324] One of the four men common to both sets was William Pickenham; we have already discussed him at some length. The three others were Sir Roger Townshend, John Sulyard and John Jermy the younger. Townshend and Sulyard were as important as Pickenham; when they came to Blythburgh in 1477–8 with William Jenny they had just been made sergeants-at-law; they went on to become justices in Richard III's reign: Townshend of the Common Pleas, Sulyard of King's Bench. They were just the men to have as feoffees in the 1470s; they were also good men to have as kin. Both, to be accurate, were closer to Thomasin than to John. Roger was her son-in-law, having married Eleanor, her daughter by William Lunsford; John Sulyard was her nephew, being the son of her sister.[325] He had been a feoffee of hers even before her marriage to Hopton.[326] From their late arrival on the scene at Blythburgh (Townshend was more important there after Hopton's death than before it, even though he had been John's steward since 1470) we might not be wide of the mark if we took them to be more Thomasin's nominees as feoffees than John's.

---

[324] See for example *CPR 1476–85*, pp142–4. They were his feoffees by 1471: see the Michaelmas courts at Blythburgh and Westleton, the first held in their names: SRO, HA 30/312/198; HA 30/312/425.

[325] Wedgwood, p828; see Thomas Barrington's will of 1469: PRO, PCC 6 Wattys. To complete the chain of evidence which binds Barrington, Sulyard and William Pickenham together, John Sulyard speaks of Picken-ham in his will as 'cognatus meus': PRO, PCC Probate 11/8.

[326] BL, Harley Charter 56 B26.

She, John Sulyard and William Pickenham were not only related, but were also, one imagines, old friends, while Townshend, as we have noted earlier,[327] had some affection for his mother-in-law, his 'moder Hopton'.

As successful lawyers Sulyard and Townshend are typical figures, and between them now it is not easy to detect those diversities of character which would have made all the difference to their contemporaries. Yet different they would have been to Thomasin and John; therefore we might pause for a moment to mark the similarities and divergencies of their wills, which reveal so much of themselves and their society. After all these men were judges; they were used to delivering judgment; when faced with its delivery upon themselves they might not any longer be able to hide behind the paraphernalia of word, gesture, and appearance those in authority cultivate to deflect the judgment of those whom they judge. In the prospect of a judgment from which there was no appeal, a few cracks may appear, a nervous tic might develop. We cannot hope for a total breakdown: men who become judges are not likely to admit to feet of clay. Still, a few burst seams in the black robes, letting the stuffing show through, we may hope for.

If they are most evident in Sir Roger Townshend's will that could be because he also lent money, and at interest.[328] The Pastons had to mortgage two estates to him, one of them, Sporle, twice over,[329] for sums he lent them. East Beckham, which they mortgaged to him for 100 marks in November 1469, they did not recover from him until 1503 on payment of £100.[330] While

---

[327] See p127.

[328] So I interpret the £10, £20, or £30, beside the 400 marks, Sir John Paston speaks of repaying Townshend in November 1474: Davis I, p477. Townshend, through the agency of Sir John Howard, also lent £100 to the Duke of Norfolk in 1467, for which he received again 160 marks during 1468–9, that is 10 marks more than he had given: Howard account books (entries in Sir John's own hand) in *Manners and Expenses*, pp462, 581.

[329] Redeemed in November 1474 (Davis I, p477), at mortgage for 400 marks again – payable in three years – in August 1477 (Davis I, p505). By October 1479 Townshend would not loan Sir John Paston any more money (Davis I, p515).

[330] Original indenture of 6 November 1469 (Davis I, p410); award of 1503

borrowing from him Sir John Paston was also drawing upon his legal advice in his attempt to recover Caister.[331] It seems an unusual combination, moneylender and solicitor, particularly when clients made use of him in both capacities at the same time. Did John Hopton? He may have done, as he was paying (or repaying) Townshend 400 marks, at 50 marks a year, in the early 1470s, the last instalment being paid on 20 January 1476.[332] Had this, however, been a loan? Might not the 400 marks which John paid Roger have been Eleanor's marriage portion, the price of an alliance with this promising young lawyer? The time, around 1470, would suit very well: Roger had crossed the threshold of his career and it was apparent that it would be a successful one. Though he was about thirty,[333] he was probably not a man to rush at things, particularly such a thing as marriage. We may note, nonetheless, that Roger did not marry an heiress, calculation did not carry him that far.

It is at this remove somewhat esoteric to ponder that the self-same money John Hopton paid him may have been lent to the Pastons: the funds which kept their case for Caister going being

---

(Davis II, p612). £100 and the rents of thirty-four years appear a good return on 100 marks captal outlay. As an afterthought the arbitrators added that Sir John should, after a year's occupation, pay another 10 marks to Sir Roger 'because th'arrerages have ben long in the tenauntes handes'. As at Michaelmas 1493 the bailiff there was only £1 in arrears (Norfolk RO, Bradfer-Lawrence v, no. X 13), and at Michaelmas 1482 (ibid., no. X 32) there had been no arrears, the award seems to have favoured Sir Roger more than Sir John, though on 2 February 1479 (ibid., no. X 45) rent arrears had stood at nearly £3, and the farmer Simon Gunnor owed just over £12. Townshend's lease of East Beckham to Simon Gunnor for seven years at £10 6s 8d per annum, dated 23 December 1476, survives (with much other important East Beckham material relating to its disputed acquisition by Judge William) in the Ketton-Cremer collection at the Norfolk Record Office: WKC 1/45. I hope to discuss this material on another occasion.

[331] Davis I, pp559, Gairdner v, p94; Davis I, p486. As early as 1467 William Paston advised his nephew to 'take avyse of Townsend' (Davis I, p168); presumably 'the wryghtyng betwen Townsend and me' which Sir John wanted his brother to send him in February 1470 was the East Beckham indenture of the previous November; John called it an indenture when he sent it up by return: Davis I, pp413, 556.

[332] BL, Harley Charter 57 A21–4.

[333] He had entered Lincoln's Inn in 1454 (Wedgwood, p864). Eleanor was not much younger, her father having died in 1445.

supplied, through Townshend, by John and Thomasin Hopton.
Yet so it may have been. As middle man Roger at any rate was
bound to gain. We might, therefore, supplement Leland, who
commented 'The father of Townshend now living got about a
hunderith pound of land by the yere with much travelling yn the
law,'[334] by adding 'and with some traffic in money'. Sheep were
yet a third source of wealth to this versatile man of the law.
In 1479 he had a dozen flocks, nearly 8000 beasts in all. Ten years
later he had well over 9000.[335] Hopton's sheep farming would
have been small-scale to him. Still, sheep may have been one of
the few things the country gentleman and the careerist lawyer had
in common, and if it was sheep they discussed from time to time,
as landlord and steward they must have done, Roger no doubt
did most of the talking. Hopton we cannot imagine voluble,
Townshend was (we are told)[336] 'ryght loose in the tongue'.

In his will he certainly goes on at length. In the preamble, for
instance, he pleads his case with professional skill:

First and principally I bequeth my soule and commend hit to
allmygthy god my maker and the redemer of me and of all man-
kynde in the most humbly wise that I canne besechyng him for the
merytes of his bitter and gloriouse passion to have mercy oon me and
to take me into his mercy which is above all workes, unto whom it is
appropused to have mercy . . . of the wych numbre of contrite synners
I mekely and humbly besechith him that I may be oon and come of
the number predestinate to be found and the rather thorow the
meanes of our most blessid lady modre and mayde and of all the
aungells of hevyn and patriarks prophets apostels marters confessours
virgyns and all the hooly company of hevyn and in speciall of them
that I have moost in remembraunce. Now I hertly pray themme of
their soccour and help that I may be partyner of the sacramentes and
merites of all hooly church and to ende my lyff in the same to pass-
over and so fynally to be oon of the Numbre at the dredefull day of
dome that shall stond and be oon of his right hand . . .[337]

334 *Itinerary* II, p12. Roger's father, says Leland 'was a meane man of substance'. Like Judge William Paston's father no doubt.
335 K. J. Allison, 'Flock Management in the Sixteenth and Seventeenth
   Centuries', *EcHR*, Second Series, XI (1958), pp98–112, especially tables
   I and II.
336 So wrote Sir John Paston, Davis I, p477.
337 PRO, Probate 11/10 f11, dated 14 August 1492.

It is a remarkable opening, but we cannot doubt it is his authentic voice.

The provisions which he made for his soul on its journey towards the terrible moment of reckoning were what we would anticipate after such a beginning. While he was being buried at East Raynham masses were to be said in twenty towns around; every priest was to have 4d, every clerk 2d, every child 1d, every poor man 1d, each husband (who was neither a poor man nor a child) 4d if that could be managed, or 2d worth of bread if it could not. The bells were to be rung and the ringers everywhere rewarded; and each of the churches was to have 6s 8d. He required a thousand masses to be sung within seven days, their purpose being exhaustively described:

I will that all this be doon to the honour and worship of almyghthy God our blessed lady all aungels and sayntes of hevyn and for the release socour and help of my poure soule my frendes and all the soules that I am bounde to pray fore and for the soules that almyghty god wold shuld be sooe prayed and for all the soulys in the payne of purgatory and most nede and lest helpe.'

To this temporary concentration but geographic diffusion – countless pleas being raised to God from north Norfolk during one week – he made the complementary addition of prayers in a single place over a long time: two priests were to pray for his soul, and the souls of others, his catalogue extending ultimately to all christian souls, for eighty years. Every Friday during that time 5d was to be given to five poor people in honour of Christ's passion and his wounds, and on the eve of every feast of the Virgin over the same period 5d to poor folk in memory of the five joys of Mary. Eighty years, we may note, was enough; he did not desire to establish a perpetual chantry. Nor, five or so years earlier, had John Sulyard, when he had made his will, in which too the thousand masses and the prayers for eighty years featured.

It is not surprising that there should be this similarity between them. They were both from East Anglia and were almost exact contemporaries, their careers following a virtually identical course. They had in fact gone up to Lincoln's Inn together in 1454.[338]

From such an early association, one which clearly continued thereafter, we should expect a closeness of some kind to have arisen,
even if Townshend may have found it not always easy to cope
with Sulyard being one 'of the best barristers in the Inn'.[339]

If Sulyard's superiority of talent was noticeable then, it is not
now, though it is not difficult to imagine the apprehension of those
against whom this clever man was reported to be intending 'to
make as wise and as crafty labour as he can'.[340] His early patrons
were probably the de la Poles: his family came from Eye, in
August 1454 either he or his father turned out to support Duchess
Alice there in her dispute with Thomas Cornwallis,[341] and by
1457–8 he was already steward of Eye, a post he held until his
death in 1488.[342] Nonetheless, with his talent he would soon
enough have been making his own way.[343] We need not mark the
successful stages of his career,[344] for it is unlikely to have concerned
John Hopton at all, certainly not until the 1470s and probably not
even much then. Moreover, here it is not John Sulyard's life which
interests us, but how, at the point of taking leave of it, he made
provision for his soul in that other which was to follow.[345]

Sulyard, like Townshend, wanted a thousand masses to be sung,
but he was at once more vague and more demanding: a thousand
different priests were to do the singing, and all within three or four
days of his death, if that was possible. Was it? Can his executors
– headed by William Pickenham – have seriously tried in so short
a time to communicate to a thousand priests the need to sing a

[339] *Ibid.*, p828, from *The Black Book of Lincoln's Inn*, p26.
[340] *Stonor Letters and Papers* II, p113.
[341] BL, Egerton Charter 8779. William Harleston, one of the most influential of de la Pole councillors in the 1450s and 1460s, was John's uncle: *The Stonor Letters and Papers* I, pp139–40.
[342] SRO, Eye Chamberlains' Accounts, EE 2/L/ 1/1 and EE 2/L 2/2/24.
[343] He was employed in the mid-1460s, for example, by Sir John Howard, and thus worked with James Hobart; on 6 February 1465 they drank a quart of wine together: *Manners and Expenses*, pp271, 481, 485, 486, 500 for 1464; p298 for 1465; p402 for 1467.
[344] His acquisition of a landed estate is beautifully documented in the case of the important properties of Stratford St Mary and Wetherden, Suffolk: see the deeds among the Sulyard papers in the Stafford Collection at the Staffs RO, D641/4. His feoffees included Roger Townshend, William Harleston, and William Pickenham.
[345] His will, dated 8 October 1487, proved 11 June 1488, is PRO, Probate 11/8 f168v.

mass for John Sulyard? John's desire for masses over a longer period was also very like Roger Townshend's. They both wanted priests to sing for eighty years, but whereas Roger specified two priests, John stipulated only one; and here he was much less vague, indeed he was in one respect curiously precise. Not only did he set the priest's salary at 8 marks, not only did he say the priest should be honest and virtuous, he also stated that he should be more than forty years old. Here, no doubt, the executors were more easily able to comply with his wishes.

Where, however, the two judges are most different (so far as their religious bequests go) is in their charity. There is no such preamble to Sulyard's will as there is to Townshend's, there is in fact no preamble at all: Sulyard at once gets down to the business of his body's burial, with only the most perfunctory mention of his soul. The contrast may be significant, but less so than that where their charity is concerned, for while Townshend requires the distribution of money to the poor, both at the time of his funeral and throughout the eighty years that masses have to be said for his and others' souls, Sulyard makes no reference to such things. What John does refer to, and Townshend, somewhat unusually, does not, is the memorialization of himself and his family which so conveniently and quite properly was included in the enhancement and enrichment of church buildings. John desired to be buried in his own parish church of Wetherden, Suffolk, in the new south aisle; this was the aisle he had himself begun.[346] Adorned with his coats of arms it, and the porch incorporated in its western end, survive: Pevsner awards them the tribute 'spectacular'. What has lasted less well has been his tomb: the tomb chest in poor condition is all that remains. He also left to Hugh Lee, the rector of Wetherden, 20 marks towards the repair of the chancel, described as Hugh's chancel; it is unusual to find one of the laity, however distinguished, leaving money for the upkeep of the part of the church with which he would have had so little to do. The Early English and Decorated chancels (onto which so often are fitted East Anglian Perpendicular naves) show just how little rectors

[346] Probably unfinished at his death; Pevsner, *Suffolk* (2nd edition), *sub nomine*, see the footnote.

cared, or could afford to care, to be up-to-date, and how equally little parishioners were concerned to do anything to help them out. Why should they? There would be plenty of masses being said at the altars in their parts of the church. To the guardians and vicar at Eye John left a further 10 marks for the glazing of an east window in the new south aisle of their church, to the honour of God and in memory of John his father, Alice his mother, and all his other ancestors. If the work was even done it has not come down to our day.

One wonders how many of those things testators wanted their executors to do for them actually got done. We have raised this question earlier; it crops up again here because of the grand religious bequests of Townshend and Sulyard. They are grand: a thousand masses each, bread for the poor for eighty years, a marble tombstone, bells to be rung for miles around; but did they come off, were they more than gestures, for they are mostly vaguely enough expressed to be interpreted as no more than gestures. With these great men there was none of that careful thought which informs Walter Fulbourne's will, and so gives us the confidence to believe his wishes came true. He knew what he was about, and went about it methodically; things had not been left to chance while he lived, he took every precaution to see that they would not be left to deceit or laziness when he was dead. Sulyard and Townshend by contrast appear generous, even flamboyant, but barely practical. Are we left to believe that all we should really draw from such wills is intention? After all Sir Roger Townshend's will was not proved.[347]

Sir Thomas Montgomery's 'amazing will'[348] we must suppose was. It is not for us, however, to comment on. We mention it only because Sir Thomas was one of John Hopton's feoffees.[349] What this very great man is doing at the head of one group of trustees of our unimportant Suffolk gentleman is hard to say. Or is it? He was an Essex man,[350] he was at the height of his powers, and

[347] An ominous blank follows the word 'Probatum': PRO, Probate 11/10.
[348] The words are Mr James Oxley's: *The Reformation in Essex* (1965), p22.
[349] *CPR 1476–85*, p143.
[350] According to Wedgwood (p606), a steward of Rayleigh, which brings him even nearer home to Thomasin.

in the latter half of the 1470s he was at his most influential. If Thomasin had any say in these matters, and we can be sure she did, for there were the interests of herself and her children to protect, then Montgomery looks like her choice. He is never encountered before this in association with the Hoptons. Was he any more than a figurehead, the distinguished name which stands at the head of the list to give it the appearance of weight and depth and reach? It looks as though there was more to it than that: in December 1480 Montgomery was granted the wardship and marriage of Edward Knevet,[351] the son of Thomas Knevet and Elizabeth Lunsford, and a favourite grandson of Thomasin's. As Sir Thomas, childless himself, married Edward off to Katherine, daughter of Sir Henry Marny,[352] that grant of his wardship can only have been, and been felt to have been by Thomasin, to Edward's advantage. Of what other part, or parts, Sir Thomas was expected to play as a Hopton feoffee we are ignorant.

Two other feoffees were of a younger generation than those whom we have so far discussed – of a different generation, and of a different character. Pickenham, Townshend, Sulyard, Montgomery *par excellence*, were men of the world; that is the very last thing John Jermy the younger was, for he made no mark in it, while Robert Clere, though his second wife Alice Boleyn would in the reign of Henry VIII bring him out, seems to have had a refinement which was not suited to the rough and tumble a Townshend or a Montgomery took in their stride. They also had something else in common: they both married Hopton girls.

John Jermy (or Jermyn)[353] of Metfield, Suffolk who was

---

[351] *CPR 1476–85*, p238. One wonders whether he made a corner in Essex minors during Edward IV's reign. In 1475 he had been granted the wardship and marriage of John Harleston, the son of Alice Bruyn, wife of Sir John Heveningham, after her death in 1473: *CPR 1467–77*, p538.

[352] *CIPM Henry VII* vol III, p319.

[353] John's father, who died 24 October 1487 (*CIPM Henry VII* vol I, p140), called himself in his will John Jermy (see above, chapter 3, p144), but whatever he preferred, others liked Jermyn, and that seems the commoner form. Moreover, while he called himself of Buckenham Ferry, Norfolk, he desired burial at Metfield, and his *IPM* returned only the two manors of Metfield and nearby Withersdale as being his. He seems to have been either perverse or out to cover his tracks; both may perhaps have been a reaction to his experiences as sheriff of Norfolk and Suffolk in 1450–1, for which see Gairdner II, pp183, 203–4, 235, 241–3, 251. He was a JP from

included in both groups of feoffees, was about thirty in 1478; he was married to Isobel, John Hopton's daughter. He peers out of the gloom at us just once, some thirteen years before when as 'younge Jermyn' Margaret Paston lists him, with Sir Thomas Brews, Micklefield, and others as among those partisans of William Jenny, who turned out prepared to back him and the Debenhams in holding a court at Caldecott Hall. The Pastons had taken precautions and the court was not held. We cannot help feeling that John Jermy who probably got a dinner out of it, was not displeased at the outcome.[354] He died in 1504, his light so far as we are concerned always hidden under a bushel; but for his father-in-law in 1478 or thereabouts it shone out. Or was he merely at hand at the time?

Robert Clere of Ormesby, Norfolk, was younger than John Jermy in 1478: he was probably nearer twenty-five than thirty, and he was, or shortly would be married to Anne, daughter of Sir William Hopton. He had been admitted to Lincoln's Inn in 1467,[355] but in 1478 his service in local government seems only just to have got under way.[356] Perhaps it was as Sir William's representative that he was one of John's feoffees, for with Sir William and with Sir George Hopton, his brother-in-law, he was most closely associated. He was, for example, on the commission of the peace for Suffolk only during Richard III's reign – though he had some thirty years as JP for Norfolk yet to serve, and whereas for that county too he was on the commission of the peace in Richard's reign, he was omitted on the accession of Henry VII and did not return until 1494. In that respect perhaps, his connection with Sir William Hopton did not stand him in good stead. During that interval he was nonetheless busy, and on behalf of Hopton's family. He was first an executor of Sir William, and then of Sir George; moreover he was guardian of the infant Arthur Hopton, and in that role is to be discovered at Blythburgh

1450 until 1458; he may not have relished that position either: *ibid.* III, p68.
[354] Davis I, p319.
[355] *Admissions Register* I, p17. He was in London c.1470; was he then still at the Inn?:Davis I, p348.
[356] Wedgwood, p190.

in 1490–1.[357] Once he has been encountered in the Paston correspondence, it is entirely understandable why both Sir William and
Sir George should have had so much faith in him: he appears, in
those pages, an obliging and straightforward fellow.

He was particularly accommodating over the repayment by the
Pastons in 1475 of £100 they had borrowed from him and his
mother. The whole transaction was a complicated and delicate
one, and it was raising the last £20 that had to be repaid which
caused a flurry of letters, containing not a few harsh words, to
pass between Margaret and her son, for it was her plate which was
pledged for its repayment.[358] Whatever Sir John's behaviour in
this affair (and he did not tell his mother everything), we have to
bear in mind he was struggling to keep solvent, to keep pressure
to bear on the Duke of Norfolk, who was pigheadedly hanging
onto Caister, and to keep withal a brave face turned towards the
world; he was also, we should not forget, trying to get a divorce.
However this harassed yet wonderfully sanguine man behaved,
Robert Clere's manner was impeccable. Even when some of the
money which had been paid to him turned out to be 'ryght on-
rysty and he cowd nowt havyt chaungyd' Margaret was still able
to write to Sir John, 'I fynd hym ryght kindly dysposyd to yow
and to me bothe'.[359] Three years later, in 1478, Margaret had
other good things to say of him, and again in a letter to her eldest
son. 'He ys', she wrote, 'a man of substaunce and worchyp, and so
wylle be taken in thys schyre.' For this reason she was unhappy to
see a servant of her son's causing trouble between them and so
losing her son Robert's goodwill: 'I wolde that iche of yow xulde
do for othere, and leue as kynnysmen and frendys; for suche
seruawntys may make trobyll by-twyxe yow, wheche where
a-geynste cortesey, so nyhe newborys as ye be.'[360] Neighbourly
might be the proper word to use of the one letter of Robert's which

---

[357] SRO, 30/369/281, see also HA 30/312/424. He was frequently entertained at Walberswick in the 1490s: *Walberswick Churchwardens'*
Accounts, pp69, 73, 78, 81.

[358] Davis I, nos. 95, 221, 222, 223, 224, 291. This was not the first time
Elizabeth Clere had lent them money: in 1471 they had borrowed 100
marks from her: *ibid.*, pp352–3. Robert's eldest son William married John
Paston's daughter Elizabeth: *Cal Anc Deeds* IV, A7773, see also Blomefield V, p1574. [359] Davis I, pp372, 374. [360] Davis I, p380.

survives in the Paston collection, or to be exact, good neighbourly; it is reminiscent of numerous similar letters among the Stonor papers;[361] it strikes, so to say, the tone of that collection, a more harmonious note than the dissonance we have ringing inside our heads after a brief acquaintance with the Pastons and the world they created for themselves. Robert, in the face it seems of provocation, writes with calm, with dignity, perhaps even with poise:

And also it is enformed yov that I schuld sey that ye schuld hangge vp-on many busches. As touchyng that, I seyd not so. I prey yov bryngge forthe my accevsar, that I may com to myn aunswere in that to knov hym that wold make varians be-twex yov and me, the qwech I wold be sory as ony pore gentilman on lyve.[362]

Would not such a man have made, among other things, an admirable feoffee? For his qualities John Hopton no doubt admired him. Did he love him? The years which divided them are likely to have prevented him doing that. We are therefore still in search of a real friend for John.

These feoffees of his late years are not bound to be his friends, not at any rate, or necessarily, the friends of his youth, or even the companions of his middle age. A man as he ages loses friends. In that there is a sadness which in Hopton's life we cannot detect, but can we detect the happiness of having old friends? Among these feoffees we found the professionals, who even if they were also in some sense, perhaps in many senses, friends of the family, were first and foremost selected to do the job: Pickenham, Townshend, Sulyard. We have noticed too Sir Thomas Montgomery, a man whom no doubt it was probably wise not to leave out, and we have discovered also two younger men, John Jermy and Robert Clere: among feoffees young men are needed to keep

---

[361] *The Stonor Letters and Papers*, nos. 115, 119, 242, for example.

[362] Davis II, p454: 'Probably autograph'. Robert's good temper is the more to be applauded in that he held none of the family property (in his own right) until his mother's death in 1493: his father, Robert Clere esquire, willed that Elizabeth his wife 'should have all his manors, lands and tenements without any exception for term of her life', and in addition he made no provision for his children nor did he charge his widow with their maintenance, 'having full confidence that if they bore themselves well and humbly to her she would maintain them becomingly': *Cal Anc Deeds* IV, A7778. At his father's death in 1446 Robert was not the heir; that was William, but William had died by January 1468: *ibid.*, A7885.

up the numbers as the older ones die. There are, however, three men whom we have not discussed, who were not men of the law, who were not grand in society or great in politics, and who were not young. Were they John's old friends? Were they the men he liked to be with, whose company tired him least, whose personalities most nearly resembled his own and thus pleased him best? Could it be that among them was the man whom, if pressed, he would have singled out as his best friend? We cannot be sure, but we suggest that these three may have been able to say in 1478 that they knew him better than anyone else did.

Sir Thomas Brews of Fressingfield was an almost exact contemporary.[363] He was already John's feoffee in the 1440s.[364] They were appointed to the commission of the peace together in February 1444, and were also often together on other commissions.[365] As we have seen, Thomas married his son and heir William to John's daughter Elizabeth.[366] Moreover, young William Brews and young William Hopton went about in company.[367] One of their companions was young Calthorp; presumably this was John, son of Sir William Calthorp, the second of our last three feoffees.[368] Sir William too was about the same age as John Hopton, though he survived him and Thomas Brews (who died in 1482) by many years, dying only in 1494.[369] He was, according to John Paston in

363 Wedgwood, p108.
364 For Cockfield Hall, SRO, HA 30/369/24.
365 *CPR 1429–36*, p524; *CPR 1441–6*, p463; *CPR 1446–52*, p479; *CPR 1452–61*, pp344, 402, 409, 560, 606; *CPR 1467–76*, p249; *CFR 1461–71*, p100.
366 See chapter 3, p142. They were married before 1456, as Thomas Brews' mother Eleanor in her will of 6 October that year made a bequest to William Brews' wife: NRO, Norwich Cons. Court, Reg. Brosiard, f23.
367 Davis II, p104.
368 William Hopton and John Calthorp had married Wentworth sisters, the daughters of Roger Wentworth: William, Margaret, John, Elizabeth: Wedgwood, p148, see also HMC *Eleventh Report*, appendix VII, p93. Thus the four young men who rode together with 24 horse to Cowhaugh in autumn 1454 were all connected by marriage (or all just about to be): Brews with Hopton, Hopton with Wentworth, Wentworth with Calthorp.
369 *CIPM Henry VII* vol I, pp416–18. For his will (PRO, PCC 23 Vox), see above chapter 2, p99. One of his daughters was married to William Gurney: to them he left 200 sheep. Gurney was another of Hopton's feoffees of the 1470s. He was escheator of Norfolk and Suffolk in 1465–6 (*CFR 1461–71*, p169), and on the Duke of Norfolk's council in 1472 (Davis I, pp453, 579). He was no doubt the William Gurney who had been

1467, a good fellow.[370] Ten years later Paston probably had the
same opinion of Thomas Brews, if, that is, one can ever view a
father-in-law with quite that detachment; Sir Thomas, even if
'so hard' at first,[371] came round in the end and allowed John and
Margery to marry. With Brews and Calthorp therefore John
Hopton may have enjoyed good fellowship for many years. Yet, if
he shared with them whatever it took in fifteenth century East
Anglia to be accounted a good fellow by one's fellows, he did not
share their involvement, their greater involvement, in local and
public affairs. In the hectic years around 1450 they were more
closely associated with those members of the nobility who opposed
the government, than he had ever been in the 1440s with those
who had supported it.[372] They also were knights: indeed they were
knighted at the coronation of queen Elizabeth in May 1465,[373]

admitted to Lincoln's Inn in 1454 (*Admissions Register* I, p12). He was on
excellent terms with the Pastons, even when acting in opposition to them
over the estate at Saxthorpe (Davis I, pp552, 556). The following passage
deserves reflection:
'Item, yerstyrday W. Gornay entryd in-to Saxthorp, and ther was he
kepyng of a coort, and had the tenauntys attorynd to hym. But er the
coort was all doon I cam thedyr, wyth a man wyth me and no more,
and ther be-for hym and all hys felawchep, Gayne, Bomsted, Hoppys,
and iij or iiij mor, I chargyd the tenauntys that they shold proced no
ferther in ther coort vp-on peyn that myght falle of it; and they lettyd
for a season, but they sye that I was not abyll to make my pertye good,
and so they prosedyd forthe. And I sye that, and set me downe by the
stward and blottyd hys book wyth my fyngyr as he wrot, so that all the
tenauntys afermyd that the coort was enterupte by me as in yowyr
ryght; and I reqweryd them to record that ther was no pesybyll coort
kepet, and so they seyd they wold. W. Gornay and I dynyd to-gedyr the
same daye, and he told me that he had spokyn to yow of the same
mater.'
Whatever modifications to our view of fifteenth century England this
episode may (or ought to) make, it shows us clearly enough that William
Gurney was a peaceable and courteous man; to Margery Paston he was in
addition a wise man (Davis I, pp665–6). He does therefore suit very well
the company of Pickenham, Sulyard and Clere.
[370] Davis I, p532.
[371] Davis I, p606.
[372] For Brews, see Gairdner II, pp163–6 and also pp275–6; for Calthorp, see
Davis II, p50. Sir William Calthorp became in the later 1460s steward of
the Duke of Norfolk's household; this appears not to have prevented him
becoming in June 1469 a sworn man of the Duke of Gloucester's: HMC,
Eleventh Report, appendix VII, p94; Davis I, p545.
[373] Wedgwood, pp109, 149.

the very occasion when John preferred to be fined rather than receive the honour.[374] These differences between them perhaps made little difference, nonetheless differences they were. With Henry Wentworth esquire, the third and last of his feoffees, John did not have even these differences; indeed Wentworth seems to have kept out of things even more successfully than did Hopton.

In 1478 he was called Henry Wentworth the elder[375] to distinguish him from his nephew, who was knighted that year. Sir Henry was the son and heir of Henry's elder brother Sir Philip Wentworth, the head of the family, whose commitment to the Lancastrian regime we have noted before.[376] Henry was not, in this respect, at all like his brother. He was on a single commission before 1461: it was in May 1459 to enquire into riots and disorders in East Anglia.[377] Ten years later he was briefly and for the only occasion in his life a Justice of the Peace – in June and July 1470 in Suffolk.[378] A few weeks later, on 27 October 1470, he was a commisisoner of oyer and terminer, also in Suffolk.[379] The circumstances of 1470 however – of the summer, and, after Henry VI's return, of the autumn – were peculiar: the government, whether Edward's or Henry's, was casting about for commissioners and drew in some odd, old fish like Edward Grimston,[380] like Henry Wentworth. The remaining twelve years of his life were untroubled by any similar calls upon his time, though one suspects that even in 1470 his name was used to fill out a list and nothing was actually expected of him. In his avoidance of the public eye Henry Wentworth was much like John Hopton; Henry

---

[374] I make this connection from the Blythburgh accounts of 1464–5: SRO, HA, 30/134/18 m2.

[375] *CPR 1476–85*, pp142–4. Called of Codham (Hall, in Wethersfield), Essex, in the pedigrees; I wonder whether that place was not acquired by him, but by his son, Sir Roger, through his wife, a Tyrell: see Morant, *Essex* II, p373, who comments 'How he came to be fixed at this place I cannot learn.' There is no surviving Essex inquisition for Henry. The tomb chest with alabaster effigies, 'not' (according to Pevsner, p387) 'of high quality', and said (*ibid.*) possibly to be his and his wife's, would then not be.

[376] See above, p161.   [377] *CPR 1452–61*, p516.

[378] *CPR 1467–77*, p631.   [379] *CPR 1467–77*, p248.

[380] On the commission of 27 October 1470. He had been out of affairs since 1451: M. J. Constantine, 'Edward Grimston, the Court Faction and the political crisis of 1450 to 1453', unpublished Keele BA dissertation 1973, especially chapter 4.

was more successful than John: he escaped more of the tasks of local government than he had a right to expect to do. Neither of them, however, made any mark at all in public affairs. Did they have anything else in common?

They were not as close in age as were Hopton, Brews and Calthorp. Although Henry died only a few years after John, in 1482,[381] he was a younger man, possibly by as much as twelve or fifteen years.[382] They were related. John married his son and heir William to Henry's sister Margaret;[383] it was an important alliance for both families: as kin they stuck together.[384] Yet what tempts us to believe that Henry Wentworth, and not Thomas Brews or William Calthorp, was John's dearest friend is that he was of a Yorkshire family, a West Riding family at that.[385] If we are correct in thinking this meant something (perhaps much) to John, the Yorkshireman in exile, then it tells us a good deal about him. Does it not also tell us a great deal about John that the man he may have loved best was, like himself, not out to make a name for himself, to cut a figure in society, to heave and shove.[386] Even

[381] Writs of *diem clausit extremum: CFR 1471–85*, pp234, 259, According to the inquisition he died 22 or 23 March 1482: PRO, C140/82/11.
[382] Wedgwood, p934 has Henry's elder brother Philip as born c.1424, which seems about right.
[383] So say the pedigrees (for instance BL, Add MS 5524, f55), and so I have assumed throughout, but I have as yet found no clear contemporary evidence, unless the escutcheons in the roof of the south chapel at Yoxford parish church are considered 'contemporary'. They date from after 1520, probably from after 1555, and they celebrate Hopton marriage alliances; one of them is of the Hopton and Wentworth arms: Parr III, p64ff.
[384] HMC, *Eleventh Report*, appendix VII, p93, where Henry's mother, Henry himself and William Hopton are disclosed as a team in negotiation with Sir John Wingfield for the marriage of John Calthorp's son and heir. William Hopton was Henry's feoffee (PRO, C140/82/11), and Henry was close to his mother, for during her lifetime she granted him and his heirs – in 1482 his heir was his young son Roger (for whom see Wedgwood, p935) – Suffolk properties which included the manors of Cavendish and Poslingford, and on her death she made him, with his clerical brother Thomas, her executor; she left him her silver plate: PRO, Probate 11/6, f253, dated 30 August 1477, proved 28 May 1478.
[385] The family was of North Elmsall, near Pontefract. Henry was by blood only half a Yorkshireman; his mother was Margaret, daughter and heir of Sir Philip Despencer of Nettlestead, Suffolk: Wedgwood, p934.
[386] Is this not indicated also by their being frequently electors but never members of parliament? For Hopton's presence at shire elections see above, chapter 3. Henry was present over a period of thirty years: in 1447, 1453,

though we dare not go beyond that 'may have', simply to find the elder Henry Wentworth among his feoffees enables us to know John Hopton slightly better. Or, perhaps we ought to say, to think we know him better.

1459, 1467 (for 1468), 1472, and 1477 (for 1478); he headed the list in 1453, which may be significant: PRO, C219/15 part 4 no. 58, 16 part 2 no. 58, 16 part 5 no. 30, 17 part 1 no. 79, 17 part 2 no. 61, 17 part 3 no. 70.

CONCLUSION

...gave me the idea that a person does not (as I had imagined) stand motionless and clear before our eyes with his merits, his defects, his plans, his intentions...exposed on his surface, like a garden at which, with all its borders spread out before us, we gaze through a railing, but is a shadow which we can never succeed in penetrating, of which there can be no such thing as direct knowledge, with respect to which we form countless beliefs, based upon his words and sometimes upon his actions, though neither words nor actions can give us anything but inadequate and as it proves contradictory information – a shadow behind which we can alternately imagine, with equal justification, that there burns the flame of hatred and of love.

> Marcel Proust,
> *Remembrance of Things Past*, vol 5
> (Chatto and Windus paperback edition, 1967), pp83–4

It is easier to say what John Hopton was not than what he was. He was not a 'courtier civil servant'.[1] He was not the author of the *Morte D'Arthur*: cattle rustling, extortion, robbery with violence, rape, and attempted murder did not fill his life as they did Sir Thomas Malory's.[2] He was not a knight and he did not want to be. He did not want to be a leader of Suffolk society. He was no magnate's man. He was not, it seems, much like other fifteenth century gentlemen. Yet, no two of them were alike, nor have we been describing *them*.

He was wealthy, enterprising, sensible, and responsible. The marriage portion of his eldest daughter, the purchase of Cockfield Hall and Easton Bavents, the expansion of the demesne at Blythburgh, Yoxford, and Westleton, the agreement with Thomasin of 1457, the estate set aside for his younger son Thomas, the educa-

---

[1] 'The courtier civil servant is the important man, and the growth of this class the key to the history of the later middle ages': E. F. Jacob, *Essays in Later Medieval History* (1968), p150.

[2] P. J. C. Field, 'Sir Thomas Malory, M.P.' *BIHR*', xlvii (1974), pp24–35.

tion provided for the boys of the family, these all demonstrate those qualities. He was easy to get on with: the long service of his auditor, Walter Fulbourne, of his legal advisor, William Bondes, of his supervisor, John Ulveston, of his brother Robert, testify to that. Moreover, he kept his friends for twenty or thirty years: William Scargill, Thomas Brews, William Calthorp, Henry Wentworth. The harmony within his family and with his friends extended to include his neighbours. The conflict with Dunwich was neither new nor necessarily undertaken on his initiative; its resolution in his favour was more to the advantage of his tenants at Walberswick and Blythburgh than to him. The itch of acquisition did not irritate John: not after 1430 at any rate. No wonder politics meant nothing to him, and he meant nothing to politicians: if he did not want anything, how could they use him?

Political frameworks were not everything. Still, we should not rush to the other extreme: Justice Hopton as Justice Shallow. John Hopton, the country gentleman sunk in rural pursuits, does not fit either. His presence at parliamentary elections, his visits to Yorkshire and London, the lawyers he knew, the church he chose to be buried in, the woman he chose to be his wife, the sons at school, university, and inns of court, his eldest boy's marriage and career, the scope of his social life, the networks of relatives and friends, spreading across not only East Anglia, but also the West Riding, Sussex and Surrey too, all this (and much else) suggests no ill-informed, out-of-touch, bumpkin. Thomas Saville would not have married his daughter to a dim young fellow, even a dim young fellow with prospects.

Nor should we dwell on the elderly John Hopton, surrounded by a younger generation of clever men like Townshend and Sulyard, or his sons William and John, and protected, possibly even managed by a determined wife. If we have shewn him thus it is because so much of our evidence comes from after 1460, when John was over fifty. The Hopton of the 1430s and 1440s there is difficulty in discerning. For preference I see him, a vigorous man in his forties, the man Thomasin was shortly to find attractive, at Westwood with Robert his brother, John Ulveston and Henry Wentworth, at dinner and discussing the king's collapse. It is

August 1453. Or: that same afternoon, he stands with Nicholas Greenhagh, the bailiff, looking out across the marshes; they talk about fattening bullocks; John has on his straw hat.

What more should we say: *laudabiliter vixit.*

INDEX

John Hopton's name appears throughout the text and is, therefore, not indexed. Some other names and places appear very frequently in the text and are indexed selectively.